TRIBAL LIFE AND FORESTS

TRIBAL LIFE AND FORESTS

(TRIBAL LIFE IN INDIA—1)

Edited by

DEVENDRA THAKUR
D. Litt.
Former Professor, L.N. Mishra College of Business Management,
B.B.A. Bihar University, Muzaffarpur

and

D.N. THAKUR
Ph.D.

SECOND REPRINT EDITION

DEEP & DEEP PUBLICATIONS PVT. LTD.
F-159, Rajouri Garden, New Delhi - 110027

Tribal Life and Forests
(Tribal Life in India—1)

First Published: 1994
Second Reprint Edition: 2009

ISBN 978-81-8450-104-9 (Vol. 1)
ISBN 978-81-8450-114-8 (Set)

Typeset by THE LASER PRINTERS, 8/15, 3rd Floor, Subhash Nagar, New Delhi-110027.

Printed in India at MAYUR ENTERPRISES, WZ-Plot no. 3, Tihar Village, New Delhi-110 018.

Published by DEEP & DEEP PUBLICATIONS PVT. LTD., F-159, Rajouri Garden, New Delhi-110027. Phones: 25435369, 25440916.
E-mail: ddpbooks@yahoo.co.in • ddpubs@gmail.com
Sales Showroom: 2/13, Ansari Road, Daryaganj, New Delhi-110002
Phone/Fax: 23245122

Contents

Preface

The tribal people being the original inhabitants of India, constitute a significant part of this vast Nation. They have been dwelling in the forests surrounded by hills for a long period. Their social structure, their culture and their language are quite different from the general people of India. In course of time, in the post-Independence age, a lot of changes have taken place in the tribal areas due to immense endeavours of the Government for their socio-economic development. But, inspite of all endeavours, they are still poor as well as illiterate and are far from the mainstream of Indian society.

Keeping in view these facts and figures, we have tried to present a systematic study of different aspects of tribal life in different volumes so that their problems can be easily understood and fresh endeavours can be made for their socio-economic development, protecting their civilisation, culture, language and literature. It is a bare fact that with change in their socio-economic status, they are parting away from their original culture. So, protection of tribal culture is as essential as their economic development.

The present volume comprises the study of tribal life and their relation to forest in historical as well as in modern perspective. This volume consists of eleven chapters having an appendix including the forest statistics. The treatise starts with general description of the tribes in India with special reference to Southern, Central and Eastern Indian tribes.

Forest is the second aspect of this study, but it does not mean that it has got secondary position in the book, rather it occupies primary position, because it is closely inter-related with tribal life.

So, the study of the forest is inter-woven with tribal life and economy of the tribe and consequently, it also deals with tribal development.

Our goal of preparing these volumes is, obviously, the welfare of the tribal people of India in true sense of the term and if they serve the purpose in any way, it will give us immense pleasure. We are thankful to all those scholars and friends whose support and sympathy encouraged us to complete this work.

Muzaffarpur

DEVENDRA THAKUR
D.N. THAKUR

Introduction: Tribes in India

THE DEFINITION OF TRIBE

The term tribe commonly signifies a group of people speaking a common language, observing uniform rules of social organisation, and working together for common purpose.[1] The other typical characteristics of tribe include a common name, a contiguous territory, a relatively uniform culture or way of life and a tradition of common descent.[2] According to another contention tribe is generally used to denote group of primitive or barbarous clans under recognised chiefs.[3]

The term tribe was taken over by the anthropologist from ordinary uses, and like all such terms it had a variety of meanings. In general, it was applied to people who were considered primitive, lived in backward area, and did not know the use of writing. Sometimes, it was considered synonymous with the term race, which in scientific uses, has an entirely different meaning. In the beginning, nobody bothered to give a precise meaning to the term tribe. This did not create much confusion so long as the groups which were dealt with could be easily located and differentiated from groups of other types. By and large, this was the case in Australia, in Malenesia and in North America, the regions which were first studied by the anthropologists.

In India, and also to a certain extent in Africa, the situation is conspicuously different. In this country, groups which correspond closely to the anthropologist's conception of tribe, have lived in long association with communities of an entirely different type. Except in a few areas, it is very difficult to come across communities which retain all their pristine tribal characters. In fact, most such tribal groups show in varying degrees elements of community with the larger society of India. It becomes necessary, therefore, to have a set of attributes in terms of which groups more or less, corresponding to the tribe can be distinguished from other communities. There are two ways of setting about in the search of a definition of the term tribe. The first is to examine the existing definitions which have been worked out on general considerations. The second is to analyse the specific conditions in India and to find out the attributes which are distinctive of groups conventionally regarded as tribes. The difficulty here would lie in making the two definitions meet. This, as has been indicated above, is because specific historical conditions have made tribal groups in this country deviate considerably from the ideal type.

Let us take first the definition of tribe on a purely theoretical level. Such a definition should be based on the empirical characteristics of a particular mode of human grouping found in different parts of the world. It should also take into account the fact that such a made of grouping represents a particular historical stage in social evolution. The concept has to be define in such manner as to include all human groups of a particular type, irrespective of conditions of time and place.

A tribe is, in an ideal State, a self-contained unit. It constitutes a society in itself. This has to be explained a little further. The anthropologist, Nadel, defines a society in this way, "... Societies are made of people; societies have boundaries, people either belonging to them or not; and people belong to a society in virtue of rules under which they stand, and which impose on them regular determinate ways of acting towards and in regard to one another."[4]

We shall first undertake to outline the characteristics of a tribe as a society and then proceed to determinate between tribes and societies of other types.

In the definition of society mentioned above, a very

important point is that which relates to its boundaries. It should be noted that a society includes within it various sub-systems and is not itself subsummed under any wider category. In other words, a society is a self-contained unit and its boundaries demarcate certain limits of inter-action in legal, political, economic and other spheres. This, of course, does not mean that no interaction takes place across the boundaries of different societies. These, however, are of a separate character. The boundaries of the tribe as society have been defined politically, linguistically and culturally by various authors. To take the first point, it is frequently said that the tribe is a society, the members of which have a common government and share a common territory. The possession of a common government sets the frame for legal action within the society and for political action with other societies. The boundary maintaining functions of a government are significant and deserve consideration. But for certain difficulties, in fact, to be pointed out presently, a society might have been defined simply in terms of its political boundries.

Most societies are characterised by the presence of a government whose form and functions may be objectively ascertained. This, however, is not true of all societies, particularly certain tribal societies. Many people conceive of tribal societies as being in a state of total anarchy. In reality, this is far from the truth, and many tribal societies have well established systems of government. On the other hand, there are certain tribal societies which do lack government in the ordinary sense of the term. This, however, must be taken to mean that they exist in a state of anarchy. Such societies which 'lack government' have been studies in some detail in certain parts of Africa. In the language of social anthropology, they are spoken of as having segmentary political systems. Examples of such societies are provided by the Nuer and the Dinka of Sudan, and the Tallensi of the Gold Coast.[5] A paper by Eisenstadt shows that societies of this type have a fairly wide distribution in the world.[6] Now, the peculiar thing about segmentary systems is that there is neither any centralised authority nor any clearly defined area or group which can be considered as constituting a fixed political unit. The social system is maintained by a balance of powers, and by other institutional mechanism. In such cases, therefore, the political boundary—

which is vague and very relative—cannot be used as a decisive criterion in delineating a tribal society.

We next come to the proposition that a tribe as a society has a linguistic boundry. It has to be pointed out that not all societies possess linguistic boundaries. A nation, for example, many including several linguistic groups and, conversely, more than one nation many have a single common language. But in the case of simpler societies it is almost always true that a common mode of speech serve to distinguish one society from another. In fact, the possession of a common dialect is considered by many as a decisive test in demarcating the boundaries of tribal societies.

Finally, we come to the definition of a tribe as collection of individuals sharing a common culture. This definition has been accepted either explicitly or implicitly, by a wide range of anthropologists, Kroeber, for instance writes, "The conception of a culture and of the tribes as its social correlate, coincides very closely with actual anthropological usage as this has developed through general consensus rather than explicit definition.[7]

It hardly needs to be mentioned that the term culture is not used here to refer to any particular sophisticated or ideally desired style of living. It is used in its widest anthropological sense to donate those traditional beliefs, art and practices which an individual acquires as a member of a particular society. Unfortunately, the definition of a tribe in terms of its cultural homogeneity is much more elusive than its definition in terms of the boundaries previously discussed. Field workers throughout the world have realised that no iron wall exists where one culture comes to an end another begins. Commonness of culture is very much a question of degree. It many include in its sway a tribe, a group of tribes, a culture area, or a whole continent, each sharing common culture traits in varying degrees. Clearly, than, the possession of a 'common culture' can hardly be considered as a primary criterion in demarcating the boundary of a tribe, or of any society for that matter.

Summing up what has been said so far, we may state: the tribe is a society having a clear linguistic boundry and generally a well defined political boundary. It is within the latter that 'regular determinate ways of acting' are imposed on its members. The tribe also has a cultural boundary, much less well-defined, and this is the general frame for the formal and informal interactions of these members. This definition agrees fairly well with the usual text-book definition of a tribe.

Now, although the statements made above, tells us a good deal about the characteristics of a tribe, they fall short of an adequate definition for one important reason. They do not tell us anything as to the distinctive feature of a tribe as a specific type of society. Most of what has been said would apply equally well to societies of an entirely different type, for instance, a nation. We must, therefore, isolate certain additional attributes in terms of which a tribe as society may be discriminated from other societies. Anthropologists have paid very little attention in their conventional definitions to features which might be considered as distinctive of tribal societies. Perhaps they appeared too obvious to merit serious attention. Some or most of these features have, however, been discussed from time to time by various people. But very little attempt has been made to systematically analyse them. Quite often, one bears the statement that ribal societies are less advanced, that their arts and crafts are of a primitive type. This, of course, does not take us very far. For it merely begs the question as to what constitutes 'primitive' and what is more advanced. Some people are more specific and say that tribal groups practice totemism, animism, or that they are characterised by the presence of clans. This also is somewhat misleading since none of these attributes is universal among tribal societies or, for that matter, exclusive to them. The same may be said of the ecological characterisation of tribes. It may be true to say that very often the tribes of India live in isolated hills and forests. But in other places and at other times, tribal societies have been known to flourish under all kinds of ecological conditions.

Differences between tribal and more advanced societies are apparent even to the casual observer. It should be difficult to sum up these differences systematically, although in a very broad and general way. Earlier, anthropologists regarded tribes as not merely societies of particular type, but societies representing a particular stage of evolution fell out of fashion. One need not, however, fear to use it, provided sufficient caution is exercised. The advanced societies are then seen to be distinguished from by the presence of certain emergent characters which the latter tribes lack. These emergent characters are, evidently, differentiation and specialisation.

Differentiation and Specialisation both exist in tribal societies, but these have a particular character. To begin with, they are based upon such purely biological factors as age, sex and kinship. The sexual division of labour appears to be inherent in the biological nature of man. Some sort of division of functions according to age would appear to be equally inevitable. In addition to these is the specification of roles according to positions in the kinship structure. Finally, one finds a few instances of functional specialization in terms of particular skills. But these almost always pertain to specific individuals and not to self-perpetuating groups or classes. The most typical examples are the priest and medicine-man.

Of an entirely different nature are the divisions which exist in the more advanced non-tribal societies. One of the most important spheres in which these divisions are apparent is in the relations of production. In all historically known forms of society which have grown beyond the tribal stage, there are divisions into social categories based upon the relations of production. Such categories have the further attribute that they tend to be self-prepetuating. In tribal societies, on the other hand, the relations of production are homogenous. Whatever the mode of production followed, whether hunting, gathering, or primitive agriculture, there is no conspicuous separation of social categories on the basis of their differential position in the system of production. As a corollary to above, it follows that tribal societies are unstratified. It is also easy to understand that the tribal economy is undeveloped, for where specialisation is absent this has to be so. Similarly, tribal economy by its very nature is based on a domestic economy, where producers are themselves the consumers, the role of money does not exist.

In speaking of tribal societies as being unstratified, one's attention is drawn to another characteristic of tribal societies. A tribe has been described as a kinship group that constitutes a society. It is almost proverbial that members of a tribe consider each other to be related by ties of kinship. In Australia, it is said that any member of a tribe could demonstrate his exact kinship relation with any other member. The restriction of kinship ties within the tribal boundary is maintained by the law of endogamy. So strong is the force of kinship that in most cases an outsider can be admitted into the tribe only through the legal fiction of adopting him as kin to some member of it.

Let us pause here and review the definition of tribe that we have attempted to formulate. We have described tribe as a society with a political, linguistic, and somewhat vaguely-defined cultural boundary. Further, as a society based upon kinship, where social stratification is absent. Now, it has to be emphasised that like so many definitions of social categories, this also is the definition of an ideal type. If we make a classification of societies, they will arrange themselves in a continuum. In many of these, stratification and differentiation will be present, but only in an incipient manner The exact point along which one should draw the line between tribal and more advanced societies will, in a sense, have to be arbitrarily decided.

In the case of India today, the situation is even more complicated. Hardly any of the tribes exist as a separate society. They have been absorbed, in varying degrees, into the wider society of India. And this is a future which can hardly be described as new. The process of absorption has been going on for centuries, in fact, since the beginning of history. If we now re-examine our definition, its inadequacies will at once become apparent. No tribe in India today has a completely separate political boundary. In some cases, in the NEFA, for instance, a certain amount of political separateness has been retained within the wider structure. In most cases, even this is absent. The larger tribes of Chhotanagpur, the Santhals and the Oraons, are territorially dispersed. In several instances, the boundaries of different States cut across tribal divisions.

The linguistic boundary has been somewhat move impermeable, but this too, has been steadily breaking down. The Bhils who constitutes one of the largest tribes in India have been using a dialect of Hindi for many years. Several tribes in Middle and South India—speak Dravidian languages which have close affinities with the languages spoken by the advanced communities of South India. The abandonment of tribal dialects in favour of one of the regional languages appears to have been accelerated during the last few decades.

If we examine the second part of definition, it also appears inadequate. We might here leave aside the question of differentiation that had grown up in tribal societies internally, although this too is important. Apart from this, there is the articulation between the tribal economy and the regional or national economy which has been rapidly increasing over the last few decades. Large sections of tribal population have been entering into productive system of the country as such. Again, this is not a new development, although the effect of industrialisation has been to give it a new identity, and even a new character. The result of entering into a complex system of production has been to break down the homogenous nature of tribal society. Distinctions on the basis of wealth have begun to appear. Something in the nature of stratification has been observed in most of the larger tribes of Chhotanagpur and Central India. Again, it has to be emphasized that this is not an entirely new phenomenon.

In today's India, therefore, tribes which answer to the anthropologist's conception of the ideal type are rarely to be found. What we find are tribes in transition. On the other hand, we are committed by the nature of our policy to regard certain communities as tribal. There is no harm in trying to locate such groups provided we are cautious in our approach, and not too pedantic. If there are no 'real' tribes in India, there are many groups which have been tribes in the recent past, and which still approximate to them in several ways. In India, we cannot have a ready made definition with which one can go into the field and locate a tribe. The greatest emphasis has to be placed on an historical perspective. The process by which tribes have been transformed is a historical process. And only by going into the antecedents of a group can we say with any confidence whether or not it should be considered as a tribe.

However, the purest of the tribal groups which have been resisting acculturation or absorption, possess certain features which can be considered as common features if possessed by all the tribal groups. They are as follows:

(i) They live away from the civilised world in the most inaccessible part of both forests and hills.
(ii) They belong either to one of the three stocks—Negritos, Austroloids or Mongoloids.
(iii) They speak the same tribal dialect.
(iv) They profess a primitive religion known as 'Animism' in which the worship of ghosts and spirits is the most important element.
(v) They follow primitive occupations such as gleaming,

hunting and gathering of forest produce.

(vi) They are largely carnivorous or flesh or meat eaters.

(vii) They live either nacked or semi-nacked using tree barks and leaves for clothing.

(viii) They have nomadic habits and a love for drink and dance.[8]

TRIBES IN INDIA

The Constitution of India has defined "Scheduled Tribes" as such tribes or tribal communities or parts of or groups within such tribes or tribal communities as are deemed under Article 342 to be Scheduled Tribes for the purpose of this Constitution. The 212 tribes declared by the President in exercise of the powers conferred by clause (1) of Article 342 of the Constitution of India in the different States of India, constitute 5.36 per cent of the total population of the country in early fifties.

The tribal habitation in India can be demarcated in three tribal zones: North-eastern, Central and Southern. The north-eastern zone consists of sub-Himalayan region and the mountain ranges of north-eastern India. This zone is inhabited by tribes like the Gurung, Limbu, Lepeha, Garo, Khasi, Naga and others. The Central zone consists of the plateaus and mountainous belts between the Indo-Gangetic Basin to the north and Krishna river in the south. The main tribes found in this zone are the Santhal, Munda, Oraon, Ho, Bhil, etc. The southern zone consists of the peninsular India, south of the river Krishna. Tribes like Chanchu. Kota, Toda, Malayam, etc., inhabit in this zone.

The tribes sometimes called aboriginals because of their being the earliest inhabitants of this country, not only belong to different stages of culture, but they vary from area to area in regard to size of the population language, racial types, socio-economic organisation, etc.

The largest concentration of tribal people anywhere in the world except perhaps Africa, is in India and it is interesting to note that there are six hundred and thirteen tribes inhabited all over India. There are as many as thirty tribes only in Bihar, but among them four tribes can be treated to be significant; Munda, Oraon, Santhal and Ho. An alphabetical list of the tribes of Bihar, is as follows:

An Alphabetical List of the Scheduled Tribes of Bihar.

1. Asur	16. Kheria
2. Baiga	17. Kharwar
3. Banjara	18. Khona
4. Bathudi	19. Kisan
5. Bedia	20. Kara
6. Bhumej	21. Karwa
7. Binjhia	22. Lohara, Lohra
8. Birhor	23. Mahli
9. Birjia	24. Mal Paharia
10. Chero	25. Munda
11. Chik Baraik	26. Oraon
12. Gond	27. Parhaiya
13. Gorait	28. Santhal
14. Ho	29. Sauria Paharia
15. Karmali	30. Savar

Source: Scheduled Tribes and Scheduled Area in India, Government of India, 1978, p. 6.

In Table 1.1, we have tried to arrange the State-wise figures of tribal population in India from different sources. In this table when we look at the figures of tribal population in India as a whole we find that the number of tribal people in India in 1951 was 2,25,11,854 and it was 3,01,72,221 in 1961. The growth in tribal population was 76,60,367. The percentage of growth was 32.23 percent. But in the following decade i.e., 1961-71, the growth in tribal population was 78,94,997 and the percentage of growth was 26.17 percent. This fact obviously reveals that there is a decreasing trend in the growth rate of tribal population in India which is chiefly concerned to the economic conditions of the tribal people.

The impact of migration and resettlement on the growth rate of the States like Himachal Pradesh, Karnataka, Tamil Nadu, Tripura, Nagaland and Lakshadweep during 1951-61 is almost obvious. A large scale migration of the tribal people from one State to the other seems to have occurred as a result of distress, growing poverty and allied factors (the so-called such factors). It might have also occurred on account of better opportunities in other States and abroad (the so-called pull factors). But the decreasing

TABLE 1.1

Tribal Population in India

Sl. No.	State/U.T.	1951	1961	%age of growth 1951-61	1971	%age of growth 1961-71	1981	%age of growth 1971-81
1	2	3	4	5	6	7	8	9
1.	Andhra Pradesh	1149919	1324368	15.17	1657657	25.17		
2.	Assam	1554801	2064816	32.80	1606648	—22.19		
3.	Bihar	3880097	4204784	8.37	4932767	17.31	5810867	17.80
4.	Gujarat	2092556	2754446	31.63	3734422	35.58		
5.	Himachal Pradesh	27925	108194	287.40	141610	30.89		
6.	Karnataka	80402	192096	138.92	231268	20.39		
7.	Kerala	132767	212762	57.89	269356	26.60		
8.	Madhya Pradesh	4844128	6678410	37.87	8387403	25.59		
9.	Maharashtra	1650852	2397169	45.21	2954249	23.27		
10.	Manipur	194239	249049	28.22	334466	34.30		
11.	Meghalaya	NA	NA	—	814230	—		
12.	Nagaland	2633	343697	66.33	457602	33.14		
13.	Orissa	3009580	4223757	40.34	5071937	20.08		
14.	Rajasthan	1774278	2351470	30.16	3125506	32.92		
15.	Sikkim	NA	NA	—	52056			
16.	Tamli Nadu	136376	251991	84.78	311515	23.62		
17.	Tripura	192293	360070	87.25	450544	25.13		

(Contd.)

TABLE 1.1 (*Contd.*)

1	*2*	*3*	*4*	*5*	*6*	*7*	*8*	*9*
18.	Uttar Pradesh	NA	NA	—	198565			
19.	West Bengal	1566868	2054081	31.00	2532969	23.31		
20.	Andaman & Nicobar	NA	14122	—	18102	—		
21.	Arunachal Pradesh	NA	NA	—	369408	—		
22.	Dadar & Nagar Haveli	NA	51269	—	64445	25.70		
23.	Goa, Daman & Diu	NA	NA	—	7654	—		
24.	Lakshadweep etc.	13486	23391	73.45	29540	26.29		
25.	Mizoram	NA	NA	—	313299	—		
	India	2511854	30172221	32.23	38067218	26.17		

Sources: (i) A Statistical Hand Book of Tribal Welfare and Development, (ii) Tribal Sub-Plan Area, and (iii) Census of India, 1981, Series 4, Bihar, Paper of 1982.

trend in general population of the Indian tribes is, certainly surprising which draws the attention of the population experts, planners and policy-makers. The growth rate of the tribal people of Bihar during the years 1961-71 and 1971-81 is 17.31 and 17.80 per cent respectively. It apparently discloses the fact that our endeavours in the field of tribal development was not satisfactory.

TRIBAL WAY OF LIVING

Many tribes, very often, live by hunting, fishing or gathering But they do not depend upon these exclusively for satisfying their needs. The aboriginal inhabitants of the Andaman Islands, however, depend upon these entirly for their livelihood. They have no trade relation with others; and are much isolated from one another that the Onge of little Andaman do not understand the language of the Jarawas of the great Andaman or of the inhabitants of the North Sentinel Island, all of which are close by. Each of these groups satisfies all its needs completely with the help of local resources and exercises considerable ingenuity in maintaining themselves on these island although technologically they are very poorly equipped.

The Andamanese fish very little with nets. They use bows and arrows and spears for the purpose. There are coral reefs round some of the island where the water is shallow and crystal clear, it is easy to spot the fish and turtles from their canoes in shallow water, while turtles' eggs can be collected easily from the beaches of a few of the lonely island. Shell-fish of various kinds and crabs are also gathered for food. But it is interesting that so far as the Onge are concerned, they do not shoot birds for meat, although the bird population is not small. It has been suggested that they do not do so for fear of losing their arrow in the thick vegetation which cover the island.

The food which the Andamanese eat by simple boiling is never enriched by salt. If meat cooked with salt is offered to them they reject it forth-with. Honey is one of their favourite foods and from January to March. They spend long time in gathering honey from hives. There is some kind of leaf, called tongee. The juice of which is mixed with saliva and besmeared over the body. This prevent the bees from stinging men who come to loot their hives.

In the midst of warm, rain drenched forests of Tripura,

Manipur, Nagaland, Mizo district and NEFA, there live a number of tribal communities who depend principally upon a rather simple form of cultivation. The same method is also applied in vogue among some of the tribes of Orissa and Madhya Pradesh, while, outside India, it is practiced in northern Burma, Sumatra, Borneo and New Guinea, as well as in parts of African continent.

In areas where it is practised in India, a village community control a certain measure of land, consisting of mountains and valleys, and puts a small parts of it every year under cultivation. Ploughs and cattle are not employed, but axes or bill-hooks and digging sticks are the only implements used for the purpose. After winter, a portion of the hill-side or jungle is first marked off for cultivation. It is cleared by lopping off the undergrowth and branches of trees, which are allowed to dry in the sun for some time. Shortly before the rains set in, the dry leaves and bushes are set on fire. Farmers take care that the fire does not spread into the forest. When the fire dies down, the ashes are lightly spread over the ground where necessary. The fire kills the weeds and insects, and the ashes fertilise the ground. Then the farmer walks over the field with a digging stick or bill-hook in hand, makes a hole in the ground, sows a few seeds and covers it over with earth by pressing it down with his toes. As the rains come, the seeds begin to sprout and the harvest is gathered as each crop ripens.

In Nagaland or NEFA, the land may, thus, be used for only one season or two, while in more crowded places like Orissa, it may be used three seasons and then left for a number of years to recuperate. The period of recovery may vary from three or four to ten years; it all depends upon the needs of the farmer and the pressure of population in the locality.

This process of shifting the area of cultivation has many names. In Assam, it is known as Jhum or Jum; in Orissa as Podu, dahi or Kamana: penda in Madhya Pradesh and so on. Those who practice this form of cultivation do not themselves move from place to place to form new settlement. What they do is, every family goes on adding a fresh patch of forest every year, while a patch which has been used several times is left free to recuperate. The villages themselves remain in the same place, generation after generation.

Shifting cultivation of the tribal people in India has become tied up with the economy of the market, i.e., with the requirement of the peasant population, of both tribal and non-tribal origin, which live nearby and which pays for goods and services in cash. Unlike the hunting and gathering of the Andamans, it has become ancillary to a larger peasant economy and lost its independent status. Yet, wherever possible, the tribal communities continue to practice it for many of the hill sides, this is, more or less, the only practicable method of land utilisation. When we consider the thin population of the area for which it is not possible to convert the hill slopes into terraced field for growing wetland paddy.

The process of slow and continuous contact between the tribal communities, who practised a comparatively simple form of production, with peasants and artisans with greater specialisation must have gone on for centuries. There is no doubt that the chief attraction for the tribes, when their system began to fail them, as in the case of the Juangs in Orissa,[9] was greater promise of food which the more advanced method held.

Among the Apatani tribes in NEFA, fields have been terraced and igneniously irrigated by diverting bills streams. But the Apatani, like the Newar of Nepal, use only the hoe and no plough or animals for cultivation. In the mountanous regions of Himachal Pradesh terraced farming is carried on with plough and bullocks. In some of these areas, there are no specialised castes of artisans; in others such castes are present.

Although such basic information is not available, we know from our specific knowledge about such tribes as the Juangs of Orissa, or the Gonds of Madhya Pradesh or the Santhals of Bihar and Bengal, how the majority of them have eventually come within the orbit of the present civilisation of the Hindus; and how also they have finally come to be largely classified under the categories of cultivators, agricultural labourers and workers in certain other primary types of occupation.

In the census of 1961, 11.59 per cent among the workers belonging to the Scheduled Tribes were classified as 'cultivators' who owned some land, 10.58 per cent were 'Agricultural labourers' who owned land; while 11.08 per cent were engaged in the primary occupation of mining, quarring, forestry, gardening, fishing, hunting, rearing of livestocks, etc. The Santhal of Bihar, Orissa and Bengal, the Mundas and Oraons of Bihar and the Gonds of Central India have, thus, largely given up their attachment to more primitive forms of production and taken to work which affiliated them with the more prosperous communities living in the neighbourhood. These tribes are thus, no longer self-contained, as primitive Andamanese fishing and gathering people happen to be.

SOCIAL INSTITUTIONS

Men do not live alone; and in order to meet their needs of food and shelter, companionship and love, recreation and play, they form into associations, build institutions through which such needs and satisfied.

The first institution which one should name is of course, the family. It is present among all people in the world. Family is formed through marriage; and each tribe or community has its own rules regarding the choice of mates. There are rules of preference and of avoidance. Whom to marry and whom not to marry. And the rules vary from one tribe to another in a wide variety of ways. There are, however, a number of special or exceptional examples which may be described on account of their uniqueness.

As a rule, most families consists of husband, wife and children. But among some tribes in the Himalayas, one wife may have several husbands. The same custom was prevalent among the Todas of the Nilgiri in Tamil Nadu. Their shortage of women was formerly due to the customs of female infanticide. That custom no longer exists there and the original practice of some men having a common wife is reported to have been replaced by some men having more than one wife in common. This does not imply, however, that sexual relations are promiscuous. Actually, strict rules are observed by parties concerned; and when a child is born, its paternity is established by means of social ceremony instead of on biological considerations.

The reason why such an extraordinary example of marital relationship has been described is for the purpose of emphasizing the fact that the code of sexual conduct which one community believes to be natural may be very different from that of another, which may consider its custom to be the most natural one instead. All codes of moral or approved behaviour are man-made i.e., artificial. And one of benefits which one derives from a study of the lives of people other than one's own, is this prejudices are loosened and one begins to realise that there are hardly any accepted codes of behaviour which are common to all people in the world. The tribal folk of Chhotanagpur, Orissa, Madhya Pradesh and Assam share a certain institution unrelated to the family, but which has a great bearing upon the sexual life of tribes like the Oraon, Juang, Maria, Gond, Naga and the like. These tribes have an organisation of the youth of the village where they club together, and have certain rights and duties in relation to the rest of the community. Among some tribes there are two dormitories, one for boys and another for girls; while among the Oraons, for example, there is only one for boys.

The youth's dormitory serves several purpose in the village. The hut in which it is housed may serve to accommodate guests, while the old and the young frequently meet there for gossip and recreation. Riddles are often exchanged while the ancient lore of the tribe may also be passed on from one generation to another in the evenings. The dormitory, thus, serves as informal kind of school. But it is chiefly used by the boys and sometimes also by the girls to seek one another's company in singing, dancing, and love-making. Pre-marital sexual intimacy is not forbidden among quite a few tribes provided the rules of avoidance in the choice of mates are not transgressed. Young men and women thus, grow up without many of the inhibitions and repressions to which sophisticated communities are generally subject. This is perhaps the reasons why most tribal communities in India have been able to preserve their joy of life, in spite of the appalling poverty from which some of them suffer.

One interesting point may be referred to here. Small tribal communities have often come under the influence of their more powerful Hindu neighbours. This sets up a desire among them to fall in step with the practices of the latter. As a result, some of them have already given up a few of their customs and taken to the imitation of Brahminical people. Some are now ashamed of admitting the existence of their youth's dormitories, and some have even given up the beautiful dances of their men and women because the superior Hindus look askance at them on that account.

There are a few more elements in the family life of tribal communities to which attention should be drawn. Young men and women may choose their own mates; but this can also be the responsibility of parents. When a bride is selected, a compensation has to be paid to her parents, as they are on the point of losing a working hand in the family. Among a few tribes, the so-called 'bride price' may be high and may entail an amount of hard labour before one can accumulate the necessary funds. There are three ways in which the difficulty can be overcome. The bridegroom may elope with his chosen bride, in the hope of securing the approval of the elders concerned later on. Or, he may serve in the house of his prospective father-in-law as a labourer, and thus, in the course of a few years, earn his right to the hand of the daughter. Another possibility is the arrangement of two marriages simultaneously when the sister of the bridegroom is married to the brother of the bride. In such cases, the dues may be largely written off against each other.

Marriages can be of long or of short duration. Divorce or separation is not uncommon marriages of widows and of divorced men and women may be quite frequent. So, the partnership of men and women in a family is of a looser nature than in an orthodox Hindu home. Yet there is no reason to believe that the emotional relationship between husband and wife in any tribal society suffers in quality on that account.

Next to the family comes the clan. The clan is composed of a number of families, often bearing a common designation and which believe that they have all sprung from a common ancestor. Marriage is usually forbidden with a clan. Among some tribes, a custom is to regard certain others as Bandhu or friendly or related clans; and no marriage takes place between the two. There are other clans from which spouses are chosen according to prescribed rules. When a clan is described as a friendly or related clan, something like the rules of incest which are applicable in the cases of the family is, thus, extended to a larger unit of organization.

Clan organization has much to do with marriage but it also ensures co-operation between members when economic assistance is needed, or when a death takes place in the house. Among the Jung of the highlands of Kemjbar in Orissa who practice shifting cultivation, villages are usually inhabited by members of a single clan. But when they adopt the more advanced technique of plough cultivation, change naturally begins to take place.

The Munda tribe of Chhotanagpur had a simple kind of political organization of its own. Two officers—one secular and the other religious, looked after the affairs of the village. There was, moreover, a bigger chief the Manki, whose jurisdiction extended over a larger territory, and to whom the village chief was subordinate. This arrangement survived for sometime even after the land came under British rule; and then the power of these chiefs became considerably reduced.

It is believed that the Bhumis of the neighbouring districts of Manbhum were originally of Munda affiliation. When in the past they came fully under the economic influence of their Hindu neighbours, the upper class among the Bhumej formed place in Hindu society as Kshatriyas. They claimed royal decent and married among neighbouring royal families. In a similar manner, it has been reported by anthropoligists from several parts of eastern and middle India that sections of tribal people thus branched off and political do dominance over their compatriots, and this by following the model set by Hindu society. The growth in members and an accentuated contact at many levels with a politically better organized community thus led to developments in tribal society, different from those which bad been found sufficient when numbers were small, and distinctions into classes on account of differences in wealth and power were of a feeble nature.

CULTURAL ASPECTS OF TRIBAL LIFE

The tribal population in India belongs to various stages of cultural development. Dr. Elwin divides the tribes into four classes according to their stages of cultural development. The purest of tribal groups comprising about two or three millions have been placed in the first class. These Highlanders do not merely exist like so many villagers, they really live. Their religion is characteristic and alive, their tribal organisation is unimpaired, their artistic and choreographic traditions are unbroken, their mythology still vitalizes the healthy organisation of tribal life. Geographical considerations have largely protected them for the debasing contact of the plains.[10]

The second category of tribes, according to Elwin's classification has been experiencing contact with the plains and consequently has been undergoing change. This group, though retaining their tribal mode of living exhibits the following characteristics in contract to the first group: (i) instead of communal life, this group live a village life which has become individualistic. Their communal life and traditions, are only preserved through their village dormitories; (ii) in contrast to the Class I Tribe, the members of those Class II do not share things with one another; (iii) axe cultivation has ceased to be a way of life for them; (iv) the members of these tribes are more contaminated by the life outside. They come in contact with the groups living on the periphery, who live a more complex, viz., civilized life; and (v) the members of these tribes are less simple and less honest than the members of the tribes belonging to Class I.[11]

The tribes who belong to the third category constitute the largest section of the total tribal population, about four-fifth of it. Members of this class of tribal groups are in a peculiar state of transition. According to some investigations, they are tribal in name but have become 'backward Hindus' constituting a sizeable section of the lower rung of Hindu society; one section is described as Christian. These tribes have been appreciably affected by external contacts. They have been exposed to the influences of economic and socio-cultural forces of Hindu society. They have been also subjected to missionary influences.

The tribals of fourth category according to Elwin consist of the old aristocracy of the country represented today by great Bhil and Naga chieftains, the Gond Rajas, a few Binshevar and Bhuyia landlords, Karku nobleman, wealthy Santhal and Uraon and some highly cultured Mundas. They retain the old tribal names and their clan and totem rules and observe elements of tribal religion though they generally adopt the full Hindu faith and live in modern and even European style.[12] According to Elwin, tribal of this class have won the battle of culture contacts. It means that they have acquired aristocratic traditions, economic stability, affluence, outside encouragement, a certain arrogance and self-confidence characteristics alike of ancient families and modern enterprise.[13]

Though tribal culture differs from tribe to tribe. The Sauria Paharia observe many a ritual which mark important stages in the Agricultural clander. During the latter half of the months of the Bhado (August-September), on getting the maize crop from the field villagers worship in the 'Jaher-than'. The whole village contributes for a he-goat and one or two chickens. These are sacrified to the village deities by the 'Kotwar'. Only after observing this ritual can they eat maize. It is similar to 'Nabanna' observed by Hindus after harvest of Aghani paddy, the main crop like maize of Sauria Paharia. The most important annual worship of the Suria Paharia is the 'Sailani Puja' in honour of 'Kando Gosain' in the month of 'Magh' (December-January-February) or 'Chait' (March-April). The god is taken out from his abode and sacrifices are offered to him. It is also similar to 'Debothan' in Hindus. Every sixth year, the villagers offer a buffalo to this deity, the ritual being known as 'Karra Puja'.

Festivals connected with hunting are observed among the Hill Kharia and the Oraon. The 'Phagun' or the spring festival among the Hill Kharia consists of two parts; one is the ceremonial hunting expedition and the other is the ceremonial consecration of the first fruits, the first flowers and the edible leaves and other products of the season. Before the performance of this ceremony, no fruits of the new season my be eaten. All the adults male population of a Hill Kharia settlement join in a ceremonial hunting expedition under the leadership of the Dehuri. In the evening, when the party returns, the hunters are entertained to a feast cooked by women. The game is divided between different Kharia families of the settlement in proportion to the number of members in each family and the whole night is spent in singing, dancing and merry-making. The morning following, the Dehuri and the villagers worship at the seat of the village deity. The expenses of the worship and the sacrifices are met by contributions made by the entire village community.

Each of the Chhotanagpur tribes has a series of festivals. For the Oraon the first festival is 'Sarhul' which is celebrated in the month of 'Chait' (March-April). It is the festival of the spring and is celebrated at the time when the Sal tree blossoms. Until the celebration of this rite, no Oraon of the village may gather, or eat or use the new fruits, flowers and edible leaves of the seasons. The 'Sarhul' festival is so important that its date is fixed by the Village Panchayat and its ceremonies extend over several days. All the villagers take part and go in procession to the sacred grove of the village where the village deities are worshipped. The 'Pahan' and his assistant officiate at the rites and the leader of the youths dormitory has important duties to perform on this occasion. The expenses of such communal festivals are large but all the villagers contribute in cash and kind. Singing and dancing continue at the village Akhra for several days.

The next important festival is the 'Karma' which is celebrated by tribals and non-tribal with equal enthusiasm in the month of September. A branch of 'Karam' tree is planted in the Akhra and offerings are made to it. The day as well as the preceding night are spent in fasting but in the evening every one meets at the 'Akhra' and spends the night in dancing and singing round the 'Karam' sapling brought from nearby jungle. The story of the two brothers Karam and Dharam is recited by the 'Pahan'. People in the village on this occasion, give themselves up completely to merry-making.

The Santhal and the Kharia hold village festivals on the occasion of the sowing of rice. The Hindus have similar festival for first transplantation of paddy seedlings by the head of the family. The Ho also publicly worship the village deity Dessauli and his consort before sowing rice. The Oraon and the Santhal observe the Hariari or festival of green rice plants in the month of Asarh (July) after the rice, millet and cotton seeds have been sown in the field. There can be no transplantation of seedlings, till this ceremony has been performed. The village elders fix a day for its celebration and fowls for sacrifice are collected from the villagers. On the day of Hariari festival, the Pahan and his assistant offer sacrifices and make offerings to the village deities on behalf of the village community.

The Kadleta or Kadlota festival is celebrated by the Munda in Asarh (July), just before the transplantation of rice seedings and on this occasion sacrifices are offered to the village deities in the sacred grove in the presence of the assembled villagers. Among the Oraon this festival is celebrated one month later.

The Kharihan Puja is celebrated among the Munda, Oraon and Kharia just after the harvest. This ceremony is intended toward off the evil eye from heaps of harvested grain. The ritual is performed by village priest on behalf of the village community.

The chief festival of the Santhai called 'Soharal' is celebrated after the rice harvesting in December-January. This festival lasts for five days and the ritual includes the sacrifice of fowls to the village deities by the Naek. The gods of the cattle-shed are also worshipped at this village festival and so are the ancestral spirits During the five days of the 'Soharai' festival, the Santhal indulge in a veritable Saturnalia, giving themselves up to dancing, eating, drinking, singing and sexual license.

Among the Ho, the chief festival is the 'Maghe Parab'. It is celebrated in December-January and also extended for five days. The Deuri performs all the rituals. All the offerings are sacrificial. Animals are contributed by the villagers. Each Ho village fixes a different date for the celebration of 'Maghe Parab' so that guests from other village may arrive. This festival, which is an occasion for dancing and singing provides opportunities for youngmen and women of different villages to come together and seek amorous adventures. Older writers like Dalton have written of the licentiousness and debauchery indulged in during this festival, but the picture they have drawn is exaggerated.

In some villages influenced by Hindu contact some Hindu festivals are also celebrated with great eclat. Somewhere the 'Phagu' festival coincides with the 'Holi' festival of the Hindus. Besides the Hindus of the village, the tribals sprinkle coloured water over their friends and neighbours. In the evening a gola dance is organised in the Akhra in which persons of different communities participate, some as dancers and others as spectators. Similarly, 'Dasahra' festival is celebrated by all the communities. Recently the Munda have come to join the *Ramanavmi* festival. On this occasion the 'Mahabiri Jhanda' is taken out in a procession.

Thus, we see that all the people in a tribal village combine for the performance of rites and for the worship of their gods on village basis. Only the village with its hierarchy of secular and sacredotal functionaries provides a framework for enactment of the great seasonal rites and times of danger and stress for the propitiation of gods and spirits and the protection of its inmates.

More than the tribe as a whole or even the exogamous clan, the village is animated by a spirit of ready co-operation in the service of the gods and it is through such constant co-operation that it assumes a certain mystic unity. Most of the deities worshipped during the seasonal rites are the gods of the village territory rather than gods of its individual inhabitants and it is probably on account of this that they can be worshipped through the traditional machinery operated by hereditary priests and headman, who again act not in their individual capacity but as representative of the village community.

The tribal concept of pleasure—their pre-occupation with

pleasure activities such as singing, dancing, drinking, story telling, etc., realized through cycles of festivals and their happy-go-lucky spontaneous nature sharply contrast than their non-tribal counterparts. Many anthropologists have praised them for their commitment to such persuits of pleasure. Archer is full of praises for the Santhal when he states "free from sickness, the Santhals have poise, buoyancy and a quite extraordinary zest for life. An air of exhilaration surrounds all that they do."[14] But some have wrongly equated the tribal concept of pleasure with hedonism which is obvious from man's comment on the Santhal. "They seem to carry out to the full the principle to eat, drink and be merry and care not for the morrow."[15] But tribal concept of pleasure is an invaluable possession of tribals. It is responsible for their optimistic nature, extraordinary zest for life and their freedom from psychosis and neurosis. It constitutes their main source of strength which serves as a cushion to absorb the suffering and frustration arising from poverty and exploitation.

Most of the tribals in India have rich tradition of oral literature. Many of the songs of tribal communities of India as well as their folk-tales have been published by anthropologists. Sarat Chandra Roy, who was one of the earliest among them presented a number of Mundari songs, along with their English translations, in his book entitled, "The Mundas and their Country" in 1912. The recent translations and transcreations of their poems by some great poets and scholars have brought to general notice their great aesthetic and literary values. Some of these poems are at par with the poems of some of the greatest poets of the world. Their folktales and their myths of creation have also been praised all over the world. Frazer, for instance, praised the Santhal myths of creation as it combines the principles of creation and evolution and found in it the confirmation of his thesis.

RELIGIOUS ASPECTS OF TRIBAL LIFE

Tribal religion in India seems to have a common feature, that all beings are endowed with a living spirit. Animals, plants, rivers, mountains are no exception to this rule. The dead who have apparently left us are yet with us, and it is through remembrance of offering that we have to renew our relationship with them on due occasions. The dead are again reborn in the shape of offsprings in the present generation. The span of mans' comradeship is thus, extended to encompass all that he sees around him, as well as those whom he loved and has apparently lost. All these are common with Hindu religion.

What is significant in the tribal religions or 'animistic' beliefs of our brethren, the Mundas, the Oreons or the Santhals, is that the whole world, peoples by spirits thus, rendered holy. In the forests where some of the more isolated communities live, a few trees are never touched or cut, for they represent the primal grove. Pipal tree is also considered sacred and abode of Basudeo, a Hindu god. It is never cut down. They are symbolic of the whole forest which men, under the pressure of needs, have had to cut down. The mountains are holy; and there are reeks of extraordinary shape or even colours, which are taken as proofs of their sacredness.

If the spirits dwell everywhere and is all are at peace with them, men enjoy freedom from illness and a long life. If anyone falls ill, the general belief is that some relationship has been violated, when, by means of trances or particular magical ceremonies men or women skilled in the art decide what should be done by sufferers. And when this is done, health is once more believed to be restored.

Among more sophisticated communities, certain places, probably enclosed by a well and covered by a roof, are marked off as specially sacred. But among the 'animistic' tribals of India, all places are holy as they are the seats of spirits. Some have accused the so-called animists of living in perpetual fear of ghosts and spirits. But there does not seem to be any particular justification for this. All men have their hopes and fears, and to single out a few elements of tribal religions and say that the latter are born only of fear is doing grave injustice to them.

A faith which establishes man's kinship with all that he sees around him, a faith which releases some of the creative forces within him, which burst forth in simple, loving ceremonies or occasionally in beautiful, lyrical poems or songs, or in art which is direct, and not trammelled by sophistication, can hardly be accused of being barren and destructive in its influence upon the human spirit.

There is one thing which has happened to tribal folk after their contact with men of other faiths. It is true that these tribes are poor, devoid of formal education, and oppressed by fears which arise out of lack of modern knowledge. But in this respect they suffer from disabilities similar to those which the poorer classes among the non-tribal people are also subject. Christian missionaries have worked these for more than a century. Firstly, because they offer a more fertile field for developing a truly religious life than nominally Christian and poverty-striken classes in the countries from which the missionaries themselves come. For many missionaries, work in their home country is less rewarding than work among the simpler and more responsive inhabitants of tribal India.

Christianity has undoubtedly brought the message of a richer life, wider companionship and a new sense of dignity to converts. But it is interesting that the Christian religion has always been attended by the benefits of modern western civilization. And this was particularly so during the period of British rule when the converts felt closer to the British rulers than to their benighted country-men. The western way of life spread among those who could afford to do so, while education, improved habits of living and reliance upon modern medicine got introduced wherever Christianity was able to enter. Yet it might be worthwhile asking the question whether Christianity and westernization in India were necessarily identical with each other. Perhaps they are not. For there can be Christian religion which does not necessarily draw men and women away from their own civilization. Yet, up-till-now, the principal agent of westernization, often regarded as modernization, among the tribal folk has been Christian missionary enterprise. It is only after independence that Christianity has been swinging round to a point of view when allegiance to one's native culture is being encouraged.

Obviously, a relation of tribal folk to Hinduism or Christianity has been quite different. For, at least Hinduism has not been a proselytizing religion. The indigenous population of India is supposed to have contributed in the past generously to the building up of what is known as Hinduism. The tribes retained the principal elements of their faith and practice, though these were modified to a greater or less extent. In addition, they shared some of gods and goddesses, and even participated in the social festivals and ceremonies of their Brahminical neighbours, without any effort on the part of the latter for convertion. That participation did not turn them into Hindus. One might indeed say that tribes can be regarded as being fully absorbed in the Hindu-fold if Brahmin priests perform Brahminical ceremonies for them during the three critical events of birth, marriage and death. If the latter are still celebrated by tribal rituals, then the communities are still true to their own faith in spite of the fact that, in outer fringes of their culture, they participate in some of the ceremonies of their Hindu neighbours.

A parallel might be drawn from the example of relationship between Hindus and Muslims in India in the past. Even now there are a large number of shrines dedicated to Muslims saints in Bihar, Uttar Pradesh, Delhi and Rajasthan where both Hindu and Muslim devotees offer worship without any detriment to their religious affiliations. In the past and not so very long ago, Muslims used to join in the celebration of the spring festival called 'Holi'. And, Hindus in similar manner used to play prominent part in the performance of the Muharram by carrying the 'Tazia' or by an exhibition of their skill in play with 'lathi' or quarter-staff. Such participation was largely in common festivals, i.e., on a social plane, and did not mean that one community had adopted the faith of another.

The relationship of many tribal communities to either Hinduism or Buddhism is of this nature unless they have been very deeply drawn into the Hindu social system. In Kinnaur in Himachal Pradesh, or the Mompas of Kaneng in Arunachal, many of the Scheduled Tribes, i.e., those who have been listed special treatment under the Constitution, have thus, come very close to either Hinduism or Buddhism or to both. Yet they have retained a custom like polyandry which marks them off from the rest of their neighbours.

After independence, when tribes, listed in a scheduled under the Constitution, have gained access to certain statutory benefits, a new movement has started among even the westernized converts to Christianity to re-discover and re-affirm their tribal identity and separateness from those who are not included in the schedule. There is nothing wrong in such endeavour. But while describing the religions of the tribal communities in India, we have to indicate not only the character of their indigenous faiths and practices, but also the many-sided changes to which they have been subject through the contact and influence of their more prosperous neighbours. Sometimes they have been attracted towards westernism through the devoted help of western missionaries. And now a new trend has begun among them of new unification between Christian and non-Christian or 'animist', so that their 'tribal' identity may be re-affirmed, and in the process a salvage takes place of as much of their tribal culture and religious faith is consistant with the demands of modern life.

CIVIC ASPECTS OF TRIBAL LIFE

Among all tribes of India, especially Bihar, the village is a well defined political and administrative unit. The unity and solidarity of the village emerge most clearly in relation to government. Whether it is a large permanent settlement among the Santhal, Munda, Oraon, or Ho or a small frequently shifted settlement as among the Hill Kharia or Suria Paharia, it is governed by an administrative mechanism which not only regulates life within the village, but orders the villagers' relations with the world outside.

This mechanism functions through its officers who are known by different designations among the various tribes under review. In the simpler societies the ordering of the social, political and ritual relations of the village are in the hands of one man. But in the more complex societies, we find a differentiation of function and authority vested in two headmen each with its own field of interest and prescribed duties. A primary differentiation of function splits village affairs into secular and sacredotal spheres of activity with a headman responsible for each and among some tribes, differentiation is further emphasized by the assistants to help each headman in the discharge of his duties.

In Hill Kharia villages, there is only one village headman who combines in his person the social as well as religious leadership of the village. He maintains peace and order within his settlement. Unlike among other tribes his position has not been recognised by Government. He is also the priest in whose hands rests the maintenance of harmonious relations with supernatural powers. His position and functions will be dealt with at the appropriate place.

Earlier authorities on the Suria Paharia mention four officers viz., the Sinyare (Headman), Bandari (Messenger), Kotware

(Incharge of arrangements for the Punch) and Giri (the most influential ryot).[16] Now-a-days we find only the headman called the Manjhi. He is responsible for all secular affairs. The Manjhi is generally elected by the villagers and is often the most influential man of the village. The Manjhi is responsible to the divisional headman called the Sardar.

Among the Oraon and the Munda, the differentiation of functions is more pronounced that among the Sauria Paharia. The secular headman known among the Oraon, as *Mahto* and among the Munda as 'Munda'. Previously the religious headman or the Pahan was the head of the village and performed both secular and religious duties. His assistant was the 'Mahato' among the Oraon and 'Munda' among the Munda.

In most Oraon villages, the *Mahto* is elected once every three years by villagers assembled at the Akhara. The *Mahto* is the representative of the village. In some villages, the post of the *Mahto* is hereditory. Everywere the *Mahto* enjoys rent free service land during the tenure of his office. The *Mahto* settles all disputes over the amount of rent due to the landlord. Formerly, the Pahan as the representative of the village community could together with the *Mahto* settled all uncultivated vacant land within the village border of which the village community was the joint owner. But now-a-days such settlements are made by Government Revenue Officials and the *Mahto* or his agent has no right to settle such lands.

All that has been said for the Oraon village headman holds true more or less of the village headman of the Munda. The Ho headman is known as the Munda and the office is generally hereditary but if a Munda is dismissed his heir loses his right of succession and a new Munda is selected. The Munda weilds great influence in the social life of the village. All disputes other than those relating to worship and the tribal group as a unit are heard by him. With the assistance of clan elders, he decides the dates for village festivals. He attends marriage parleys and advises villagers on their duties and rights. If the village is a single-clan village, the importance of the Munda is considerable, but in multi-clan village, he must exercise great caution and tact in securing the smooth working of the village machinery.

Among the Santhal, as among the other tribes, headmanship is an indigenous institution. The Santhal headman is known as

Manjhi. The Manjhi is the head of the village people. All the people will have to follow his lead. In ordering and inviting, in calling and restraining, at the name giving, at the initiating festivals, at marriages, when hunting and chasing, at feast and festivals, at religious instruction and worship, in connection with rice and curry, with bear and liquor, with spirits and mountain spirits, in quarrelling and squabbling, in strife and dispute, when there is hunger and thirst, with landlords and money lenders, when crime and misdeeds occur, in connection with theft and stealing, with medicine and witchcraft, with wenches and strumpets, when there is a fighting and killing, murder and wickedness, in grief and sorrow, in calmities and danger, in illness and pain, at dying and falling away, in ceremonies connected with death and disease, at cremation and at final funeral ceremonies, in connection with all this the Manjhi has responsibility.[17]

Traditionally the Manjhi is elected by the entire village community. He is the representative of the village in both internal and external matters. Sometimes the officially recognised Manjhi is a non-Santhal and then villagers elect an official called Handi-Manjhi who is responsible for social matters in the village life while official duties are left to the Government nominee. The Manjhi is considered so important that in certain villages deceased Manjhis are worshiped at a shrine called Manjhithan.

In local usage the headman is variously known as Manjhi, Pradhan or Mustagir, but these terms are now used synonymously. The appointment of the Manjhi now lies with the Deputy Commissioner, who must satisfy himself that his nominee will be acceptable to the villagers.

The first and foremost duty of the Manjhi is the collection and punctual payment of the village revenue to the Government. The duty of keeping irrigation works in repair, maintaining village roads, boundary marks, camping and grazing grounds in the joint responsibility of the Manjhi and the villagers.

The Santhal Manjhi has two assistants. The principal assistants, the Parmanik is chosen by the Manjhi himself. If the Manjhi dies without any male issue or brother, the Parmanik may succeed him. The second assistant is the Jog-Manjhi. His duties lie in the social sphere. He is the guardian of tribal morality; and is held responsible or clan incest of the sexual union of a Santhal with a non-Santhal. in addition to Parmanik and Jog-Manjhi, there is a 'Gorait' who is the village messenger of the Santhal. He summons the villagers at the call of the Manjhi.

Thus we see that the different tribes with their villages of varying size and character are administered by a number of officers each with clearly prescribed duties. The corporate unity of the tribal village is maintained and strengthened by the existance of village officers who not only organize village affairs on a community basis and assist Government in the collection of revenue and in the maintenance of law and order at the village level, but also acts as a liaison between the authorities and the people in the village. Tribal custom has endowed these functionaries with influence and authority and even where they have not been grafted on the present administrative machinery, their influence and prestige often exceeds that of the officially recognised head of the village.

ECONOMIC ASPECTS OF TRIBAL LIFE

It is almost obvious that the tribal communities in India is extremely backward and poverty striken. It is because a number of communities have continued in the pastoral or shifting cultivation stage of economy even till today. As the pressure of population further grew agriculture advanced the forest receded into the background. With larger land-mass coming under settled cultivation it was possible to grow a variety of crops in different fields. But, in spite of all, the economic condition of the tribal people cannot be said to be much improved. The area under cultivation as a proportion of the total reported area in some of the districts of Bihar reveals this fact. The reported area of cultivation is 50.5 per cent in Ranchi, 18.9 percent in Singhbhum and 13.2 per cent in Palamau which is decidedly much lower. Agricultural productivity is according to one study,[18] between Rs. 750 to 1000 of output in value terms per hectare. Productivity per worker varies below Rs. 500 per annum and during 1960's productivity per worker is estimated to have declined by as much as Rs. 140 per worker. The gross annual agricultural income per head of agricultural population is, therefore, extremely low.

Agriculture in the tribal region has remained backward due to natural, technological as well as institutional factors. Whereas the acidic soil certainly act as a constraint on increasing productivity by indigenous methods, inadequacy of irrigation facilities, lack of adequate extension facilities and concentration of land ownership, etc., hold the realisation of the potential that exists in its, agriculture. The main agricultural produce in the area is rice. The share of rice in the total agricultural income in Palamu was 49 per cent, in Ranchi 92 per cent and 96 per cent in Singhbhum in 1971. The yield per hectare in the three districts in 1970 was 677 kgs, 762 kgs and 863 kgs, respectively.[19]

Tribal economy is intimately connected with the forests and their economy. The forest regions are, generally, inhabited by the tribal communities who are at one of the earlier stages of economic development compared to other communities in the country. These regions, therefore, are comparatively under-developed though they have rich natural resources.

As the population engaged in collection of minor forest produce is believed to be essentially tribal and dependent mostly on agriculture for major part of its income, the low level of agricultural income makes it furthermore dependent upon the forest produce.

Forest in Bihar covers about 17 per cent of total land area against the all-India average of 23 per cent. In Bihar, the bulk of these forest lies in the Chhotanagpur region. In Ranchi district, forest covers 18.2 per cent of total reported area whereas in Singhbhum and Palamau the proportions go up to 33 per cent and 44 per cent respectively. However, the share of forest in total land area has been dwindling, yet the per head forest area in these three districts is about four times of the average per head forest area in the State.

Timber and fuel are the major forest product in Bihar. At present the standing stock of timber is estimated at about Rs. 600 crores, at current prices. Among the minor forest produce, which includes every thing other than timber, the production of lac in value terms is very important. In 1978-79 when the production of stick lac in Bihar touched its historically lowest level, the value of stick lac production was estimated at about Rs. 2 crores. Distributed over about 5 lakh workers it would amount to an average of about Rs. 40 per worker for the year. But the production of stick lac, however, has witnessed a spectacular decline unlike other forest produce.

Outlays for forest development in Bihar have been rather

meagre and it has remained a net revenue earner for the State. During 1977-78, the gross revenue of the forest department was about Rs. 17 crores of which about 10 crores was a direct contribution to the State exchequer.

Considering the above figure related to tribal economy, it can be said that tribal economy is intimately connected with forest, because their way of living is forest-based. The relationship has been recognised but has not been articulated in terms of clear policies and programmes. The tribal economy and the forest economy, therefore, have tended to drift apart with adverse implications to both. In some cases forest have suffered tremendous loss, while in others, the tribal economy has been shattered. In spite of these, tribal economy, in general, is characterised by the close relation between the economy and the habitat. Not being powerful enough to modify the surroundings, the tribal learn to adapt themselves to it. Primitive society has tried to work out some kind of adjustment between material needs and the potentialities of the environment.[20] This is now here more clearly evident than in the adjustment of the tribal needs and effort to the forest that we set them. The tribal dependence on forest for food, fuel, house building materials, agricultural implements and minor produce of barter and market exchange also is considerable.

Here is also a points of consideration in this respect. The forest regions are sparely populated generally inhabited by the tribal communities who are at the earlier or pre-stages of economic development compared to the other. Community in the country. These regions, therefore, are comparatively underdeveloped, though they have rich natural resources. These dormant resources have to be activised for faster regional growth.

As in a rough division tribals were partially nomadic and partially settled one. Nomadics dependence on forest is vital. They maintain their little material needs through minor forest products. Semi-settled and semi-nomadic tribe utilises inside forest semi-open land for their shifting or settled cultivation, but the settled tribals who settle generally near the forest utilises minor forest products and they are agricultural also. Besides this they have traditional undeveloped animal husbandry and poultry Farms. If land is owned by the community, then animal husbandry is personal, even in the case of nomadic or semi-nomadic tribal. Animal rearing is related to draft animal for animal power rarely of which is mostly in primitive stage. Bullock is the only draft animal in the tribal belt of Bihar. For milking purposes, cows and goats are reared. They are mostly traditional of low variety. The purpose of animal rearing for protein purpose lies in rearing of besides cow, goat, pig, sheep and cock.

Minor forest products which are used by tribal are forest leaves, fire-wood, mahua flower, sabni grass, munje chirannje, fruit's flowers and other ingredients. For self-consumption and also for barter and exchange, Karujia. For only exchange. Non-edible and edible mahua seed for self-consumption and sale purposes.

Besides this there are two rare minor product which are most closely related with the tribal economy. They play and will also play increasing dominant role in future. They are lac and tasar silk cocoons. Lac is a rare forest product by some insect. It is grown on forest trees.

Lac is a versatile industrial intermediate good, a unique natural resin. Besides inner consumption it is a exportable goods also Export earning out of it is 5 to 24.3 crores rupees. It is evident from lac export earning figure from 1970-71 to 1974-75 (see Kamal Narain Kabra, *Dependence and Dominance,* Indian Institute of Public Administration, New Delhi, p. 20). Tribal share in collection of raw lac is around 82%. The another important forest produce is tasar silk cocoon. According to the report of District Industrial Centre, Ranchi, the tasar silk cocoon is annually collected of Rs. 121 lakhs annually from the forest belt of Chhotanagpur and Santhal Pargana. Tasar cocoon is reared on sul tree. State Government under the scheme of Tribal development and silk development plan have started 12 seed rearing centre of tasar silk insects. It appears from the report of the State Government of Bihar, 1983 that rearing through silk cocoon is increasing year by year. Tasar silk cocoons are counted in Kahu, 80 per cent tribals are responsible for its total collections, 20 per cent collection work is in hands of non-tribals, but the raw silk cocoons trade is still in the hands of big traders of Bangalore, Bombay and Ahmedabad. Thus, it appears that tribals are distressed to sell this product and are exploited heavily.

Industry occupies the second position in terms of employment in the tribal region. A little more than 9 per cent of the work force is engaged in industrial activities, in both household and non-house-hold sectors. The work force employed in other than house-hold industries varies from 1.2 per cent in Palamau to 11.85 per cent in Singhbum. Ranchi has only as little as 4.13 per cent employment in non-house-hold sector. These employment figures, however, include a good number of migrant workers.

On the other hand, Ranchi accounts for 45 per cent of the regional work force in house-hold industries, whereas Palamau employs only about one-sixth of the total work force of this region in this sector. The total employment in manufacturing and processing activities, however, is only 3 per cent of the total work force in Palamau: 7 per cent in Ranchi and 13.3 per cent in Singhbhum.

Trade and commerce along with transport employ about 5 per cent of total work force-concentration being in Singhbhum district (50.75 per cent) followed by Ranchi (35 per cent) and Palamau (14.25 per cent).

Collection of local produce is carried out through 'haats', 'mandis', 'melas', etc., which are held over more than 500 centres within the tribal region of Bihar. State regulation of market is confined to looking after law and order and the collection of auction prices. Only Ranchi town has a regulated market. A sizeable number of markets are controlled by local bodies as well.

The tribal region of Bihar exports agricultural commodities, forest produce, minerals, iron and steel, engineering goods, some manufactured articles and transports equipments. Its imports consists of foodgrain, vegetable, oil, sugar, manufactured and processed consumer, goods, and raw materials such as coal, steel alloys, etc.

The forest area and its surroundings are rich in minerals while economy starts to dig it economic activities in that area increases and the economic activities in tribals are benefited. The benefits in the shape of employment both regular and irregular increase their standard of living. It also has impacts on their social way of living. Their ethnic aloof character starts diminishing and becomes under and common with the main stream of the country. With the start of living activities naturally industrial belts emerges which generally invites and attracts tribal labour force to participate. Participation in industrialisation and mining operations may be migratory from both sides and seasonal in nature. But it definitely adds in their employment potentiality and consequently in their earning. Industrial towns and mining centre brings a new way of life in modernity in the tribal areas.

Surfaced road mileage per lakh of population in Bihar, is 20.61 miles whereas it is 36.72 in Ranchi, 41.01 in Palamau and 22.31 in Singhbhum. However, road mileage per 1000 km of area is below the average of 6.68 miles for Bihar ranging between 4.04 for Singhbhum to 5.23 miles in Ranchi. This indicates the large area of the tribal region of Bihar commands, its low population density and poorer road coverage.

As on March 31, 1971, only 2.96 per cent of villages in Bihar were reported to have electricity whereas in Ranchi it was 3.08, Palamau 8.60 and Singhbhum only 1.70 per cent.

From the above-mentioned facts it is almost obvious that the tribal region of Bihar is extremely backward with a large proportion of the population depending upon backward agriculture and for subsidiary employment on forest produce. The organised sector in industries though well developed in areas of the tribal region of Bihar and using modern techniques is not integrated with the economy of the region and provides employment to only a small section of local work force. The industrial sector uses local fuels and mineral resources, but their location in the region does not seem to have affected the economy of the local people in any significant way. As a result, the bulk of population remains unemployed and underemployed with low incomes and dependent on backward agriculture and forest produce. To improve the economic condition of the tribal people, development of agriculture and social forestry need to get the topmost priority. The development of industries is also required which utilize the local produce as Sabai grass, cocoons, wood, leafs, etc., and thereby increase employment as well as the demand of the forest produce. Such a development strategy instead of creating pockets of highly sophisticated industries, will be integrated with the principal resources and sectors of the tribal economy and hence, will be more effective in raising the standard of living of the tribal population.

GENERATION GAP—A COMPARATIVE REVIEW

Indian tribal life a few generation ago, was well adjusted in their own social forms. It cannot be said whether is was happy. Today, there is neither adjustment nor happiness in the life pattern of the Indian tribes. Their culture soil has been constantly eroded by the dangerous floods of Christianity and Hinduism. The entire tribal India is thus, passing through the critical stage of transition. The sum total of coercion, conversion, and the willing adoption of new ways meant the giving up of the traditional ways of life. This every body has not been ready to do, leading to a social cultural schism in tribal society. Further, those who changed over, willingly or through coercion, to new ways were faced with problems to some of which they could find solutions and some others which could either not perceive and comprehend or perceiving could not solve.[21]

The problem of the tribal people can be solved neither by isolation nor by assimilation but by integration. By integration is meant the combining of several elements into a complex entirely in which the elements can be clearly distinguished. The Santhal, Munda, Gond, Naga and the rest may maintain their own culture and identity and yet be an integral part of then Indian nation and society. Our country abounds in many heterogenous cultural patterns and social groups. It is only through integration, and that can be done only by allowing maximum freedom to the different groups to maintain and develop their identity and individuality that the emergence of a free social democratic life in India is possible.

The tribal people should be made to understand that efforts are being made to change their life for better without uprooting them from their cultural moorings. Pandit Jawaharlal Nehru, the first Prime Minister once pointed out: "We must approach the tribal people with affection and friendliness and come to them as a liberating force. We must let them feel that we come to give and not to take something away from them. That is the kind of psychological integration India needs."[22]

The integration of tribal people in Indian society is a great task. Administrators, social workers and social scientists have to evolve an integrated plan for integration of the tribal people in Indian society.

NOTES AND REFERENCES

1. The New Encyclopaedia Britanica, Vol. X, p. 115.
2. *Ibid.*
3. Everyman's Encyclopaedia, Vol. XII, p. 44.
4. *Ibid.*, p. 46.
5. Thaper Ramesh, "Tribe Caste and Religion in India", p. 10.
6. *Ibid.*
7. *Ibid.*, 11.
8. Mamoria, C.B., "Tribal Demography in India, pp. 21-22.
9. Guang is a miner tribe in Orissa. Originally they were semi-settled tribe. Traditionally their aquired land won a Community land in which they were cultivating jointly with very poor capital but with the start of developmental effort the old tradition had been broken. Tribal and their Development—A study of two tribal Development Blocks in Orissa, National Institute of Community Development, Hyderabad, p. 13.
   For further reference see L.P. Vidyarthi and B.K. Ray, "Tribal Culture in India", pp. 109-10, Concept Publication, New Delhi.
   For Further reference see J.N. Sinha, "Rural Employment Planning Dimensions and Constraints," *The Economic and Political Weekly*, Vol. XIII, Nos. 6 and 7, Annual No. 1978, p. 297.
10. Elwin, Verrier, The Aboriginals Bombay, 1943, p. 8.
11. *Ibid.*, pp. 8-10.
12. *Ibid.*, pp. 10-11.
13. *Ibid.*, p. 11
14. Archer, W.G., "The Hill of Flutes, Life, Love and Poetry in Tribal India, a Portrait of the Santhals", p. 290.
15. Man, E.G., "Santhalia and the Santhals," p. 17.
16. Bainbridge, R.B., "The Surias of the Rajmahal Hill Memoirs of the Asiatic Society of Bengal," Vol. I, No. 2, 1907, p. 84.
17. Bodding, P.O., "Tradition and Institution of Santhal", p. 104.
18. Draft Sub-Plan for Tribal Region of Bihar, 1974-79, p. 15.
19. *Ibid.*, p. 14.
20. Majumdar, D.N., "Races and Culture of India", Allahabad, p. 67.
21. Majumdar, D.N. and Madan, T.N., "An Introduction to Social Anthropology," p. 270.
22. Nehru, Jawaharlal, "Tribal Folk", p. 5.

2

Scheduled Tribes and Scheduled Areas in India*

I

STATE/UNION TERRITORY-WISE LIST OF SCHEDULED TRIBES

1. Andhra Pradesh

1. Andh
2. Bagata
3. Bhil
4. Chenchu, Chenchwar
5. Gadabas
6. Gond, Naikpod, Rajgond
7. Goudu (in the Agency tracts)
8. Hill Reddis
9. Jatapus
10. Kammara
11. Kattunayakan
12. Kolam, Mannervarlu
13. Konda Dhoras
14. Konda Kapus

*Government of India, Ministry of Home Affairs, New Delhi.

15. Kondareddis
16. Kondhs, Kodi, Kodhu, Desaya Kondhs, Dongria Kondhs, Kuttiya Kondhs, Tikiria Kondhs, Yenity Kondhs
17. Kotia, Bentho Oriya, Bartika, Dhulia, Dulia, Holva, Paiko, Putiya, Sanrona, Sidhopaiko
18. Koya, Goud, Rajah, Rasha Koya, Lingadhari Koya (ordinary), Kottu Koya, Bhine Koya, Rajkoya
19. Kulia
20. Malis (excluding Adilabad, Hyderabad, Karimnagar, Khammam, Mahbubnagar, Medak, Nalgonda, Nizamabad and Warangal districts)
21. Manna Dhora
22. Mukha Dhora, Nooka Dhora
23. Nayaks (in the Agency tracts)
24. Pardhan
25. Porja, Parangiperja
26. Reddi Dhoras
27. Rona, Rena
28. Savaras, Kapu Savaras, Maliya Savaras, Khutto Savaras
29. Sugalis, Lambadis
30. Thoti (in Adilabad, Hyderabad, Karimnagar, Khamman, Mahbubnagar, Medak, Nalgonda, Nizamabad and Warangal districts)
31. Valmiki (in the Agency tracts)
32. Yenadis
33. Yerukulas.

2. Assam

I. In the autonomous distícts:

1. Chakma
2. Dimasa, Kachari
3. Garo
4. Hajong
5. Hmar
6. Khasi, Jaintia, Synteng, Pnar, War, Bhoi, Lyngngam
7. Any Kuki Tribes, including:
   - (i) Biate, Biete
   - (ii) Changsan

(iii) Chongloi
(iv) Doungel
(v) Gamalhou
(vi) Gangte
(vii) Guite
(viii) Hanneng
(ix) Hao Kip, Hanpit
(x) Haolai
(xi) Hengna
(xii) Hongsungh
(xiii) Hrangkhwal, Raogkhol
(xiv) Jongbe
(xv) Khawchung
(xvi) Khawathlang, Khothalong
(xvii) Khelma
(xviii) Kholhou
(xix) Kipgen
(xx) Kuki
(xxi) Lengthang
(xxii) Lhangum
(xxiii) Lhoujem
(xxiv) Lhouvun
(xxv) Lupheng
(xxvi) Mangjel
(xxvii) Misao
(xxviii) Riang
(xxix) Sairhem
(xxx) Selnam
(xxxi) Singson
(xxxii) Sitlhou
(xxxiii) Sukto
(xxxiv) Thado
(xxxv) Thangngeu
(xxxvi) Uibuh
(xxxvii) Vaiphei

8. Lakher
9. Man (Tai speaking)
10. Any Mizo (Lusnai) tribes
11. Mikir
12. Any Naga tribes

13. Pawi
14. Syntheng

II. In the State of Assam excluding the autonomous districts:

1. Barmans in Cachar
2. Boro, Borokachari
3. Deori
4. Hojai
5. Kachari, Sonwal
6. Lalung
7. Mech
8. Miri
9. Rabha

3. Bihar

1. Asur
2. Baiga
3. Banjara
4. Bathudi
5. Bedia
6. Bhumij (in North Chhotanagpur and South Chhotanagpur divisions and Santal Parganas districts)
7. Binjhia
8. Birhor
9. Birjia
10. Chero
11. Chik Baraik
12. Gond
13. Gorait
14. Ho
15. Karmali
16. Kharia
17. Kharwar
18. Khond
19. Kisan
20. Kora
21. Korwa
22. Lohara, Lohra
23. Mahli
24. Mai Paharia
25. Munda

26. Oraon
27. Parhaiya
28 Santal
29. Sauria Paharia
30. Savar

4. Gujarat

1. Barda
2. Bavacha, Bamcha
3 Bharwad (in the Nesses of the forests of Alech, Barada and Gir)
4. Bhil, Bhil Garasia, Dholi Bhil, Dungri Bhil, Dungri Garasia, Mewasi Bhil, Rawal Bhil, Tadvi Bhil, Bhagalia, Bhilala, Pawra, Vasava, Vasave
5. Charan (in the Nesses of the forests of Alech, Barada and Gir)
6. Chaudhri (in Surat and Valsad districts)
7. Chodhara
8. Dhanka, Tadvi, Tetaria Valvi
9. Dhodia
10. Dubla, Talavia, Halpati
11. Gamit, Gamta, Gavit, Mavchi, Padvi
12. Gond, Rajgond
13. Kathodi, Katkari, Dhor Kathodi, Dhor Katkari, Son Kathodi, Son Katkari
14. Kokna, Kokni, Kukna
15. Koli (in Kutch district)
16. Koli Dhor, Tokre Koli, Kolcha Kolgha
17. Kunbi (in the Dangs district)
18. Naikda, Nayaka, Cholivala Nayaka, Kapadia Nayaka, Mota Nayaka, Nana Nayaka
19. Padhar
20. Paradhi (in Kutch district)
21. Pardhi, Advichincher, Phanse Pardhi (excluding Amreli, Bhavnagar, Jamnagar, Junagadh, Kutch, Rajkot and Surendranagar districts)
22. Patelia
23. Pomla
24. Raban (in the Nesses of the forests of Alech, Barada and Gir)

25. Rathawa
26. Siddi (in Amreli, Bhavnagar, Jamnagar, Junagadh, Rajkot and Surendranagar districts)
27. Vaghri (in Kutch district)
28. Varli
29. Vitola Kotwalia, Barodia

5. Himachal Pradesh

1. Bhot, Bodh
2. Gaddi [excluding the territories specified in sub-section (1) of Section 5 of the Punjab Reorganisation Act, 1966 (31 of 1966), other than the Lahaul and Spiti district]
3. Gujjar [excluding the territories specified in sub-section (1) of section 5 of the Punjab Reorganisation Act, 1966 (31 of 1966)]
4. Jad, Lamba, Khampa
5. Kanaura, Kinnara
6. Lahaula
7. Pangwala
8. Swangla.

6. Karnataka

1. Adiyan
2. Barda
3. Bavacha, Bamcha
4. Bhil, Bhil Garasia, Dholi Bhil, Dungri Bhil, Dungri Garasia, Mewasi Bhil, Rawal Bhil, Tadvi Bhil, Bhagalia, Bhilala, Pawra, Vasava, Vasave
5. Chenchu, Chenchwar
6. Chodhara
7. Dubla, Talavia, Halpati
8. Gamit, Gamta, Gavit, Mavchi, Padvi, Valvi
9. Gond, Naikpod, Rajgond
10. Gowdalu
11. Hakkipikki
12. Hasalaru
13. Irular
14. Iruliga
15. Jenu Kuruba
16. Kadu Kuruba

17. Kammara (in South Kanara district and Kollegal taluk of Mysore district)
18. Kaniyan, Kanyan (in Kollegal taluk of Mysore district)
19. Kathodi, Katkari, Dhor Kathodi, Dhor Katkari, Son Kathodi, Son Katkari
20. Kattunayakan
21. Kokna, Kokni, Kukna
22. Koli Dhor, Tokre Koli, Kolcha, Kolgha
23. Konda Kapus
24. Koraga
25. Kota
26. Koya, Bhine Koya, Rajkoya
27. Kudiya, Melakudi
28. Kuruba (in Coorg district)
29. Kurumans
30. Maha Malasar
31. Malaikudi
32. Malasar
33. Malayekandi
34. Maleru
35. Maratha (in Coorg district)
36. Marati (in South Kanara district)
37. Meda
38. Naikda, Nayaka, Cholivala Nayaka, Kapadia Nayaka, Mota Nayaka, Nana Nayaka
39. Palliyan
40. Paniyan
41. Pardhi, Advichincher, Phanse Pardhi
42. Patelia
43. Rathawa
44. Sholaga
45. Soligaru
46. Toda
47. Varli
48. Vitolia, Kotwalia, Barodia
49. Yerava

7. Kerala

1. Adiyan
2. Arandan

3. Eravallan
4. Hill Pulaya
5. Irular, Irulan
6. Kadar
7. Kammara [in the areas comprising the Malabar district as specified by sub-section (2) of Section 5 of the States Reorganisation Act, 1956 (37 of 1956)]
8. Kanikaran, Kanikkar
9. Kattunayakan
10. Kochu Velan
11. Konda Kapus
12. Kondareddis
13. Koraga
14. Kota
15. Kudiya, Melakudi
16. Kurichchan
17. Kurumans
18. Kurumbas
19. Maha Malasar
20. Malai Arayan
21. Malai Pandaram
22. Malai Vedan
23. Malakkuravan
24. Malasar
25. Malayan [excluding the areas comprising the Malabar district as specified by sub-section (2) of Section 5 of the States Reorganisation Act, 1956 (36 of 1956)]
26. Malayarayar
27. Mannan
28. Marati (in Hosdrug and Kasaragod taluks of Cannanore district)
29. Muthuvan, Mudugar, Muduvan
30. Palleyan
31. Palliyan
32. Palliyar
33. Paniyan
34. Ulladan
35. Uraly

8. Madhya Pradesh

1. Agariya
2. Andh
3. Baiga
4. Bhaina
5. Bharia Bhumiai Bhuinhar Bhumia, Bhumiya, Bharia, Paliha, Pando
6. Bhattra
7. Bhil, Bhilala, Barela, Patelia
8. Bhil Mina
9. Bhunjia
10. Biar, Biyar
11. Binjhwar
12. Birhul, Birhor
13. Damor, Damaria
14. Dhanwar
15. Gadaba, Gadba
16. Gond; Arakh, Arrakh, Agaria, Asur, Badi Maria, Bada Maria, Bhatola, Bhimma, Bhuta, Koilabhuta, Koliabhuti, Bhar, Bisonhorn Maria, Chota Maria, Dandami Maria, Dhuru, Dhurwa, Dhoba, Dhulia, Dorla, Gaiki, Gatta, Gatti, Gaita, Gond Gowari Hill Maria, Kandra, Kalanga, Khatola, Koitar, Koya, Khirwar, Khirwara, Kucha Maria, Kuchaki Maria, Madia, Maria, Mana, Mannewar, Moghya, Mogia, Monghya, Mudia, Muria, Nagarchi, Nagwanshi, Ojha, Raj, Sonjhari, Jhareka, Thatia Thotya, Wade Maria, Vadi Maria, Daror.
17. Halba, Halbi
18. Kamar
19. Karku
20. Kawar, Kanwar, Kaur, Cherwa, Rathia, Tanwar, Chattri
21. Keer (in Bhopal, Raisen and Sebore districts)
22. Khairwar, Kondar
23. Kharia
24. Kondh, Khond, Kandh
25. Kol
26. Kolam
27. Korku, Bopchi, Mouasi, Nihal, Nahul, Bondhi, Bondeya
28. Korwa, Kodaku
29. Majhi

30. Majhwar
31. Mawasi
32. Mina (in Sironj sub-division of Vidisha district)
33. Munda
34. Nagesia, Nagasia
35. Oraon, Dhanka, Dhangad
36. Panika (in Chhatarpur, Datia, Panna, Rewa, Satna, Shahdol, Sidhi and Tikamgarh districts)
37. Pao
38. Pardhan, Pathari Saroti
39. Pardhi (in Bhopal, Raisen and Sehore districts)
40. Pardhi; Bahelia, Bahellia, Chita Pardhi, Langoli Pardhi, Phans Pardhi, Shikari, Takankar, Takia [in (1) Bastar, Chhindwara, Mandla, Raigarh, Seoni and Surguja districts, (2) Baihar tahsil of Balaghat district, (3) Betul and Bhainsdehi tahsils of Betul district. (4) Bilaspur and Katghora tahsils of Bilaspur district, (5) Durg and Balod tahsils of Durg district, (6) Chowki, Manpur and Mohala Revenue Inspectors' Circles of Rajnandgaon district, (7) Murwara, Patan and Sihora tahsils of Jabalpur district, (8) Hoshangabad and Sohagpur tahsils of Hoshangabad district and Narsimhapur district, (9) Harsud tahsil of Khandwa district, (10) Bindra-Nawagarh, Dhamtari and Mahasamund tahsils of Raipur district]
41. Parja
42. Sahariya, Saharia, Seharia, Sehria, Sosia, Sor
43. Saonta, Saunta
44. Saur
45. Sawar, Sawara
46. Sonr

9. Maharashtra

1. Andh
2. Baiga
3. Barda
4. Bavacha, Bamcha
5. Bhaina
6. Bharia Bhumia, Bhuinhar Bhumia, Pando
7. Bhattra

8. Bhil, Bhil Garasia, Dholi Bhil, Dungri Bhil, Dungri Garasia, Mewasi Bhil, Rawal Bhil, Tadvi Bhil, Bhagalia, Bhilala, Pawra, Vasava, Vasave
9. Bhunjia
10. Binjhwar
11. Birhul, Birhor
12. Chodhara (excluding Akola, Amravati, Bhandara, Buldana, Chandrapur, Nagpur, Wardha, Yavatmal, Aurangabad, Bhir, Nanded, Osmanabad and Parbhani districts)
13. Dhanka, Tadvi, Tetaria, Valvi
14. Dhanwar
15. Dhodia
16. Dubla, Talavia, Halpati
17. Gamit, Gamta, Gavit, Mavchi, Padvi
18. Gond Rajgond, Arakh, Arrakh, Agaria, Asur, Badi Maria, Bada Maria, Bhatola, Bhimma, Bhuta, Koilabhuta, Koilabhuti, Bhar, Bisonhorn Maria, Chota Maria, Dandami Maria, Dhuru, Dhurwa, Dhoba, Dhulia, Dorla, Gaiki-Gatta, Gatti, Gaita, Gond Gowari, Hill Maria, Kandra, Kalanga, Khatola, Koitar, Koya, Khirwar, Khirwara, Kucha Maria, Kuchaki Maria, Madia, Maria, Mana, Mannewar, Moghya Mogia, Monghya, Mudia, Muria, Nagarchi, Naikpod, Nagwanshi, Ojha, Raj, Sonjhari Jhareka, Thatia, Thotya, Wade Maria, Vade Maria
19. Halba, Halbi
20. Kamar
21. Kathodi, Katkari, Dhor Kathodi, Dhor Kathkari, Son Kathodi, Son Katkari
22. Kawar, Kanwar, Kaur, Cherwa, Rathia, Tanwar, Chattri
23. Khairwar
24. Kharia
25. Kokna, Kokni, Kukna
26. Kol
27. Kolam, Mannervarlu
28. Koli, Dhor, Tokre Koli, Kolcha, Kolgha
29. Koli Mahadev, Dongar Koli
30. Koli Malhar
31. Kondh, Khond, Kandh

32. Korku, Bopchi, Mouasi, Nihal, Nahul, Bondhi, Bondeya
33. Koya, Bhine Koya, Rajkoya
34. Nagesia, Nagasia
35. Naikda, Nayaka, Cholivala Nayaka, Kapadia Nayaka, Mota Nayaka, Nana Nayaka
36. Oraon, Dhangad
37. Pardhan, Pathari, Saroti
38. Pardhi; Advichincher, Phans Pardhi, Phanse Pardhi, Langoli Pardhi, Bahelia, Bohellia, Chita Pardhi, Shikari, Takankar, Takia
39. Parja
40. Patelia
41. Pomla
42. Rathawa
43. Sawar, Sawara
44. Thakur, Thakar, Ka Thakur, Ka Thakar, Ma Thakur, Ma Thakar
45. Thoti (in Aurangabad, Bhir, Nanded, Osmanabad and Parbhani districts and Rajura tahsil of Chandrapur district)
46. Varli
47. Vitolia, Kotwalia, Barodia

10. Manipur

1. Aimol
2. Anal
3. Angami
4. Chiru
5. Chothe
6. Gangte
7. Hmar
8. Kabui
9. Kacha Naga
10. Koirao
11. Koireng
12. Kom
13. Lamgang
14. Mao
15. Maram
16. Maring

17. Any Mizo (Lushai) tribes
18. Monsang
19. Moyon
20. Paite
21. Purum
22. Ralte
23 Sema
24. Simte
25. Suhte
26. Tangkhul
27. Thadou
28. Vaiphui
29. Zou

11. Meghalaya

1. Chakma
2. Dimasa, Kachari
3. Garo
4. Hajong
5. Hmar
6. Khasi, Jaintia, Synteng, Pnar, War, Bhoi, Lyngngam
7. Any Kuki Tribes including:
   (i) Biate, Biete
   (ii) Changsan
   (iii) Chongloi
   (iv) Doungel
   (v) Gamalhou
   (vi) Gangte
   (vii) Guite
   (viii) Hanneng
   (ix) Haokip, Haupit
   (x) Haolai
   (xi) Hengna
   (xii) Hongsungh
   (xiii) Hrangkhwal, Rangkhol
   (xiv) Jongbe
   (xv) Khawchung
   (xvi) Khawathlang, Khothalong
   (xvii) Khelma
   (xviii) Kholhou

(xix) Kipgen
(xx) Kuki
(xxi) Lengthang
(xvii) Lhangum
(xxiii) Lhoujem
(xxiv) Lhouvun
(xxv) Lupheng
(xxvi) Mangjel
(xvii) Misao
(xxviii) Riang
(xxix) Sairhem
(xxx) Selnam
(xxxi) Singson
(xxxii) Sitlhou
(xxxiii) Sukte
(xxxiv) Thado
(xxxv) Thangngeu
(xxxvi) Uibuh
(xxxvii) Vaiphei

8. Lakher
9. Man (Tai speaking)
10. Any Mizo (Lushai) tribes
11. Mikir
12. Any Naga tribes
13. Pawi
14. Synteng

12. Nagaland

1. Naga
2. Kuki
3. Kachari
4. Mikir
5. Garo

13. Orissa

1. Bagata
2. Baiga
3. Banjara, Banjari
4. Bathudi
5. Bhottada, Dhotada
6. Bhuiya, Bhuyan

7. Bhumia
8. Bhumij
9. Bhunjia
10. Binjhal
11. Binjhia, Binjhoa
12. Birhor
13. Bondo Poraja
14. Chenchu
15. Dal
16. Desua Bhumij
17. Dharua
18. Didayi
19. Gadaba
20. Gandia
21. Ghara
22. Gond, Gondo
23. Ho
24. Holva
25. Jatapu
26. Juang
27. Kandba Gauda
28. Kawar
29. Kharia, Kharian
30. Kharwar
31. Khond, Kond, Kandha, Nanguli Kandha, Sitha Kandha
32. Kisan
33. Kol
34. Kolah Loharas, Kol Loharas
35. Kolba
36. Koli, Malhar
37. Kondadora
38. Kora
39. Korua
40. Kotia
41. Koya
42. Kulis
43. Lodha
44. Madia
45. Mahali
46. Mankidi

47. Mankirdia
48. Matya
49. Mirdhas
50. Munda, Mudda Lohara, Munda Mahalis
51. Mundari
52. Omanatya
53. Oraon
54. Parenga
55. Paroja
56. Pentia
57. Rajuar
58. Santal
59. Saora, Savar, Saura, Sahara
60. Shabar, Lodha
61. Sounti
62. Tharua

14. Rajasthan

1. Bhil, Bhil Garasia, Dholi Bhil, Dungri Bhil, Dungri Garasia, Mewạsi Bhil, Rawal Bhil, Tadvi Bhil, Bhagalia, Bhilala, Pawra, Vasava, Vasave
2. Bhil Mina
3. Damor, Damaria
4. Dhanka, Tadvi, Tetaria, Valvi
5. Garasia (excluding Rajput Garasia)
6. Kathodi, Katkari, Dhor Kathodi, Dhor Katkari, Son, Kathodi, Son Katkari
7. Kokna, Kokni, Kukna
8. Koli Dhor, Tokre Koli, Kolcha, Kolgha
9. Mina
10. Naikda, Nayaka, Cholivala Nayaka, Kapadia Nayaka, Mota Nayaka, Nana Nayaka
11. Patelia
12. Seharia, Sehria, Sahariya

15. Sikkim

1. Bhutia (including Chumbipa, Dopthapa, Dupka, Kagatey, Sherpa, Tibetan, Tromopa, Yolmo).
2. Lepcha

16. Tamil Nadu

1. Adiyan
2. Aranadan
3. Eravallan
4. Irular
5. Kadar
6. Kammara (excluding Kanyakumari district and Shenkottah taluk of Tirunelveli district)
7. Kanikaran, Kanikkar (in Kanyakumari district and Shenkottah taluk of Tirunelveli district)
8. Kaniyan, Kanyan
9. Kattunayakan
10. Kochu Velan
11. Konda Kapus
12. Kondareddis
13. Koraga
14. Kota (excluding Kanyakumari district and Shenkottah taluk of Tirunelveli district)
15. Kudiya, Melakudi
16. Kurichchan
17. Kurumbas (in the Nilgiri district)
18. Kurumans
19. Maba Malasar
20. Malai Arayan
21. Malai Pandaram
22. Malai Vedan
23. Malakkuravan
24. Malasar
25. Malayali (in Dharmapuri, North Arcot, Pudukottai, Salem, South Arcot and Tiruchirapalli districts)
26. Malayekandi
27. Mannan
28. Mudugar, Muduvan
29. Muthuvan
30. Palleyas
31. Palliyan
32. Palliyar
33. Paniyan
34. Sholaga

35. Toda (excluding Kanyakumari district and Shenkottah taluk of Tirunelveli district)
36. Uraly

17. Tripura

1. Bhil
2. Bhutia
3. Chaimal
4. Chakma
5. Garoo
6. Halam
7. Jamatia
8. Khasia
9. Kuki, including the following sub-tribes:
   - (i) Balte
   - (ii) Belalhut
   - (iii) Chhalya
   - (iv) Fun
   - (v) Hajango
   - (vi) Jangtei
   - (vii) Khareng
   - (viii) Khephong
   - (ix) Kuntei
   - (x) Laifang
   - (xi) Lentei
   - (xii) Mizel
   - (xiii) Namte
   - (xiv) Paitu, Paite
   - (xv) Rangchan
   - (xvi) Rangkhole
   - (xvii) Thangluya
10. Lepcha
11. Lushai
12. Mag
13. Munda, Kaur
14. Noatia
15. Orang
16. Riang
17. Santal
18. Tripura, Tripuri, Tippera
19. Uchai

18. Uttar Pradesh

1. Bhotia
2. Buksa
3. Jaunsari
4. Raji
5. Tharu

19. West Bengal

1. Asur
2. Baiga
3. Bedia, Bediya
4. Bhumij
5. Bhutia, Sherpa, Toto, Dukpa, Kagatay, Tibetan, Yolmo
6. Birhor
7. Birjia
8. Chakma
9. Chero
10. Chik Baraik
11. Garo
12. Gond
13. Gorait
14. Hajang
15. Ho
16. Karmali
17. Kharwar
18. Khond
19. Kisan
20. Kora
21. Korwa
22. Lepcha
23. Lodha, Kheria, Kharia
24. Lohara, Lohra
25. Magh
26. Mahali
27. Mahli
28. Mal Pahariya
29. Mech
30. Mru
31. Munda
32. Nagesia

33. Oraon
34. Parhaiya
35. Rabha
36. Santal
37. Sauria Paharia
38. Savar

20. Andaman and Nicobar Islands

1. Andamanese, Chariar, Chari, Kora, Bo, Tabo, Yere, Kede, Bea, Balawa, Bojigiyab, Juwai, Kol
2. Jarawas
3. Nicobarese
4. Onges
5. Sentinelese
6. Shorn Pens

21. Arunachal Pradesh

All tribes of the Union Territory including:

1. Abor
2. Aka
3. Apatani
4. Dafla
5. Galong
6. Khampti
7. Khowa
8. Mishmi
9. Momba
10. Any Naga tribes
11. Sherdukpen
12. Sinpho

22. Dadra and Nagar Haveli

1. Dhosia
2. Dubla including Halpati
3. Kathodi
4. Kokna
5. Koli Dhor including Kolgha
6. Naikda or Nayaka
7. Varli

23. Goa, Daman and Din

1. Dhodia

2. Dubla (including Halpati and Talavia)
3. Naikda (including Nayaka)
4. Siddi
5. Varli

24. Lakshadweep

Through the Union Territory:
Inhabitants of the Laccadive, Minicoy and Amindivi Islands who, and both of whose parents, were born in those islands.

25. Mizoram

Throughout the Union Territory:

1. Chakma
2. Dimasa (Kachari)
3. Garo
4. Hajong
5. Hmar
6. Khasi and Jaintia (including Khasi, Synten or Pnar, War, Bhoi or Lyngngam)
7. Any Kuki tribes, including:
   (i) Baite or Biete
   (ii) Changsan
   (iii) Chongloi
   (iv) Doungel
   (v) Gamalhou
   (vi) Gangte
   (vii) Guite
   (viii) Hanneng
   (ix) Haokip or Haupit
   (x) Haolai
   (xi) Hengna
   (xii) Hongsungh
   (xiii) Hrangkhwal or Rangkhol
   (xiv) Jongbe
   (xv) Khawchung
   (xvi) Khawathlong or Khothalong
   (xvii) Khelma
   (xviii) Kholhou
   (xix) Kipgen
   (xx) Kuki

(xxi) Lengthang
(xxii) Lhangum
(xxiii) Lhoujem
(xxiv) Lhouvun
(xxv) Lupheng
(xxvi) Mangjel
(xxvii) Missao
(xxviii) Riang
(xxix) Sairhem
(xxx) Selnam
(xxxi) Singson
(xxxii) Sitlhou
(xxxiii) Sukte
(xxxiv) Thado
(xxxv) Thangngeu
(xxxvi) Uibuh
(xxxvii) Vaiphei

8. Lakher
9. Man (Tai-Speaking)
10. Any Mizo (Lushai) tribes
11. Mikir
12. Any Naga tribes
13. Pawi
14. Synteng.

II
ALPHABETICAL LIST OF SCHEDULED TRIBES

Sl. No.	*Schedule Tribe*	*State/Union Territory where Scheduled*
1	*2*	*3*
		A
1.	Abor	Arunachal Pradesh.
2.	Adiyan	Karnataka, Kerala, Tamil Nadu.
3.	Advichincher	Gujarat, Karnataka, Maharashtra.
4.	Agaria	Madhya Pradesh, Maharashtra.
5.	Agariya	Madhya Pradesh.
6.	Aimol	Manipur.
7.	Aka	Arunachal Pradesh.

1	2	3
8.	Anal	Manipur.
9.	Andh	Andhra Pradesh, Madhya Pradesh. Maharashtra.
10.	Andamanese	Andaman and Nicobar Islands.
11.	Angami	Manipur.
12.	Apatani	Arunachal Pradesh.
13.	Arakh	Madhya Pradesh, Maharashtra.
14.	Araduan	Kerala, Tamil Nadu.
15.	Arrakh	Madhya Pradesh, Maharshtra.
16.	Asur (Gond)	Bihar, West Bengal, Madhya Pradesh, Maharashtra.
		B
1.	Baiga	Bihar, Madhya Pradesh, Maharshtra, Orissa and West Bengal.
2.	Baite (Kuki)	Mizoram.
3.	Balawa (Andamanese)	Andaman and Nicobar Islands.
4.	Balte (Kuki)	Tripura.
5.	Bamcha (Bavacha)	Gujarat, Karnataka, Maharashtra.
6.	Banjara	Bihar, Orissa.
7.	Banjari (Banjara)	Orissa
8.	Barda	Gujarat, Karnataka, Maharashtra.
9.	Barela (Bhil)	Madhya Pradesh, Rajasthan.
10.	Barmans	Assam.
11.	Barodia (Vitolia)	Karnataka, Maharashtra.
12.	Bartika (Kotia)	Andhra Pradesh.
13.	Bathudi	Bihar, Orissa.
14.	Bauacha	Gujarat, Karnataka, Maharashtra.
15.	Bea	A and N Islands.
16.	Bedia	Bihar, West Bengal.
17.	Bediya (Bedia)	West Bengal.
18.	Belalhut (Kuki)	Tripura.
19.	Bentho Oriya (Kotia)	Andhra Pradesh.
20.	Bhagalia (Bhil)	Gujarat, Karnataka, Maharashtra. Rajashthan.
21.	Bhaina	Madhya Pradesh, Maharashtra.
22.	Bhar (Gond)	Madhya Pradesh, Maharashtra.
23	Bharia (Bharia, Bhumia)	Madhya Pradesh.

1	2	3
24.	Bharia Bhumia	Madhya Pradesh, Maharashtra.
25.	Bharwad	Gujarat.
26.	Bhatola (Gond)	Madhya Pradesh, Maharashtra.
27.	Bhattra	Madhya Pradesh, Maharashtra.
28.	Bhil	Andhra Pradesh, Gujarat, Karnataka, Madhya Pradesh, Maharashtra, Rajashthan, Tripura.
29.	Bhil Garasia (Bhil)	Gujarat, Karnataka, Maharashtra, Rajasthan.
30.	Bhil Mina	Madhya Pradesh, Rajashthan.
31.	Bhilala (Bhil)	Gujarat, Karnataka, Madhya Pradesh, Maharashtra, Rajashtan.
32.	Bhimma (Gond)	Madhya Pradesh, Maharashtra.
33.	Bhine Koya (Koya)	Andhra Pradesh, Karnataka, Maharashtra.
34.	Bhoi (Khasi)	Assam, Meghalaya, Mizoram.
35.	Bhot	Himachal Pradesh.
36.	Bhotia	Uttar Pradesh.
37.	Bhottada	Orissa.
38.	Bhuinhar Bhumia (Bharia Bhumia)	Madhya Pradesh, Maharashtra.
39.	Bhuiya	Orissa.
40.	Bhumij	Bihar, Orissa, West Bengal.
41.	Bhuta (Gond)	Madhya Pradesh, Maharashtra.
42.	Bhumiya (Bharia, Bhumia)	Madhya Pradesh.
43.	Bhumia	Orissa.
44.	Bhunjia	Madhya Pradesh, Maharashtra, Orissa.
45.	Bhutia	Sikkim, Tripura, West Bengal.
46.	Bhuyan (Bhuiya)	Orissa.
47.	Biar	Madhya Pradesh.
48.	Biate (Kuki)	Assam, Meghalaya, Mizoram.
49.	Biete (Kuki)	Assam, Meghlaya, Mizoram.
50.	Birhor (Birhol)	Madhya Pradesh, West Bengal.
51.	Binjhal	Orissa.
52.	Binjhia	Bihar, Orissa.
53.	Binjhoa (Binjhia)	Orissa.

1	2	3
54.	Binjhwar	Madhya Pradesh, Maharashtra,
55.	Birhor	Bihar. Madhya Pradesh (Birhol). Maharashtra (Bisul). Orissa, West Bengal.
56.	Birhul	Madhya Pradesh, Maharashtra.
57.	Birjia	Bihar, West Bengal.
58.	Bisonhorn Maria (Gond)	Madhya Pradesh, Maharashtra.
59.	Biyar (Biar)	Madhya Pradesh.
60.	Bo (Andamanese)	A and N Islands.
61.	Bodh (Bhot)	Himachal Pradesh.
62.	Bojigiyab (Andamanese)	A and N Islands.
63.	Bondeya (Korku)	Madhya Pradesh, Maharashtra.
64.	Bondhi (Korku)	Madhya Pradesh, Maharashtra.
65.	Bondo Poraja	Orissa.
66.	Bopchi (Korku)	Madhya Pradesh, Maharashtra.
67.	Boro	Assam.
68.	Barodia (Vitola)	Gujarat, Maharashtra.
69.	Borokachari (Boro)	Assam.
70.	Buksa	Uttar Pradesh.
71.	Bada Maria (Gond)	Madhya Pradesh, Maharashtra.
72.	Badimaria (Gond)	Madhya Pradesh, Maharashtra.
73.	Bagata	Andhra Pradesh, Orissa.
74.	Bahelia (Pardhi)	Madhya Pradesh, Maharashtra.
75.	Bahellia (Pardhi)	Madhya Pradesh, Maharashtra.

C

1.	Chimal	Tripura.
2.	Chakma	Assam, Meghalaya, Mizoram, Tripura, West Bengal.
3.	Changsan (Kuki)	Assam, Meghalaya, Mizoram,
4.	Charan	Gujarat.
5.	Chari (Andamanese)	A and N Islands.
6.	Chariar (Andamanese)	A and N Islands.
7.	Chattri (Kawar)	Madhya Pradesh, Maharashtra.

1	2	3
8.	Chaudhri	Gujarat.
9.	Chenchu	Andhra Pradesh, Karnataka, Orissa.
10.	Chenchwar (Chenchu)	Andhra Pradesh, Karnataka.
11.	Chero	Bihar, West Bengal.
12.	Cherwa (Kawar)	Madhya Pradesh, Maharashtra.
13.	Chhalya (Kuki)	Tripura.
14.	Chik Baraik	Bihar, West Bengal.
15.	Chiru	Manipur.
16.	Chitapardhi (Pardhi)	Madhya Pradesh, Maharashtra.
17.	Chodhara	Gujarat, Karnataka, Maharashtra.
18.	Cholivalanayaka (Naikda)	Maharashtra.
19.	Cholivalanayaka (Naikda)	Karnataka, Rajasthan, Gujarat.
20.	Chongloi (Kuki)	Assam, Meghalaya Mizoram.
21.	Chotamaria (Gond)	Madhya Pradesh, Maharashtra.
22.	Chothe	Manipur.
23.	Chumbipa	Sikkim.
		D
1.	Dafla	Arunachal Pradesh.
2.	Dal	Orissa.
3.	Damaria (Damor)	Madhya Pradesh, Rajasthan.
4.	Damor	Madhya Pradesh, Rajasthan.
5.	Dandami Maria (Gond)	Madhya Pradesh, Maharashtra.
6.	Daroi (Gond)	Madhya Pradesh.
7.	Dasaya Konds (Kondhs)	Andhra Pradesh.
8.	Deori	Assam.
9.	Desua Bhumij	Orissa.
10.	Dhangad (Oraon)	Madhya Pradesh, Maharashtra.
11.	Dhanka (Oraon)	Gujarat, Madhya Pradesh, Maharashtra, Rajasthan.
12.	Dhanwar	Maharashtra, Madhya Pradesh.
13.	Dharua	Orissa.
14.	Dhoba (Gond)	Madhya Pradesh, Maharashtra.
15.	Dhodia	Gujarat, Maharashtra, Dadra and Nagar Haveli, Goa, Daman and Diu.

1	2	3
16.	Dholi Bhil (Bhil)	Gujarat, Karnataka, Maharashtra, Rajasthan.
17.	Dhor (Koli)	Maharashtra.
18.	Dhora	Andhra Pradesh.
19.	Dhor Katkari (Karhodi)	Rajasthan, Gujarat, Karnataka, Maharashtra.
20.	Dhor Kathodi (Kathodi)	Gujarat, Karnataka, Maharashtra, Rajasthan.
21.	Dhotada (Bhottada)	Orissa.
22.	Dhulia (Gond)	Madhya Pradesh, Maharashtra, (Kotia) Andhra Pradesh.
23.	Dhuru (Gond)	Madhya Pradesh, Maharashtra.
24.	Dhurwa (Gond)	Madhya Pradesh, Maharashtra.
25.	Didayi	Orissa.
26.	Dimasa	Assam, Meghalaya, Mizoram.
27.	Dongar Koli (Koli)	Maharashtra.
28.	Dongria Konds (Kondhs)	Andhra Pradesh.
29.	Dopthapa	Sikkim.
30.	Dorla (Gond)	Madhya Pradesh, Maharashtra.
31.	Doungel (Kuki)	Assam, Meghalaya, Mizoram.
32.	Dubla	Gujarat, Karnataka, Maharashtra, Dadra and Nagar Haveli, Goa, Daman and Diu.
33.	Dulia	Andhra Pradesh.
34.	Dukpa (Bhutia)	Sikkim, West Bengal
35.	Dungri Bhil (Bhil)	Gujarat Karnataka, Maharashtra, Rajasthan
36.	Dungri Garasia (Bhil)	Gujarat, Karnataka, Maharashtra, Rajasthan.
		E
1.	Eravallan	Kerala, Tamil Nadu.
		F
1.	Fun	Tripura.
		G
1.	Gadaba	Madhya Pradesh, Orissa.

1	2	3
2.	Gadabas	Andhra Pradesh.
3.	Gadba (Gadaba)	Madhya Pradesh.
4.	Gaddi	Himachal Pradesh.
5.	Gaiki (Gond)	Madhya Pradesh, Maharashtra.
6.	Gaita (Gond)	Madhya Pradesh, Maharashtra.
7.	Galong	Arunachal Pradesh.
8.	Gamalhou (Kuki)	Assam, Meghalaya, Mizoram.
9.	Gamit	Gujarat, Karnataka, Maharashtra.
10.	Gamta (Gamit)	Gujarat, Karnataka, Maharashtra.
11.	Gandia	Orissa.
12.	Gangte (Kuki)	Assam, Meghalaya, Manipur, Mizoram.
13.	Garasia	Rajasthan.
14.	Garo	Asssam, Meghalaya Mizoram, Nagaland, West Bengal.
15.	Garoo	Tripura.
16.	Gatta (Good)	Madhya Pradesh, Maharashtra.
17.	Gatti (Gond)	Madhya Pradesh, Maharashtra.
18.	Gavit (Gamit)	Gujarat, Karnataka, Maharashtra.
19.	Ghara	Orissa.
20.	Gond	Andhra Pradesh, Bihar, Gujarat, Karnataka, Madhya Pradesh, Maharashtra, Orissa, West Bengal.
21.	Gond Gowari (Gond)	Madhya Pradesh, Maharashtra.
22.	Gondo	Orissa.
23.	Gorait	Bihar, West Bengal.
24.	Goud	Andhra Pradesh.
25.	Goudu	Andhra Pradesh.
26.	Gowdalu	Karnataka.
27.	Gujjar	Himachal Pradesh.
28.	Guite (Kuki)	Assam, Meghalaya, Mizoram.

H

1.	Hajang	West Bengal.
2.	Hajango (Kuki)	Tripura.
3.	Hajong	Assam, Meghalaya, Mizoram.
4.	Hakkipikki	Karnataka.
5.	Halam	Tripura.

1	2	3
6.	Halba	Madhya Pradesh, Maharashtra.
7.	Halbi	Madhya Pradesh, Maharashtra.
8.	Halpati (Dubla)	Gujarat, Karnataka, Goa, Daman and Diu.
9.	Hannedg (Kuki)	Assam, Meghalaya, Mizoram.
10.	Haokip (Kuki)	Assam, Meghalaya, Mizoram.
11.	Haolai (Kuki)	Assam, Meghalaya, Mizoram.
12.	Hasalaru	Karnataka.
13.	Haupit (Kuki)	Assam, Meghalaya, Mizoram.
14.	Hengna	Assam, Meghalaya, Mizoram.
15.	Hill Maria (Gond)	Madhya Pradesh, Maharashtra.
16.	Hill Pulaya	Kerala.
17.	Hill Raddis	Andhra Pradesh.
18.	Hmar	Assam, Manipur, Meghalaya, Mizoram.
19.	Ho	Bihar, Orissa, West Bengal.
20.	Hojai	Assam.
21.	Holva (Rotia)	Andhra Pradesh, Orissa.
22.	Hongsungh (Kuki)	Assam, Meghalaya, Mizoram.
23.	Hrangkhwa (Kuki)	Assam, Meghalaya, Mizoram.
	I	
1.	Irulan (Irular)	Kerala.
2.	Irular	Karnataka, Kerala, Tamil Nadu.
3.	Iruliga	Karnataka.
	J	
1.	Jad	Himachal Pradesh.
2.	Jaintia (Khasi)	Assam, Meghalaya, Mizoram.
3.	Jamatia	Tripura.
4.	Jangtei	Tripura.
5.	Jarawas	A and N Islands.
6.	Jatapu	Orissa.
7.	Jatapus	Andhra Pradesh.
8.	Jaunsari	Uttar Pradesh.
9.	Jenu Kuruba	Karnataka.
10	Jongbe (Kuki)	Assam, Meghalaya, Mizoram.
11	Juang	Orissa.

1	2	3
12.	Juwai	A and N Islands
		K
1.	Kabui	Manipur.
2.	Kacha Naga	Manipur.
3.	Kachari	Assam, (Dimasa) Meghalaya, Nagaland.
4.	Kadar	Kerala, Tamil Nadu.
5.	Kadu Kuruba	Karnataka.
6.	Kagatay (Bhutia)	Sikkim, West Bengal.
7.	Kalanga (Gond)	Madhya Pradesh, Maharashtra.
8.	Kamar	Madhya Pradesh, Maharashtra.
9.	Kammara	Andhra Pradesh, Karnataka, Kerala, Tamil Nadu.
10.	Kanaura	Himachal Pradesh.
11.	Kandh (Kondh)	Madhya Pradesh, Maharashtra.
12.	Kandha (Konnd)	Orissa.
13.	Kandha Gauda	Orissa.
14.	Kandra (Gond)	Madhya Pradesh, Maharashtra.
15.	Kanikkar (Kanikaran)	Kerala, Tamil Nadu.
16.	Kaniyan	Karnataka, Tamil Nadu.
17.	Kannikaran	Kerala, Tamil Nadu.
18.	Kanwar (Kawar)	Madhya Pradesh, Maharashtra.
19.	Kanyan (Kaniyan)	Karnataka, Tamil Nadu.
20.	Kapadia Nayaka (Naikda)	Gujarat, Karnataka, Maharashtra, Rajasthan.
21.	Kapu Savaras (Savaras)	Andhra Pradesh.
22.	Karku	Madhya Pradesh.
23.	Karmali	Bihar, West Bengal.
24.	Ka Thakar (Thakur)	Maharashtra.
25.	Ka Thakur (Thakur)	Maharashtra.
26.	Kathodi	Gujarat, Karnataka, Maharashtra, Dadra and Nagar Haveli, Rajasthan.
27.	Katkari (Kathodi)	Gujarat, Karnataka, Maharashtra, Rajasthan.
28.	Kattunayakan	Andhra Pradesh, Karnataka, Kerala, Tamil Nadu.
29.	Kaur (Munda)	Tripura.

1	2	3
30.	Kaur (Kawar)	Madhya Pradesh, Maharashtra.
31.	Kawar	Madhya Pradesh, Maharashtra. Orissa.
32.	Kede (Andamanese)	A. and N. Islands.
33.	Keer	Madhya Pradesh.
34.	Khairwar	Madhya Pradesh, Maharashtra.
35.	Khampa (Jad)	Himachal Pradesh
36.	Khampti	Arunachal Pradesh.
37.	Khareng (Kuki)	Tripura.
38.	Kharia	Bihar, Madhya Pradesh, Maharashtra, Orissa, (Lodha) West Bengal.
39.	Kharian (Kharia)	Orissa.
40.	Kharwar	West Bengal.
41.	Khasi	Assam, Meghalaya, Mizoram.
42.	Khasia	Tripura.
43.	Khatola (Gond)	Madhya Pradesh, Maharashtra.
44.	Khawchung (Kuki)	Assam, Meghalaya, Mizoram.
45.	Khawathlang (Kuki)	Assam, Meghalaya, Mizoram.
46.	Khelma (Kuki)	Assam, Meghalaya, Mizoram.
47.	Khephong (Juki)	Tripura.
48.	Kheria (Lodha)	West Bengal.
49.	Khirwar (Gond)	Madhya Pradesh, Maharashtra.
50.	Khirwara (Gond)	Madhya Pradesh, Maharashtra.
51.	Kholhou (Kuhi)	Assam, Meghalaya, Mizoram.
52.	Khond	Bihar, (Kondh) Madhya Pradesh, (Kondh) Maharashtra, West Bengal, Orissa.
53.	Khothalong (Kuki)	Assam, Meghalaya, Mizoram.
54.	Khowa	Arunachal Pradesh.
55.	Khutto Savaras (Savaras)	Andhra Pradesh.
56.	Kipgen (Kuki)	Assam, Meghalaya, Mizoram.
57.	Kinnara (Kanaura)	Himachal Pradesh.
58.	Kisan	Bihar, Orissa, West Bengal.
59.	Kochu Velan	Kerala, Tamil Nadu.
60.	Kodaku (Korwa)	Madhya Pradesh.
61.	Kodhu (Kondha)	Andhra Pradesh.
62.	Kodi (Kondhs)	Andhra Pradesh.

1	2	3
63.	Koilabhuta (Gond)	Madhya Pradesh, Maharashtra.
64.	Koilabhuti (Gond)	Madhya Pradesh, Maharashtra.
65.	Koirao	Manipur.
66.	Koireng	Manipur.
67.	Koitar (Gond)	Madhya Pradesh, Maharashtra.
68.	Kokna	Gujarat, Karnataka, Maharashtra, Rajasthan, Dadra and Nagar Haveli.
69.	Kokni	Gujarat, Karnataka, Maharashtra, Rajasthan.
70.	Kol	Madhya Pradesh, Maharashtra, Orissa, (Andamanese) A. and N. Island.
71.	Kol Loharas (Kolah Loharas)	Orissa.
72.	Kolah Loharas	Orissa.
73.	Kolam	Andhra Pradesh, Madhya Pradesh, Maharashtra.
74.	Kolcha (Kolidhor)	Gujarat, Karnataka, Maharashtra, Rajasthan.
75.	Kolgha (Kolidhor)	Gujarat, Karnataka, Maharashtra, Rajasthan, Dadra and Nagar Haveli.
76.	Kolha	Orissa.
77.	Koli	Gujarat, Orissa.
78.	Koli Dhor	Gujarat, Karnataka, Maharashtra, Rajasthan, Dadra and Nagar Haveli.
79.	Koli Mahadev	Maharashtra.
80.	Koli Malhar	Maharashtra.
81.	Kom	Manipur.
82.	Kond (Khond)	Orissa.
83.	Kondadora	Orissa.
84.	Konda Dhoras	Andhra Pradesh.
85.	Konda Kapus	Andhra Pradesh, Karnataka, Kerala, and Tamil Nadu.
86.	Kondar (Khairwar)	Madhya Pradesh.
87.	Kondareddis	Andhra Pradesh, Kerala, Tamil Nadu.
88.	Kondh	Madhya Pradesh, Maharashtra.
89.	Kondhs	Andhra Pradesh.

1	2	3
90.	Kora	Bihar, Orissa, West Bengal. (Andamanese) A. & N. Islands.
91.	Koraga	Karnataka, Kerala, Tamil Nadu.
92.	Korku	Madhya Pradesh, Maharashtra.
93.	Korua	Orissa.
94.	Korwa	Bihar, Madhya Pradesh, West Bengal.
95.	Kota	Karnataka, Kerala, Tamil Nadu.
96.	Kotia	Andhra Pradesh, Orissa.
97.	Kottu Koya (Koya)	Andhra Pradesh.
98.	Kotwalia (Vitolia)	Gujarat, Karnataka, Maharashtra.
99.	Koya (Gond)	Andhra Pradesh, Karnataka, Madhya Pradesh, Maharashtra, Orissa.
100.	Kucha Maria (Gond)	Madhya Pradesh, Maharashtra.
101.	Kuchaki Maria (Gond)	Madhya Pradesh, Maharashtra.
102.	Kudiya	Karnataka, Kerala, Tamil Nadu.
103.	Kuki	Assam, Meghalaya, Mizoram, Nagaland, Tripura.
104.	Kukna (Kukna)	Gujarat, Karnataka, Maharashtra, Rajasthan, Dadra and Nagar Haveli.
105.	Kulia	Andhra Pradesh.
106.	Kulis	Orissa.
107.	Kuki	Assam, Meghalaya, Mizoram, Nagaland, Tripura.
108.	Kunbi	Gujarat.
109.	Kuntei (Kuki)	Tripura.
110.	Kurichchan	Kerala, Tamil Nadu.
111.	Kuruba	Karnataka.
112.	Kurumans	Karnataka, Kerala, Tamil Nadu.
113.	Kurumbas	Kerala, Tamil Nadu.
114.	Kuttiyakondus (Kondhs)	Andhra Pradesh.

L

1.	Lahaula	Himachal Pradesh.
2.	Laifang (Kuki)	Tripura.
3.	Lakher	Assam, Meghalaya, Mizoram.
4.	Lalung	Assam.
5.	Lamba (Jad)	Himachal Pradesh.

1	2	3
6.	Lambadis (Sugalis)	Andhra Pradesh.
7.	Lamgang	Manipur.
8.	Langoli (Pardhi)	Madhya Pradesh, Maharashtra.
9.	Lengthang (Kuki)	Assam, Meghalaya, Mizoram.
10.	Lentei (Kuki)	Tripura.
11.	Lepcha	Sikkim, Tripura, West Bengal.
12.	Lhangum (Kuki)	Assam, Meghalaya, Mizoram.
13.	Lhoujem (Kuki)	Assam, Meghalaya, Mizoram.
14.	Lingadhari Koya (Koya)	Andhra Pradesh.
15.	Lodha	Orissa (Shabar), West Bengal.
16.	Lohara	Bihar, West Bengal.
17.	Lohra (Lohara)	Bihar, West Bengal.
18.	Lhouvun (Kuki)	Assam, Meghalaya, Mizoram.
19.	Lupheng (Kuki)	Assam, Meghalaya, Mizoram.
20.	Lushai	Tripura.
21.	Lyngngam (Khasi)	Assam, Meghalaya, Mizoram.
		M
1.	Madia (Gond)	Madhya Pradesh, Maharashtra, Orissa.
2.	Mag (Kuki)	Tripura.
3.	Magh	West Bengal.
4.	Mahali	Orissa, West Bengal.
5.	Maha Malasar	Karnataka, Kerala, Tamil Nadu.
6.	Mahli	Bihar, West Bengal.
7.	Majhi	Madhya Pradesh.
8.	Majhwar	Madhya Pradesh.
9.	Malai Arayan	Kerala, Tamil Nadu.
10.	Malai Pandaram	Kerala, Tamil Nadu.
11.	Malai Vedan	Kerala, Tamil Nadu.
12.	Malaikudi	Karnataka.
13.	Malakkuravan	Kerala, Tamil Nadu.
14.	Malasar	Kerala, Karnataka, Tamil Nadu.
15.	Malayali	Tamil Nadu.
16.	Malayan	Kerala.
17.	Malayarayar	Kerala.
18.	Malayekandi	Karnataka, Tamil Nadu.

1	2	3
19.	Maleru	Karnataka.
20.	Malis	Andhra Pradesh.
21.	Maliya Savaras (Savaras)	Andhra Pradesh.
22.	Malpaharia	Bihar, West Bengal.
23.	Man	Assam, Meghalaya, Mizoram.
24.	Mana (Gond)	Madhya Pradesh, Maharashtra.
25.	Mangjel (Kuki)	Assam, Meghalaya, Mizoram.
25.	Mankidi	Orissa.
27.	Mankirdia	Orissa.
28.	Manna Dhora	Andhra Pradesh.
29.	Mannan	Kerala, Tamil Nadu.
30.	Mannervarlu (Kolam)	Andhra Pradesh, Maharashtra.
31.	Mannewar (Gond)	Madhya Pradesh, Maharashtra.
32.	Mao	Manipur.
33.	Maram	Manipur.
34.	Maratha	Karnataka.
35.	Marati	Karnataka, Kerala.
36.	Maria (Gond)	Madhya Pradesh, Maharashtra.
37.	Maring	Manipur.
38.	Mavchi (Gamil)	Karnataka.
39.	Mru	West Bengal.
40.	Ma Thakar (Thakur)	Maharashtra.
41.	Ma Thakur (Thakur)	Maharashtra.
42.	Muthuvan	Kerala, Tamil Nadu.
43.	Matya	Orissa.
44.	Mavchi (Gamit)	Gujarat, Maharashtra.
45.	Mawasi	Madhya Pradesh.
46.	Mech	Assam, West Bengal.
47.	Meda	Karnataka.
48.	Melakudi (Koya)	Karnataka, (Kudiya) Kerala, (Kudiya) Tamil Nadu.
49.	Mewasi Bhil (Bhil)	Gujarat, Karnataka, Maharashtra, Rajasthan.
50.	Mikir	Assam, Meghalaya, Mizoram, Nagaland.
51.	Mina	Madhya Pradesh, Rajasthan.
52.	Mirdhas	Orissa.

1	2	3
53.	Miri	Assam.
54.	Mishmi	Arunachal Pradesh.
55.	Misao (Kuki)	Assam, Meghalaya.
56.	Missao (Kuki)	Mizoram.
57.	Mizel (Kuki)	Tripura.
58.	Mizo	Assam, Manipur, Meghalaya, Mizoram.
59.	Moghya (Gond)	Madhya Pradesh, Maharashtra.
60.	Mogia (Gond)	Madhya Pradesh, Maharashtra.
61.	Momba	Arunachal Pradesh.
62.	Monghya (Gond)	Madhya Pradesh, Maharashtra.
63.	Monsang	Manipur.
64.	Mota Nayaka (Naikda)	Gujarat, Karnataka, Maharashtra, Rajasthan.
65.	Mouasi (Korku)	Madhya Pradesh, Maharashtra.
66.	Moyon	Manipur.
67.	Mudia (Gond)	Madhya Pradesh, Maharashtra.
68.	Mudugar (Muthuvan)	Kerala, Tamil Nadu.
69.	Muduvan (Muthuvan)	Kerala, (Mudugar) Tamil Nadu.
70.	Mukha Dhora	Andhra Pradesh.
71.	Munda	Bihar, Madhya Pradesh, Orissa, Tripura, West Bengal.
72.	Munda Lohara (Munda)	Orissa.
73.	Munda Mahalis (Munda)	Orissa.
74.	Mundari	Orissa.
75.	Muria (Gond)	Madhya Pradesh, Maharashtra.

N

1	2	3
1.	Naga	Assam, Arunachal Pradesh, Meghalaya, Mizoram, Nagaland.
2.	Nagarchi (Gond)	Madhya Pradesh, Maharashtra.
3.	Nagasia (Nagesia)	Madhya Pradesh, Maharashtra.
4.	Nagesia	Madhya Pradesh, Maharashtra, West Bengal.
5.	Nagwanshi (Gond)	Madhya Pradesh, Maharashtra.
6.	Nahul (Korku)	Madhya Pradesh, Maharashtra.

1	2	3
7.	Naikda	Gujarat, Karnataka, Maharashtra, Rajasthan, Dadra and Nagar Haveli, Goa, Daman and Diu.
8.	Naikpod (Gond)	Andhra Pradesh, Karnataka, Maharashtra.
9.	Namte (Kuki)	Tripura.
10.	Nana Nayak (Naikda)	Gujarat, Karnataka, Maharashtra, Rajasthan.
11.	Nanguli Kandha	Orissa.
12.	Nayaka (Naikda)	Gujarat, Karnataka, Maharashtra, Rajasthan, Dadra and Nagar Haveli, Goa, Daman and Diu.
13.	Nayaks	Andhra Pradesh.
14.	Nicobarese	Andaman and Nicobar Islands.
15.	Nihal (Korku)	Madhya Pradesh, Maharashtra.
16.	Noatia	Tripura.
17.	Nooka Dhora (Mukha Dhoras)	Andhra Pradesh.
	O	
1.	Ojha (Gond)	Madhya Pradesh, Maharashtra.
2.	Omanatya	Orissa.
3.	Onges	A. and N. Islands.
4.	Orang	Tripura.
5.	Oraon	Bihar, Madhya Pradesh, Maharashtra, Orissa.
6.	Oriya (Kotia)	Andhra Pradesh.
	P	
1.	Padhar	Gujarat.
2.	Padvi (Gamit)	Gujarat, Karnataka, Maharashtra.
3.	Paiko	Andhra Pradesh.
4.	Paite (Kuki)	Manipur, Tripura.
5.	Paitu	Tripura.
6.	Palihal (Bharia Bhumia)	Madhya Pradesh.
7.	Palleyan	Kerala, Tamil Nadu.
8.	Palliyan	Karnataka, Kerala, Tamil Nadu.

1	*2*	*3*
9.	Palliyar	Kerala, Tamil Nadu.
10.	Pando (Bharia Bhumia)	Madhya Pradesh, Maharashtra.
11.	Pangwala	Himachal Pradesh.
12.	Panika	Madhya Pradesh.
13.	Paniyan	Karnataka, Kerala, Tamil Nadu.
14.	Pao	Madhya Pradesh.
15.	Paradhi	Gujarat.
16.	Parangiperja	Andhra Pradesh.
17.	Pardhan	Andhra Pradesh, Madhya Pradesh, Maharashtra.
18.	Pardhi	Gujarat, Karnataka, Madhya Pradesh, Maharashtra.
19.	Parenga	Orissa.
20.	Parhaiya	Bihar, West Bengal.
21.	Parja	Andhra Pradesh, Madhya Pradesh, Maharashtra.
22.	Paroja	Orissa.
23.	Patelia	Gujarat (Bhil), Karnataka (Bhil), Madhya Pradesh (Bhil), Maharashtra, Rajasthan.
24.	Pathari	Maharashtra.
25.	Pathari (Pardhan)	Maharashtra.
26.	Patharisaroti (Pardhan)	Madhya Pradesh.
27.	Pawi	Assam, Meghalaya, Mizoram.
28.	Pawra (Bhil)	Gujarat, Karnataka, Maharashtra, Orissa, Rajasthan.
29.	Pentie	Orissa.
30.	Phanspardhi (Pardhi)	Madhya Pradesh, Maharashtra.
31.	Phansepardhi (Pardhi)	Gujarat, Karnataka, Maharashtra.
32.	Pnar (Khasi)	Assam, Meghalaya, Mizoram.
33.	Pomla	Gujarat, Maharashtra.
34.	Porja	Andhra Pradesh.
35.	Potiya	Andhra Pradesh.
36.	Purum	Manipur.
37.	Putiya	Andhra Pradesh.

1	2	3
		R
1.	Rabari	Gujarat.
2.	Rabha	Assam, West Bengal.
3.	Raj (Gond)	Madhya Pradesh, Maharashtra.
4.	Rajgond (Gond)	Andhra Pradesh, Gujarat, Karnataka.
5.	Raji	Uttar Pradesh.
6.	Rajah (Koya)	Andhra Pradesh.
7.	Rajkoya (Koya)	Andhra Pradesh, Karnataka, Maharashtra.
8.	Rajuar	Orissa.
9.	Ralte	Manipur.
10.	Rangchan	Tripura.
11.	Rangkhol (Kuki)	Assam, Meghalaya, Mizoram.
12.	Rangkhole (Kuki)	Tripura.
13.	Rasha Koya (Koya)	Andhra Pradesh.
14.	Rathawa	Gujarat, Karnataka, Maharashtra.
15.	Rathia (Kawar)	Madhya Pradesh, Maharashtra.
16.	Rawal Bhil	Gujarat, Karnataka, Maharashtra, Rajasthan.
17.	Reddi Dhoras	Andhra Pradesh.
18.	Rena (Rona)	Andhra Pradesh.
19.	Riang	Assam, Meghalaya, Tripura, Mizoram.
20.	Rona	Andhra Pradesh.
		S
1.	Sahara (Saora)	Orissa.
2.	Saharia (Sahariya)	Madhya Pradesh.
3.	Sahariya	Madhya Pradesh, (Saharia) Rajasthan.
4.	Sairhem (Kuki)	Assam, Meghalaya, Mizoram.
5.	Sanrona (Kotia)	Andhra Pradesh.
6.	Santal	Bihar, Orissa, Tripura, West Bengal.
7.	Saonta	Madhya Pradesh.
8.	Saora	Orissa.
9.	Saroti (Pardhan)	Maharashtra.
10.	Saunta (Saonta)	Madhya Pradesh.
11.	Saur	Madhya Pradesh.

1	2	3
12.	Saura (Saora)	Orissa.
13.	Sauria Paharia	Bihar, West Bengal.
14.	Savar	Bihar (Saora) Orissa, West Bengal.
15.	Savaras	Andhra Pradesh.
16.	Sawar	Madhya Pradesh, Maharashtra.
17.	Sawara (Sawar)	Madhya Pradesh, Maharashtra.
18.	Seharia (Sahariya)	Madhya Pradesh, Rajasthan.
19.	Sehria (Sahariya)	Madhya Pradesh, (Seharia) Rajasthan.
20.	Selnam (Kuki)	Assam, Meghalaya, Mizoram.
21.	Sema	Manipur.
22.	Sentinelese	A. & N. Islands.
23.	Shabar	Orissa.
24.	Sherdukpen	Arunachal Pradesh.
25.	Sherpa	Sikkim, West Bengal.
26.	Shikari (Pardhi)	Madhya Pradesh, Maharashtra.
27.	Sholaga	Karnataka, Tamil Nadu.
28.	Shorn Pens	A. & N. Islands.
29.	Siddi	Gujarat, Goa, Daman & Diu.
30.	Sidhopaiko (Kotia)	Andhra Pradesh.
31.	Simte	Manipur.
32.	Singpho	Arunachal Pradesh.
33.	Singson (Kuki)	Assam, Meghalaya, Mizoram.
34.	Sitha Kandha (Khond)	Orissa.
35.	Sitlhou	Assam, Meghalaya, Mizoram.
36.	Soligaru	Karnataka.
37.	Sonjhari Jhareka	Madhya Pradesh, Maharashtra.
38.	Son Katkari (Kathodi)	Gujarat, Karnataka, Maharashtra, Rajasthan.
39.	Sonkathodi (Katbodi)	Gujarat, Karnataka, Maharashtra, Rajasthan.
40.	Sonr	Madhya Pradesh.
41.	Sonwal (Kachari)	Assam.
42.	Sor (Sahariya)	Madhya Pradesh.
43.	Sosia (Sahariya)	Madhya Pradesh.
44.	Sunti	Orissa.
45.	Sugalis	Andhra Pradesh.
46.	Suhte	Manipur.

1	2	3
47.	Sukte (Kuki)	Assam, Meghalaya, Mizoram.
48.	Swangla	Himachal Pradesh.
49.	Synten (Khasi)	Mizoram.
50.	Synteng	(Khasi) Assam, (Khasi) Meghalaya, Mizoram.
51.	Syntheng	Assam.
		T
1.	Tabo	A. & N. Islands.
2.	Tadvi (Dhanka)	Gujarat, Maharashtra, Orissa, Rajasthan.
3.	Tadvi Bhil (Bhil)	Gujarat, Karnataka, Maharashtra, Orissa, Rajasthan.
4.	Takankar (Pardhi)	Madhya Pradesh, Maharashtra.
5.	Takia (Pardhi)	Madhya Pradesh, Maharashtra.
6.	Talavia (Dubla)	Gujarat, Karnataka, Maharashtra, Goa, Daman & Diu.
7.	Tangkhul	Manipur.
8.	Tanwar (Kawar)	Madhya Pradesh, Maharashtra.
9.	Tetaria (Dhanka)	Gujarat, Maharashtra, Orissa, Rajasthan.
10.	Thado (Kuki)	Assam, Meghalaya, Mizoram.
11.	Thadou	Manipur.
12.	Thakar (Thakur)	Maharashtra.
13.	Thakur	Maharashtra.
14.	Thangluya (Kuki)	Tripura.
15.	Thangngeu (Kuki)	Assam, Maharashtra, Mizoram, Meghalaya.
16.	Tharu	Uttar Pradesh.
17.	Tharua	Orissa.
18.	Thatia (Gond)	Madhya Pradesh, Maharashtra.
19.	Thoti	Andhra Pradesh, Maharashtra.
20.	Thotya (Gond)	Madhya Pradesh, Maharashtra.
21.	Tibetan (Bhutia)	Sikkim, West Bengal.
22.	Tikiria Kondhs	Andhra Pradesh.
23.	Tippera (Tripura)	Tripura.
24.	Toda	Karnataka, Tamil Nadu.

1	*2*	*3*
25.	Tokre Koli (Koli Dhor)	Gujarat, Karnataka, Maharashtra.
26.	Toto (Bhutia)	West Bengal.
27.	Tripura	Tripura.
28.	Tripuri (Tripura)	Tripura.
29.	Tromopa	Sikkim.
		U
1.	Uchai	Tripura.
2.	Uibuh	Assam, Meghalaya, Mizoram,
3.	Ulladan	Kerala.
4.	Uraly	Kerala, Tamil Nadu.
		V
1.	Vade Maria (Gond)	Madhya Pradesh, Maharashtra,
2.	Vaghri	Gujarat.
3.	Vaiphei (Kuki)	Assam, Meghalaya, Mizoram.
4.	Valphui	Manipur.
5.	Valmiki	Andhra Pradesh.
6.	Valvi (Dhanka)	Karnataka, Maharashtra, Rajasthan.
7.	Varli	Gujarat, Karnataka, Maharashtra, Goa, Daman & Diu, Dadra & Nagar Haveli.
8.	Vitolia	Karnataka, Maharashtra.
9.	Vasava (Bhil)	Gujarat, Karnataka, Maharashtra, Rajasthan.
10.	Vasave	Gujarat, Karnataka, Maharashtra, Rajasthan.
11.	Vitola	Gujarat.
12.	Vitolia	Maharashtra.
		W
1.	Wade Maria (Gond)	Madhya Pradesh, Maharashtra.
2.	War (Khasi)	Assam, Meghalaya, Mizoram.
		Y
1.	Yenadis	Andhra Pradesh.
2.	Yenity Kondhs (Kondhs)	Andhra Pradesh.

1	2	3
3.	Yerava	Karnataka.
4.	Yere (Andamanese)	A. & N. Islands.
5.	Yerukulas	Andhra Pradesh.
6.	Yolmo (Bhutia)	Sikkim, West Bengal.
		Z
1.	Zou	Manipur.

III
STATEWISE LIST OF SCHEDULED AREAS

Andhra Pradesh

(1) Valmor, Kondnagol, Banal, Bilakas, Dharawaram, Appaipalli, Rasul Cheruvu, Pulechalma, Marlapaya, Burj, Gundal, Agarla Penta, Pullaipalli, Dukkan Penta, Bikit Penta, Karkar Penta, Boramacheruvu, Yemlapaya, Irlapenta, Mudardi Penta, Terkaldari, Vakaramamidi Penta, Medimankal, Pandibore, Singri-gundal, Lingabore, Rampur, Appapur, Malapur, Jalal Penta, Piman Penta, Railet, Vetollapalli, Patur Bayal, Bhavi Penta, Naradi Penta, Tapasi Penta, Chandragupta, Ullukatrevu, Tim-mareddipalli, Sarapalli, Tatigundal. Elpamaehena, Koman Penta, Kollam Penta, Mananur, Macharam, Malhamamdi, Venkateshwarla Bhavi, Amrabad, Tirmalapur, Upnootola, Madhavadpalli, Jangamreddi Palli, Pedra, Venkeshwaram, Chitlamkunta, Lachmapur, Udmela, Mared, Ippalpalli, Maddimadag, Akkaram Ainoi, Siddapur, Bamanpalli, Ganpura and Manewarpalli villages of Achempeth taluq of MAHBUBNAGAR district.

(2) Malai Borgava, Ankapur, Jamul Dhari, Lokari, Vanket, Tantoli, Sitagondi, Burnoor, Navgaon, Pipal Dari, Pardi, Buzurg Yapalguda, Chinchughat, Vankoli, Kanpa, Avasoda Burki, Malkapur, Jaree, Palsi, Buzurg, Arli Khurd, Nandgaon, Vaghapur, Palsikurd, Lingee, Kaphar Deni, Ratnapur, Kosai, Umari, Madanapur, Ambugaon, Ruyadee, Sakanapur, Daigaon, Kaslapur, Dorlee, Sahaij, Songvee, Khodgoor, Kobai, Ponala, Chaprala Mangrol, Kopa Argun, Soankhas, Khidki, Khasalakurd, Khasalabuzurg, Jamni, Borgaon, Sayedpur, Khara, Lohara, Marigaon, Chichdari, Khanapur, Kandala, Tipa, Hati Ghota, Karond Kurd, Karoni Buzurg, Singapur, Buranpur, Nagrala, Bodad, Chandpelli

Peetgain, Yekori, Sadarpur, Varoor, Rohar, Takli and Ramkham villages of Adilabad taluq of ADILABAD district.

(3) Hatnur, Wakri, Pardhi, Kartanada, Serlapalli, Neradiknoda, Daligaon, Kuntala, Venkatapur, Hasanpur, Surdapur, Polmamda, Balhanpur, Dharampuri, Gokonda, Bhotai, Korsekai, Patnapur, Tejapur, Guruj, Khahdiguda Rajurvadi, Ispur, Ghanpur, Jaterla, Khantegaon, Sauri, Ichora Mutnur, Gudi Hatnur, Talamedee, Gerjam, Chincholi, Surchelma, Mankapur, Narsapur, Dharampur, Harkapur, Dhampur, Nigni, Ajhar Wajhar, Chintalbori, Chintakarva, Rampur, Gangapur and Gayatpalli villages of Boath taluq of ADILABAD district.

(4) All villages of Utnur taluq of ADILABAD district.

(5) Rajampet, Gunjala, Indhani, Samela, Tejapur, Kannar gaon, Kantaguda, Shankepalli, Jamuldhari, Gundi Chorpalli, Saleguda, Wadiguda, Savati, Dhaba, Chopanguda, Nimgaon, Khirdi, Metapiari, Sakra, Sangi, Devurpalli, Khotara-Ringanghat, Nishani, Kota Parandoli, Mesapur, Goigaon, Dhanora, Pardha, Surdapur, Kerineri Murkilonke, Devapur, Chinta Karra, Iheri, Ara, Dasnapur, Kapri, Belgaon, Sirasgaon, Moar, Wadam, Dhamriguda, Dallanpur, Chalwardi, Ihoreghat, Balijhari, Sakam-gundi, Ara, Uppal Naugaon, Anksorpur, Cbirakunta, Illipita Dorli, Mandrumera, Dantanpalli, Deodurg, Tunpalii, Dhagleshwar, Padibanda, Tamrin, Malangundi, Kandan Moar, Geonena, Kuteda, Tilani Kanepalli, Bordoum Telundi, Maugi Lodiguda, Moinda-Gudipet, Chinnedari, Koitelundi, Madura, Devaiguda, Areguda, Gardepalli, Tanepalti, Choutepalli, Rane Kannepalli, Sungapur, Rala Samkepalli, Chopri, Doda Arjuni, Serwai, Rapalli, Tekamandwa and Mets Arjuni villages of Asifabad taluq ADILABAD district.

(6) Gudam, Kasipet, Dandepalli, Chelampeta, Rajampet, Mutiempet, Venkatapur, Rali, Kauwal, Tarapet, Devapur, Gathapalli, Rotepalli, Mandamari, Dharmaraopet Venkatapur, Chintaguda, and Mutiempalli villages of Lakshetipet taluq of ADILABAD district.

(7) Raiapet, Kistampet, Takalapalli, Chakalpalli, Anaram, Bhepalli, Korsni, Isgaon, Chintaguda, Ankora, Usurampalli Allagualli, Bophalpatnam, Balasaga, Pardhi, Tumrihati, Chintalmanopally Chintam, Gullatalodi, Damda, Dhorpalli, Kanki, Garlapet, Gudlabori, Gurmpet, Lomvelli, Mogurdagar, Wirdandi and Chilpurdubor villages of Sirpur taluq of ADILABAD district.

(8) Kannaiguda, Ankannaguda, Ragbavpatnam, Medarmola, Koetla Farsa Nagaram, Muthapur, Motlaguda, Venglapur, Yelpak, Kaneboenpalli, Medaram, Kondred, Chintaguda, Konda-parthi, Yelsethipalli, Allvammarighunpur, Rampur, Malkapalli, Chettial, Bhupathipur, Gangaram, Kannaiguda, Rajannapet, Bhutaram, Akkela, Sirvapur, Gangaram Bhupathipur, Pumbapur, Rampur, Ankampalli, Kamaram, Kamsettigudam, Ashnaguda, Yellapur, Allaguda, Narsapur, Puschapur, Bhattupalli, Lavnal, Vadduguda, Kothur, Pegdapalli, Sarvapur, Bhussapur, Chelvai, Rangapur, Govindraopet, Ballapalli, Dhumpallaguda, Kerbpalli, Lakhanavaram, Pasra, Gonepalli, Padgapur, Narlapur, Kalvapalli, Uratam, Kondia, Maliat, Aclapur, Dodla, Kamaram, Tadvai, Boodiguda, Bannaji, Bandam, Selpak, Kantalpalli, Sarvai Gangaguda, Tupalkalguda, Akulvari Ghanpur, Shahpalli, Gag-pelli, Chinna-beonnpalli, Venkatpur, Narsapur, Anvaram, Lingal, Ballepalli, Bandal and Thunraapur villages of Mulug taluq of WARRANGAL district.

(9) Vebelli, Polara, Bakkachintaphad, Ganjad, Thirmalguda, Gopalpur, Khistapur, Tatinari, Venpalli, Pattal Bhoopati, Chan-delapur, Battalpalli, Advarampet, Satiahnagar, Dutla, Mothwada, Mangalawarpet, Karlai, Arkalkunta, Kodsapet, Gundepalli, Masami, Battavartigudem, Mamidiudam, Pangonda, Roturai, Satreddipalli, Konapur, Kondapuram, Pogulapalli, Govindapuram, Makadapalli, Pagulapalli, Murraigudem, Yelchagudem, Tummapuram, Jangamvartigudem, Rangagludem, Peddalapalli, Yerravaram, Kundapalli, Neelampalli, Daravarinamapalli, Karnegund, Mahadevagudem, Marrigudem, Jangalpalli, Bavarguda, Oarbak, Gangaramam, Mucheria, Amaroncha, Kamaiaam, Chintagudem, Nilavancha, Kangargidds, Madagudem, Duarpet, Kothagudem, Kotapalli, Durgaram, Dubagudem, Rudravaram, Narsugudam, Komatlagudem, Katervam, Semar Rajpet, Marepalli, Goarur, Radhiapur, Gazalguden, Rajvepalli and Bollypalli villages of Narsampet taluq of WARRANGAL district.

(10) All the villages of Yellandu talug of WARRANGAL district (excluding the Yallandu, Sinugareni and Sirpur villages and the town of Kothaguda).

(11) (i) All the villages of Palocha taluq of WARRANGAL district (excluding Palondha, Borgampad, Ashwaraopet, Damma-pet, Kuknur and Nelipak villages) and (ii) Samasthan of Paloncha.

(12) Visakhapatnam Agency area excluding the areas comprised in the villages of Agency Lakshmipuram, Chidikada, Konkasingi, Kumarapuram, Krishnadevipeta, Pichigantikothagudem, Golugondapeta, Gunupudi, Gummudukonda, Sarabhupa-lapatnam, Vadurupalli, Pedajaggampeta Sarabhupathi Agraharam, Ramachandrarajupeta Agraharam and Kondavatipudi Agraharam in VISAKHAPATNAM district.

(13) East Godavari Agency area excluding the area comprised in the village of Ramachandrapuram including its hamlet purushothapatnam in the EAST GODAVARI district.

(14) West Godavari Agency area in WEST GODAVARI district.

Bihar**

1. RANCHI district.
2. SINGHBHUM district.
3. Latehar sub-division, and Bhandaria block of Garhwa sub-division, in PALAMAU district.
4. Dumka, Pakur, Rajmabal and Jamtara sub-division, and Sundar Pahari and Boarijor blocks of Godda sub-division in SANTHAL PARGANAS district.

Gujarat**

1. Uchchhal, Vyara, Mahuwa, Mandvi, Nizar, Songadh, Valod, Mangrol and Bardoli talukas in SURAT district.
2. Dediapada, Sagbara, Valia, Nandod and Jhagadia talukas in BHARUCH district.
3. DANGS district and taluka.
4. Bansda, Dharampur, Chikhali, Pardi and Umbergaon talukas in VALSAD district.
5. Jhalod, Dohad, Santrampur, Limkheda and Deogarh Baria talukas in PANCHMAHALS district.
6. Chhotaudepur and Naswadi talukas and Tilakwada mahal in VADODARA district.

**The Scheduled Area in the States of Bihar and Gujarat were originally specified by the Scheduled Areas (Part A States) Order, 1950 (Constitution Order, 9) dated 23-1-1950 and have been respecified as above by the Scheduled Areas (States of Bihar, Gujarat, Madhya Pradesh and Orissa) Order, 1977 (Constitution Order, 109) dated 31-12-1977 after rescinding the Order cited first so far as it related to the States of Bihar, Gujarat, Madhya Pradesh and Orissa.

7. Khedbrahma, Bhiloda and Meghraj talukas, and Vijayanagar mahal in SABARKANTHA district.

Himachal Pradesh*

1. KINNAUR district.
2. LAHAUL and SPITI district.
3. Pangi tahsil and Bharmaur sub-tahsil in CHAMBA district.

Madhya Pradesh**

1. JHABUA district.
2. MANDLA district.
3. SURGUJA district.
4. BASTAR district.
5. Sardarpur, Dhar, Kukshi and Manawar tahsils, in DHAR district.
6. Barwani, Rajpur, Sendhwa, Bhikangaon, Khargone and maheshwar tahsils in KHARGONE (West Nimar) district.
7. Khalwa Tribal Development Block of Harsud tahsil, and Khaknar Tribal Development Block of Burhanpur Tahsil, in KHANDWA (West Nimar) district.
8. Sailana tahsil in RATLAM district.
9. Betul tahsil (excluding Betul Community Development Block) and Bhainsdehi tahsil in BETUL district.
10. Lakhnadon tahsil and Kurai Tribal Development Block of Seoni tahsil in SEONI district.
11. Baihar tahsil in BALAGHAT district.
12. Kesla Tribal Development Block of Hoshangabad tahsil in HOSHANGABAD district.
13. Pushparajgarh and Sohagpur tahsils, and Jaisingh Nagar Community Development Block of Beohari tahsil, in SHAHDOL district.

* Specified by the Scheduled Areas (Himachal Pradesh) Order, 1975 (Constitution Order, 102) dated 21-11-1975.

** The Scheduled Area in the State of Madhya Pradesh was originally specified by the Scheduled Areas (Part A States) Order, 1950 (Constitution Order, 9) dated, 23-1-1950 and the Scheduled Areas (Part B States) Order, 1950, (Constitution Order 26) dated 7-12-1950 and has been respecified as above by the Scheduled Areas (States of Bihar, Gujarat, Madhya Pradesh and Orissa) Order, 1977, (Constitution Order, 109) dated 31-12-1977 after rescinding the Orders cited earlier in so far as they related to the States of Bihar, Gujarat, Madhya Pradesh and Orissa.

14. Kusimi Tribal Development Block of Gopadbanas tahsil in SIDHI district.

15. Jashpurnagar, Udaipur and Gharghoda tahsils, and Kharsia Tribal Development Block of Raigarh tahsil in RAIGARH district.

16. Katghora tahsil and Marwahi Tribal Development Block, Gorella Tribal Development Block and Gorella Community Development Block, and Kota Revenue Inspector Circle of Bilaspur tahsil in BILASPUR district.

17. Dondi Tribal Development Block of Balod tahsil in DURG district.

18. Manpur and Mohla Tribal Development Blocks and Chowki Community Development Block of Rajnandgaon tahsil in RAJNANDGAON district.

19. Gariaband. Mainpur and Chhura Tribal Development Blocks of Bindradawagarh tahsil, and Sihawa Community Development block of Dhamtari Tahsil, in RAIPUR district.

20. Karahal Tribal Development Block of Sheopur tahsil in MORENA district.

21. Tamia and Jamai Tribal Development Blocks, Patwari Circle Nos. 63 to 68 and Nos. 72 and 73, villages Seergaon Khurd and Kirwani of Patwari Circle No. 62, villages Mainawari and Gaulie Parasia of Patwari Circle No. 69 and village Bamhani of Patwari Circle No. 97 of Chhindwara tahsil! Harrai Tribal Development Block and Patwari Circle Nos. 26, 27, 30, 31, 32, 41 to 44, 48, 49, 50-B and 60 of Amarwara tahsil; Bichhua Tribal Development Block and Patwari Circle No. 1 to 19, 25 to 30, 32 to 37, villages Nandapur of Patwari Circle No. 20, villages Nilkantha and Dhandikhapa of Patwari Circle No. 24, villages Ramudhana, Silora and Jobni of Patwari Circle No. 31 and all villages, excluding village Muli, of Patwari Circle No. 39 of Saunsar tahsil, of CHHINDWARA district.

Maharashtra

(1) Dahanu, Talasari Jawahar, Mokhada and Shahapur taluka in THANA district.

(2) Peint, Surgana and Kalwan talukas in NASIK district.

(3) Nawpur, Akalkuwa and Akrani talukas in DHULIA district.

(4) Melghat taluka in AMRAVATI district.

(5) Ahiri Zamindaris in Sironcha tahsil; Dhanora, Dudmala, Gewardna, Jharapara, Khulgaon, Kotgal, Muramgaon, Palasgarh, Rangi, Sirsundi, Sonsari, Chandala, Bilgaon, Pai-Muranda and Potgaon Zamindaris in CHANDRAPUR district.

(6) Bendwi, Chincholi, Goigaon, Birapur, Sakri, Balapur, Manoli, Antargaon, Wirur, Dongargaon, Timbeivai, Sersi, Badora, Vmarjeeri, Lakarkot, Ergaon, Kirdi, Sondo, Devara, Khorpana, Kanargaon, Chenai, Kairgaon, Samalhira, Dhanoli, Marnagondi, Yellapur, Katalbori, Isapur, Devti, Panderwani, Wansari, Perda, Wargaon, Nokari, Mirapur, Pardhi, Kutoda, Parsewara, Mangilhra, Karki, Nokali, Manoli, Sonapur, Inapur, Mangi, Uparwai, Tutra, Lakmapur, Kirdi, Injapur, Jamni, Hargaon, Chikli, Patan, Kosundi, Kotara and Sonorli villages of Rajura taluka of CHANDRAPUR district.

(7) Satpura Hill forest area of Chopda Raver and Yawal talukas in JALGAON district.

(8) Ambari, Bodri, Chikli, Kamtala, Ghoti, Mandwa, Maregaon, Malborgaon, Patoda, Dahigaon, Domandhari, Darsangi, Digri, Sindgi, Kanakwari, Kopra, Malakwadi, Nispur, Yenda, Pipalgaon, Bulja, Varoli, Anji, Bhimpur Sirmeti, Karla, Kothari, Gokunda, Gogarwudi, Malkapur, Dhonora, Rampur, Patri, Porodhi, Boath, Darsangi, Norgaon, Unrsi, Godi, Sauarkher, Naikwadi, Sarkani Wajhera, Mardap, Anjenkher, Gondwarsa, Palaiguda, Karalgaon, Palsi, Patoda, Jawarla, Pipalgaon, Kanki, Singora, Dongargaon, Pipalsendha, Jurur, Minki, Tulsi, Machauder Pardhi, Murli, Takri, Parsa, Warsa, Umra, Ashta, Hingni, Timapur, Wajra, Wanola, Patsonda, Dhonora, Sakur and Digiri villages of Kinwat taluka of NANDED district.

Orissa**

1. MAYURBHANJ district.
2. SUNDERGARH district.

** The Scheduled Area in the State of Orissa was originally specified by the Scheduled Areas (Part A States) Order, 1950 (Constitution Order, 9 dated 23-1-1950 and the Scheduled Areas (Part B States) Order, 1950, (Constitution Order, 26) dated 7-12-1950 and has been respecified as above by the Scheduled Areas (States of Bihar, Gujarat, Madhya Pradesh and Orissa) Order, 1977, (Constitution Order, 109) dated 31-12-1977 after rescinding the Orders cited earlier in so far as they related to the States of Bihar, Gujarat, Madhya Pradesh and Orissa.

3. KORAPUT district.

4. Kuchinda tahsil in SAMBALPUR district.

5. Keonjhar and Telkoi tahsils of Keonjhar sub-divison, and Charapua and Barbil tahsils of Champua Sub-Divison, in KEONJHAR district.

6. Khondmals tahsil of Khondmals Sub-Division, and Balliguda and G. Udayagiri Tahsils of Balliguda Sub-Division in BOUDH-KHONDMALS district.

7. R. Udayagiri Tahsil, and Guma and Rayagada Blocks of Parlakhemundi tahsil of Parlakhemundi Sub-Division and Surada tahsil (excluding Gazalbadi and Gocha Gram Panchayats) of Ghumsur Sub-Division in GANJAM district.

8. Thuamul Rampur Block of Kalahandi tahsil, and Lanjigarh Block, falling in Lanjigarh and Kalahandi tahsils, in Bhawanipatna Sub-Division in KALAHANDI district.

9. Nilgiri Community Development Block of Nilgiri tahsil in Nilgiri Sub-Division in BALASORE district.

Rajasthan*

1. DUNGARPUR district except the

(i) Towns of Dungarpur, Sagwara and Galiakot,

(ii) Villages of Peeth, Aspur, Sabla and Bankoda, and

(iii) Police Station and outpost portions of the villages of Kanba, Vinya, Dewai, Bargana, Mewda, Kura, Dhamola, Ganeshpur, Sarthuna and Fatehpur.

2. BANSWARA district except the

(i) Towns of Banswara and Kushalgarh,

(ii) Villages of Garni, Ghatole, Pratabpura, Talwara, and Bagidora, and

(iii) Police station and outpost portions of the villages of Khamera, Bhagora, Bhopatpura Anas, Jagpura, Bhondia, Narwalia, Shergath, Loharia, Anthunia, Chandji-ka-Gura, Chandanwara, Dhanpur, Phalwa, Ghaditejpur, Solapat, Pipalkhunt, Mandikhera, Sadulpur, Gangror, Dungra, Patan and Khandu.

*Declared vide The Scheduled Areas (Part B States) Order 1950 (C.O. 26)—published with the Ministry of Law Notification No. C.O. 26 dated the 7th December, 1950, Gazette of India, Extraordinary, 1950, Part II, Section 3, page 975.

3. Partabgarh tehsil of CHITTORGARH district except the

(i) Towns of Partabgarh and Deogarh, and

(ii) Police Station and outpost portions of the villages of Mathunia, Sangthali, Kherat, Kotri, Suhagpur, Katanjana, Phugatalao, Salamgarh, Arnoda and Ninor.

Any reference in the preceding paragraph to a territorial division by whatever name indicated shall be construed as a reference to the territorial division of that name existing at the time of the Order.

Tribes in South India*

A. AIYAPPAN

Some of the most primitive tribes of the world are found in southern India. Among the tribes considered extremely backwards in anthropological literature, the Veddahs of Ceylon are the nearest to us, but some of the South Indian tribes such as Aranadans of the Nilambur forests of Kerala are far more primitive than the Veddahs. The Aranadans even now do not know the elements of the most primitive methods of agriculture; they depend for subsistence on roots, tubers and small game.

With the increasing penetration of the plains' people into the jungle areas, a good number of the Aranadans find employment as farm and forest labourers. As late as the last century, these miserable tribesmen did not know how to make a hut and were living in rock shelters. They are less than 200 in number and so low and despised and neglected that it is not possible to think of a more depressed little group in any part of the world. There are half a dozen other tribes in the same taluk who are only slightly better off than the Aranadans. The jungle provides them with food though the quest for tubers is time consuming and not easy, particularly in the rainy season. Contact with the plainsmen has

*From *Seminar* (14), October 1960.

increased their wants. More cloth, tobacco, tea and beedi are now in demand and the craving for rice is also on the increase. The cash to meet these new needs has to be earned by casual labour on the farms in forest valleys, and by collecting and selling barks from which rope is made. Their patrons and employers are chiefly Muslims in the local bazzars who are generally ruthless in their exploitation, but in spite of this the Aranadans prefer to work for the Muslims. The Hindus treat the Aranadans as very 'impure' and keep them at a distance. The Aranadans are almost omnivorous—they eat even pythons—and the local Hindus look on the food habits of the tribesmen with disgust and horror. Those who are well off have a general tendency in southern India—I do not know if it is so in other parts of the country—to insult the poor and to treat their poverty as though it were a crime. Nothing distresses the Aranadans so much as the insult and ridicule to which they are subjected. Some of the insulting stories have found their way even into official reports prepared by government agents who gather information about the tribes from the local bazzars! In spite of their poverty, they are a pleasant and likeable people. I have enjoyed their friendship and regard them as good as any of our best tribal groups.

Credit goes to L.N. Rao, until recently member of the Servants of India Society, for being the first social worker in India to turn his attention to the Aranadans. With great difficulty, he started a school for the tribesmen at Karulai in the Nilambur taluk of the Calicut district and made arrangements to acquire housing sites for them.

Survivals of the prehistoric stage of a food-gathering economy, as illustrated by the Aranadans, are not confined to Kerala. Sections of the Chenchus of the Andhra State are still ignorant of or averse to agriculture and eke out a living by grubbing for roots and tubers in the same way as the Aranadans; they supplement what is offered by nature by the earnings of casual work for forest contractors and others from the plains. Efforts made by the Madras and Hyderabad Governments some decades ago to settle them in 'colonies' failed miserably, as the plans were ill-conceived and did not take into account the needs of the people. The majority of the tribes of southern India are shifting cultivators. The future of these tribes is left nebulous and uncertain. The Union Home Minister is perhaps the only person in a position of authority who has expressed his sympathy for the thousands whose subsistence and survival are made problematic by the vacillations in government policy towards shifting cultivation. The matter has been discussed threadbare by national and international bodies of experts and the discussions seem endless, but meanwhile the distress of the tribesmen is welling up.

Let me try to give the reader the case history of the situation in the Attapady valley in Kerala inhabited by the three tribes, of whom the Mudugas are best known to me. The Mudugas number about 3000 and are on the friendliest terms with the other tribes, namely the Irulas and Kurumbas. Until very recently they had only minimal contacts with the people of the plains on the Malabar and Coimbatore sides, as there were no motorable roads to their valley. A few officers of the forest department, rare visitors of the revenue department and the representatives of the landlords who owned a great part of the forests were the only outsiders with whom they dealt. As several miles of good roads were constructed during recent years, and the exploitation of the forest, and the clearing of forest land for wet cultivation and for plantations, etc., gained momentum, the tribesmen were exposed to the full blast of the forces of changes. All along the roads can now be seen the settlements of the plainsmen, small traders and agents of planters and labourers from the plains, who outnumber the tribesmen. Missionaries and tractors, WHO teams of malariologists and anthropologists, make the Attapady scene typically modern. The new facility of transport enables the tribesmen in their turn to see towns and learn urban ways.

Kumri (slash-and-burn) cultivation of the hill slopes is the basis of the subsistence economy of the Mudugas. Until a few years ago, there was little restriction on the area of the jungle which they could clear and cultivate, and so the tribesmen had a fair degree of economic security. But now both government and the private owners of the forests have imposed very severe restrictions on the Mudugas' traditional right to clear and cultivate the hill slopes. The area allotted for cultivation is now strictly limited and instead of remaining fallow for future *kumri,* the cleared plots are being planted by government and the private landlords with economically important timber or fruit trees. Private landlords seem to be exploiting the needs of the tribesmen;

they get the scrub jungle cleared for their plantations in the cheapest possible manner. No one has raised the question of the tribesmen's right to the soil on which they have been living for years and whether it can be so unceremoniously alienated.

What is the kind of future that awaits our children? That was the question which a tribal friend of mine asked me, his eyes moist with tears. The average Muduga is now a highly frustrated person; he has begun to hate the roads which he thinks have brought them all these troubles. At the time of my visit (1955), the valley was under the Madras Government. The tribesmen told me that they had heard of a government department which was supposed to look after their interests, but none of them had seen any representative of that department. They had grown cynical about visiting government officials who promised sympathy which was never translated into action. The M.L.A. for whom they voted, and who in turn promised to do many things for them, did not bother to visit them.

Till December 1959, anyone who had anything to do with the Attapady valley exploited the Mudugas, and no one, not even the Government of Madras, did a thing for their welfare. However, a pilot project for tribal welfare was inaugurated in December 1959, for the tribes of the Attapady valley by the Government of Kerala. The two things for which the Mudugas in their frustration crave are land and schools. The tribesmen here, with so much of unused land about them, are now among those thousands who are described as landless and land-hungry. I can understand their craving for land, but it was not clear to me why they hankered after schools. They seem vaguely to realise the need for literate leadership.

Some of the tribes of southern India, now lying low and docile, were once spirited fighters for freedom from oppression. The Konds, one of the major tribes of southern Orissa and northern Andhra, the Konda Doras who followed the lead of the revolutionary Sitaram Raju and waged war against the British, the Kurichiyas of Wynad who under the Rajah of Kottayam fought with great heroism against the East India Company, were all heroes in their own way.

In spite of the Government's safeguards for the tribes, the half-hearted manner in which State policies were executed made it possible for money-lenders and traders (with the connivance of petty officials) to make life miserable for the tribesmen. In the Agency areas of Andhra, tribal riots or *fituris* were the only way of inviting the attention of the Government to the existence of oppression. But the Government had only one way of reacting to a riot and that was shooting down the troublesome tribesmen. The last riot in the Agencies of Andhra was the *fituri* under Sitaram Raju which took place about four decades ago. The story goes that the tribesmen's grievances were directed against a very corrupt and troublesome tahsildar who was making roads by forced tribal labour. The tribesmen were accustomed to work without wages for the local zamindars, but the latter were considerate. They demanded only a small number of workers and if a man had urgent work of his own, he was allowed to absent himself. The tahsildar in question knew no mercy; the tribesmen found the situation intolerable and rose in revolt, but the *fituri* was but down and hundreds of tribesmen and their leader were killed. Tearfully, our old Konda Dora guide showed us the place where Sitaram Raju was shot dead. The lands of several tribesmen who participated in the riot were confiscated by the British Government. After Independence, several of them appealed that their confiscated lands be restored to them, but it is doubtful if anything has yet been done in the matter.

The Kurichiya tribesmen of Kerala, who were land-owning farmers, practising both dry and wet cultivation, have during the last hundred years been reduced to the position of tenants-at-will (in most cases, of their creditors). Many of them had their lands confiscated by the Government for the crime of participating in a riot against payment of revenue in cash. Several others lost their holdings by the manipulation of revenue officials. A Kurichiya family-head told me that his ancestors lost a whole hill slope and the valley below for the simple reason that they could not deposit a small sum of money demanded by the surveyors. Others, of course, were ready to acquire the land they lost! This hill slope is now a fine tea plantation. If it were possible to gather correct information about land dealings in tribal areas, the story would not make pleasant reading. I have yet to see a government agency in southern India which is interested in restoring land to the tribesmen.

In the State of Orissa, one of the tribes started satyagraha to get back its land. The struggle was partly successful because the

Government was sympathetic and fortunate to have some officials who carried out its wishes, administering the laws in the spirit in which those laws were made. In the southern States, the tribes are so disorganised, and the land-hungry and predatory plainsmen so strongly pitted against them, that the feeble government measures for the protection of tribal interest have all proved infructuous. The point I wish to make is that government have been responsible, directly or indirectly, for the economic malaise that afflicts the tribesmen. They have failed to give the minority—the weakest of our minorities—the protection it deserves from exploitation by the stronger members of the majority communities.

Frustration and a feeling of inadequacy seem to make members of the small tribal communities in the South suffer from a severe inferiority complex. I have seen bold heroes of the jungle who, for sport, net and spear tigers, quake with fear in the presence of revenue inspectors! The threat of imprisonment is enough to shatter the resistance of any tribesmen. I know of cases where, to escape from the clutches of the police, tribesmen have sold all their belongings. Plainsmen, often unconsciously, make use of any means at their disposal to denigrate the tribes. The schoolbooks which our children study still continue to spread the stupid idea that the tribesmen are racially different and inferior. The anthropologist has made it clear that no racial line separates the jungle-dwellers from the rest of the Indian community, that they are Indians who have chosen somewhat different ways of life and have failed to make adjustments as readily as others more exposed to change. But the gap between the writers of schoolbooks and the scientists is still very wide in southern India. It is high time that something was done to remove the race prejudice against the tribesmen from the mind of the public.

While discussing their problems, I asked a Paniya—Paniyas are a large tribe of former serfs in the Wynad Taluk of Malabar district—why he did not send his children to school. His reply was: 'Can washing transform a cow into a crane? He seemed to be convinced that he and his people were created dull and no amount of education was going to be of use to them. The first tribal M.L.A. representing the tribes of the Wynad area was a Paniya.

While pessimism and depression comprise the lot of the majority of the tribes, I should not fail to mention a small number of tribes like the Todas who fell they are the best in the world and refuse to regard anyone as their equal! The Todas were the lords of the Nilgiris once upon a time, and still live in the hope that the Government of Madras will honour an old agreement and restore to them the Toda Patta land.

The Government of India is quite clear that its objective is to integrate the tribal people with the rest of the Indian community. Funds, which according to pre-Independence standards, would seem ample have been earmarked for various programmes to help the tribes to reach the level of the rest of our people. To speed up this transformation, internal leadership or, in its absence, outside leadership in which the tribesmen have trust, should be present. Unfortunately, the small scattered tribes have no leadership worth the name. There are men of character and capacity among them, but they are illiterate. Missionaries have begun work among some of them, for example, among the Todas, among the Irulas and also among the Kurichiyas.

The larger tribes of Andhra Pradesh have some leaders, but they are detribalised and 'sanskritised', caring more for the personal advantages of being a tribal than for the welfare of their fellow tribesmen. Missionaries have been doing very useful work in the Andhra tribal areas for some decades. They give some protection and security to the tribal convert. In the context of helplessness of the tribes against exploitation, Christianity plus missionary protection seem to be far more satisfactory than tribal culture and religion minus subsistence. The missionary fills a vacuum in the tribal areas and until some better agencies go and do better work than the missionary, anti-missionary talk is just hollow non-sense. It is strange that Hindu ethnocentrism would not allow missionaries to organise welfare work among the tribes in some States, while the Hindu leaders of these and other States are eager to send their own children to schools run by the missionaries and would also have them feed the patients in the large hospitals (as in Madras)!

Most of the tribal welfare work now done in the southern States is through official agencies. Any welfare in a poor country is difficult, as the needy are many and resources inadequate. Still, the leaders in New Delhi are lamenting that the funds allotted are not being spent. The district welfare officers in the tribal areas are as good as any other class of officers, but the tribesmen's capacity and readiness to accept the innovations presented to them by the welfare officers are less than those of the rural peasant. Unless government procedures are simplified work in tribal areas will continue to be difficult and slow.

The difficulties can be illustrated from the working of the Andhra Scheduled Tribes Co-operative Finance and Development Corporation started in 1956-57 as a large cooperative organisation for credit, sale and purchasing, all combined. Though well conceived and good in intention, the Corporation is poorly staffed and works without adequate consideration for the tribesmen. I am told that the money-lender is still able to do good business keeping the tribesmen away from the Corporation because he deals with them at a personal level and has no confounding forms and procedures. Unless procedures are simplified and the moneylenders banned from tribal areas, the Corporation is bound not to succeed. Government welfare work is almost like unorganised charity. Instead of creating organisations which would generate their own momentum, the government make a well here, a few houses there, and a few hostels and offer a few scholarships for students. This is just charity. It is of course, better than doing nothing, but it is no substitute for new institutions essential in the new and changing set-up.

We should send out a band of enthusiastic men and women into the tribal areas, young people who will have Schweitzer and Thakkar Bapa as their ideals. They should identify themselves with the tribes and rouse them to directed activity to rebuild their economy and culture. The speech of the Prime Minister at the Tribal Conference in Delhi, in June 1952, is almost a Magna Carta of the Indian tribes, but the unfortunate thing is that the personnel to work out his policy has not yet come into being.

At government level, something in this direction can be done by creating a special cadre of government officials trained for social work among the tribes. They will provide the on-the-spot leadership which the tribal groups require to run their cooperative and other types of new group activities. Welfare work in the tribal areas in the South has to be reorganised, but the key to the problem is personnel. Men are available but they will have to be hand-picked. The State governments are spending a lot of money organising cooperative societies, opening schools and settling some tribal families in colonies, but the tempo of the work and its impact are so slight that one's hopes, raised to a high pitch by the framers of our Constitution and our planners, are being dashed to the ground. Several friends of the tribes share this feeling with me. It is not mere evaluation that is now wanted (though it is desirable and should be done by a non-governmental body of evaluators), but rethinking and replanning.

In their statements on the general implications of tribal welfare, the Planning Commission has very wisely suggested that the administrator, the specialist, the social worker and the anthropologist should pool their experience and resources in approaching the problems of the tribes. In all the four southern States, anthropological work is conspicuous by its absence. The Union Government has been pressing these States for long to start tribal research institutes, but no action has yet been taken. The excuse in one State is that its tribal population is small, as though scientific information about a small tribe is likely to be less interesting than that about a large tribe. Numbers seem to be very important. An angry officer asked me: 'Why should I bother about the health of 600 miserable Todas? I am concerned about the health of millions of others.' If the State governments themselves are not keenly interested in the progress and welfare of the tribes, it is too much to expect their officers to show interest.

One, therefore, takes the neglect of research on tribal problems as an indication of the lack of interest of the four southern State governments in their tribes. If further proof is wanted, one has only to go through the report of the Commissioner for Scheduled Tribes and Scheduled Castes, a good part of which is devoted to a lament over things that ought to but in fact have not been done by the State governments. They do not even send the Commissioner reports in time or hold meetings of the tribal advisory councils 'for want of business'.

Tribes in Central India

TRIBAL ZONES

The tribal population of India is generally divided into three Zones according to their distribution, namely, the North-Eastern Zone, the Central Zone, and the Southern Zone. The North-Eastern Zone consists of the Himalayan region and the hill and mountain ranges of North-Eastern India. The Southern Zone consists of that part of the Peninsular India which falls South of the river Krishna. The Central Zone occupies the central belt of the older hills and plateaus along the dividing line between Peninsular India and the Indo-Gangetic Plains. The main tribes inhabiting this zone are the Santhal, Munda, Oraon, Ho, Bhumij, Kharia, Birhar, Bhuiyan, Juang, Kandh, Savara, Gond, Baiga, Bhil, Koli, Korku, etc.

SCHEDULED TRIBES IN MADHYA BHARAT

The State of Madhya Bharat falls in this Central Zone. There are five tribes in Madhya Bharat: The Bhils, the Bhilalas (including other sub-tribes), the Saharias, the Korkus and the Gonds.

The constitution (Scheduled Tribes) Order, 1950 recognised the above five tribes as the only scheduled tribes of the State.

Scheduled Areas

Eleven of the Covenanting States of Madhya Bharat had sizeable tribal populations. These state, or parts thereof, were brought together to form the Scheduled Areas, mentioned in the Schedule II of the Covenant.

More or less the same areas were declared by the President of India, as the Scheduled Areas of the State by the Scheduled Areas (Part B States) Order, 1950. The Scheduled Areas are:

(a) Revenue district of Jhabua (whole). All the five tehsils of Jhabua, Alirajpur, Petlawad, Thandla and Jobat).
(b) Tehsils Sendhwa, Barwant, Rajpur, Khargone, Bhikangaon and Maheshwar of the Revenue district of Nimar.[4]
(c) Tehsils Sardarpur, Kukshi, Dhar and Manawar of the Revenue district of Dhar.
(d) Tehsil Sailana in the Revenue district of Ratlam.

The scheduled area extends to the sixteen tehsils in the south of the State and covers an area of 10,011 square miles. Except the tehsil of Sailana in the district of Ratlam the rest of the area falls in the Hill division. Even Sailana tehsil, which does not fall in the Hill division, is geographically very akin to the hilly region of the rest of the scheduled areas. The chief features of the scheduled areas are the hilly terrain, dense forests, poor soils and lack of irrigation facilities. The Constitution (Scheduled Tribes) Order, 1950, recognised the Bhils and Bhilalas (inclusive of sub-tribes) as Scheduled Tribes *only within the confines of the Scheduled Areas*. Bhil and Bhilalas, outside the Scheduled Areas were not treated as Scheduled Tribes. On the other hand the Saharia, Gond and Korku were created as Scheduled Tribes throughout the State.

The Scheduled Areas account for nearly 86 per cent of the tribal population of the State. This 86 per cent of population lives in contiguous areas in the Scheduled Areas. This concentration of the tribes population has imparted a characteristic culture to these areas. The economy, the language, the customs, the manners—all the aspects of the social life of the areas bear a strong imprint of the aboriginal culture.

THE TRIBES OF MADHYA BHARAT

Anthropologically the tribes of Madhya Bharat can be classified in two main classes: The Munda and the Gond.

The Munda class is further subdivided into three sub-classes. The Bhil, Savara and the Korku. The Bhil group includes the Bhilala and other allied sub-tribes such as Mankar, Barela and Rathia. The Gond class consists only of the Gonds.

Geographical Distribution of the Tribes

Reference was made earlier to the characteristic geographical distribution of these tribes in the State. Except the Gonds and Korkus who inhabit the same regions of Nemawar in the district Dewas on the Plateau, rest of the tribes are found in different well defined regions. The Saharias inhabit the district Morena of the Lowlands, and the districts Guna, Shivpuri and Bhilsa of the Plateau. Looked purely from a geographical angle the Saharias live in a compact and contiguous hilly tract covering the districts of Morena, Guna and Shivpuri. The Bhils and the Bhilalas, almost exclusively, live in the Hill division of the south.

But whether in the Lowlands, the Plateau or the Hill division, their inhabitation is invariable a spur of the Vindhyas or the Satpuras, and the regions adjoining them. Godds and Korkus, although living on the Plateau, do not have the rolling plains as their habitation. Centuries of oppression have driven them to the hills where they eke out a miserable and marginal existence on the mercy of nature. The same holds true of the Saharias on the Plateau as well as the Lowland. Beit a Bhil or Bhilala, a Saharia or a Gond or a Korku; be it the north, the centre or the south of the State the tribal setting is the same. Their hearths and homes are set in the wildest forests and the hardest hills. The Vindhyan hills run like a common cord through the lives of the tribal pepole giving them a common physical environment. And, physical environment plays a very important part in the determination of the material and moral culture of the people which we term as history. Gordon East aptly remarks, "It is often said, history is all Geography, for we know that at a primitive stage of culture and for a countless millenia, folk lived on the sufference of an ommipotent nature which they were powerless either to modify or to exploit". And nature and habitat have continued to exercise on the life of the tribals an influence which is the main determinant of their present status. Under the poorest resources available they have not done very badly. They have kept their material needs to the minimum and exploited the natural resources, with the skill and tools they have, to their best.

THE BHILS

The Bhils are the third most numerous tribe of India after Gonds and Santhals. The total Bhil population of the country was 23 lakhs in 1941. In the tribal population of Madhya Bharat they constitute the largest element. And they are also the most familiar, as a consequence, no doubt, of their long and close contact with the Hindus.

History

The origin of the word 'Bhil' is still clothed with uncertainty and the various explanations put forward to unravel the mystery of the appellation are well within the realm of conjecture. It is commonly believed that "the word Bhil is derived from a Dravidian word for a bow which is the characteristic weapon of the tribe".

Venkatachar mentions that the ancient Tamil poets termed certain savages of the pre-Dravidian blood as *Villaur* (Bowman), and he suggests that possibly the modern Bhils are the tribe designated by the later term. According to this school of thought Bhil is not a tribe name at all. Venkatachar is of the opinion that Bhils are a pre-Dravidian race, probably Proto-Mediterranean, who spread "far and wide when a climatic crisis occurred in the grass steppes of Sahara, and it is this race which is responsible for the industry associated with Final Capsian culture in the Vindhyas". The Bhils are held to have occupied the Aravali hills and the Western Vindhyas between the Banas and Mahi rivers. The Dravidians, a Mediterranean race, entered India through south-west and moved towards the south, "And it would be reasonable to suppose that Gujarat was on the way of the immigrant Dravidians in their march towards the Deccan and the South". It must have been here that the first contact and clash of cultures took place and earned the Bhils their present name.

It is commonly held that the Bhils are identical with the

pygmies mentioned by Ktesias (400 B.C.) and the Phyllitae of Ptolemy (A.D. 150). Sometimes the world *Nishad* which occurs in the *Samhitas* and the *Brahmans,* is held to mean Bhilla or Bhil. But Nishad meant one who sat low (नि. + षाद्) and such is could not be taken to mean any specific tribe. It is rightly held to be a generic name applied to non-Aryans who had accepted low positions in the Vedic Society. Bose, basing his view on the *Arthasastra* and the *Dharmasastras,* is of the opinion that Nishad meant the offspring of Brahman of a sudra women.

Still others identify it with the Pulinda tribe mentioned in the *Aitreya Brahman* and the edicts of Ashoka. Venkatachar quotes Enthoven to the effect that the word Bhil occurs for the first time in the *Katha Sarita Sagar* wherein mention is also made of a Bhil chief opposing the progress of another king through the Vindhyas.

Whether Bhils are autochthonous or not, is very difficult to say. But there is no tradition to suggest that they were ever masters of the plains of Malwa. Malwa, as we know, was colonized in very early times. At the time of Buddha, Malwa was a highly developed republic. Malcolm says, "The Bhils of Malwa and neighbouring provinces have no record of ever having possessed the plains of the country; but they assert, and on authentic grounds, that they long maintained exclusive possession of the hilly tracts under their leaders, many of whom were as distinguished by their character as by their wealth and power. The accounts we have of the comparatively recent conquest of Dongurhpoor, Banswara, Jabooah, Barwanee, and other principalities fully establish the truth of this pretension".

Their Earlier Home

It may be safe to suggest that Rajasthan was the real home of the Bhils. When the Muslim invasion of India began in the 11th century the Rajputs were pressed to leave the Indo-Gangetic plain and migrated to Rajasthan, in turn expelling the Bhils from there. Thus, there was a contact between Bhils and the proud Rajputs who were not averse to accepting Bhil maidens as brides. The unions resulted into splitting the Bhil tribe into Hinduised sub-tribes such as Bhilalas, Patlias, etc. The introduction of Rajput blood led to further distinctions among the Bhils: The *Ujle* (pure) and *Mele* (impure) Bhils which do not inter-marry.

This view is strengthened by the tradition among the Rajputs to recognize the Bhil as the former residents and masters of the land by the fact that some Rajput chiefs could not assume the throne untill they were marked on the forehead with a Bil's blood. The alliance between the Bhils and the Rajputs resulting in marriages and other forms of social intercourse, however, were short lived. Hinduism became more orthodox in Rajasthan and because of their habits of beef eating, the Bhils slowly started losing the position of equality and began to be treated with contempt. This change again forced them to migrate to the Central highlands where they had preforce to wander in the most inaccessible, remote and difficult regions on the hills, where, subsequently, they had to make their homes.

Major Erskine, writing in 1908, has something very uncomplimentary to say of the Bhils, "About thirty years ago, a native student in an examination for a University degree described the tribe thus, 'The Bhil is a very black man, but more hairy. He carries in his hand a long spear, with which he runs you when he meets you, and afterwards throws your body in the ditch. By this you may know a Bhil'."

MARATHAS AND THE BHILS

However exaggerated and naive be the description, it does underline heavily the predatory and lawless habits of the Bhils during nearly two centuries of their recent past. The transformation of these former masters of the Rajasthan into free-booters and unabashed savages can be traced to the Maratha invasion of the Central India in the seventeenth century. Marathas treated the Bhils in a most cruel and merciless manner. If they found a Bhil in the disturbed part of the country, he was, without any enquiry, flogged and hanged. Hundreds were thrown over high cliffs, and large bodies of them, assembled under promise of pardon, were beheaded or blown from guns. Their women were mutilated or smothered by smoke, and their children smashed to death against stones.

Writing of the conditions in the Nimar District in the middle of the eighteenth century, Luard has also described the death and destruction heaped on the Bhils. Describing the campaigns of extermination against the Bhils, he writes, "these people were brought into Khargone and were required to give security for good behaviour. On doing so they were presented with a special collar to wear. All Bhils who did not give in were caught and beheaded at the *chabutra* in Khargone. The pillar to which the victims were bound for execution is still extant as also the axe used".

Forsyth also has given a very graphic description of the unsettled conditions then prevailing in the whole of Central India. Says he, "The hill tribes, Pindari plunderers and lawless Maratha soldiery with their daggers at each other's throats, were unanimous in robbing the husbandmen who ploughed their fields by night with swords and matchlocks tied to the shafts of their ploughts or purchased peace by heavy payments of blackmail".

It is evident that the tribal people were forced to a profession of lawlessness and savagery as a consequence of being chased from pillar to the post by a succession of invaders. First came Rajputs who deprived them of their legitimate lands in the Rajasthan plains and pursued them to the most inaccessible parts of the hills. Then came the Marathas to whom the tribal life was no more precious than a common fly. Deprived of land to cultivate and opportunity to live at peace, the struggle for existence forced upon them a mode of guerilla warfare. Unbiased towards the tribal people, Forsyth readily admits that they were greatly maligned in being described as 'savage and intractable'. Malcolm also admits that "believing themselves doomed to be thieves and plunderers they have been confirmed in their destiny by the oppression and cruelty of neighbouring governments, increased by an avowed contempt for them as out-castes. The common answer of a Bhil when charged with theft and robbery is, "I am not to blame; I am the Mahadeva's thief." This fatalism, outcome as it was of the anarchy of the times and the historical development of centuries preceding it, had however, not changed the nature and the basic character of the tribal folks. When once the conditions settled down and they found their necks safe from the knives of the marauders they took to more peaceful professions. Forsyth, playing them the tribute of an administrator who had known them well as Settlement officer, says, "they have long since gained the character of being a remarkably submissive and law-abiding people."

But the lands they lost to the Rajputs and other castes ranging high in the Hindu hierarchy were never restored to them, and to this day they cultivate the most unsuitable lands. Their overwhelming dependence on forests is also to be traced to the same facts of history.

Marriage

Bhils are not permitted to marry in their own *gotra* (sept) nor can they marry outside the tribe. Thus, the tribe is endogamous, while the sept is exogamous. No one can marry in the same sept in which he has already married for at last three generations. The same prohibition applies to marriage in the sept to which his mother belonged. There is no prohibition of a man marrying two sisters.

The marriage is generally adult. But the Hindu influence has slowly effected a marked change in this respect. Child marriage is considered more respectable and fashionable today than it ever was in the past. Even then adult marriage is the rule. Several types of marriages are prevalent among the Bhils. They are:

(i) *Lagan Mandwa* (Hinduised form of religious marriage).
(ii) *Lugda-ladi* (An abbreviated form of the conventional marriage).
(iii) *Aa bharana ar uchal jana* (marriage by intrusion).
(iv) *Ghees kar le jana* (marriage by abduction).
(v) *Ghar jamai* (matrilocal marriage).

Lagan Mandwa

In the more orthodox type of marriage reliable persons representing the two parties meet at the place of the girl's father and work out the details of bride-price which varies between Rs. 6 and Rs. 140. Besides cash, grain and *gur* are also given. When the terms of the marriage have been settled the betrothal ceremony known as *chhak* takes place.

On the day of the marriage the bridegroom's party goes to the bride's place accompanied with friends and relatives. It is customary in Bhil marriages for the ladies of the household to join the party. Generally the boy is mounted. The party is led by a person or a group of persons beating a drum in a singsong way. The bridegroom is dressed for the occasion in white *dhoti* and red *angrakha* and wears an imitation crown known as *maur*. The night is spent in an orgy of drinking and dancing to the accompaniment of wild and rousing music. After an exchange of presents the upper-garments of the boy and the girl are joined and seven times the couple goes round the nuptial fire lighted in the middle of the *mandap*. Again there is feasting and singing and dancing. Next day the party returns with the bride.

This is more or less the orthodox and Hinduized form of marriage. Greater the degree of Hindu influence, the more would be the performance of the customary rituals and the greater would be the divergence from the truly tribal form. Hinduized tribal castes which regard themselves higher in the social scale insist upon the presence of a Brahmin priest to conduct their ceremonies. This type of marriage costs anywhere between Rs. 500 to Rs. 1000 the days. This, looking to the economic condition of the tribe, is an exhorbitant sum. The poorer and more humbler people take recourse to other forms of marriage.

Lugda Ladi

This is a more economical form of marriage as compared to the religious form described earlier. The bride-price is settled as in the orthodox form and on an auspicious day the bride-price is made over to the bride's father. On a suitable day the boy's father takes the wedding party consisting of not more than five persons to the bride's place. The bride is presented with a new set of *lugra* and the marriage is over. After a day or two the party returns with the bride.

Bharana or Uchal Jana (Intrusion)

Sometimes, when tbe girl takes a liking to a boy, she enters the boy's house by the backdoor and silently starts doing the household work. Generally this happens with the full consent and knowledge of the boy. After the girl has forced her entry, the boy's father informs the girl's father of the incident and invites him to talk over the terms of settlement of bride-price, etc. The bride's father, accompanied by the *Patel* and *Panchs* of his village come to the boy's father for the talks. This is known as *jhagra todna* or setting the dispute. The bride price is settled and duly paid.

Bhaga kar le jana (or capture)

This is capture only in name. Really speaking it is an elopement with mutual consent. For the sake of her self-respect the girl insists on the boy dragging her a few steps so that she may not be accused of having taken the lead in elopement which is considered unladylike. This type of marriage generally follows the *Bhagoria* festival held during the *Holi* festival. The lovers, taking advantage of the festival, take to the jungle celebrating the honeymoon there. Later, they return to the boy's house and the usual settlement of bride-price follows.

This form of marriage is perhaps a reminder of the marriage by capture that might have existed among the Bhils at some point of their history.

Ghar Jamai (Matrilocal Marriage)

This is a very characteristic and economically very significant form of marriage. When a boy is too poor to be able to pay the bride-price, he agrees to work for a stipulated number of years at the bride's place. The stipulated period is 7-9 years. After the expiry of this period, the girl becomes his lawfully wedded wife. Even during the course of 'apprenticeship' they live like man and wife, and the children born during this period are considered legitimate. Generally, after the expiry of the term the boy sets up his own independent household, not far from that of his father-in-law's. This type of marriage is taken recourse to either in case of the poverty of the boy or when the girl's father has no brothers or sons to help in the agricultural operations.

The *ghar jamai* is a laughing stock of the whole village. The Bhils have a witty proverb about the *ghar jamai*:

Son-in-law in a distant part,
Like flowers sweet, is dear to heart,
But, should he come to stay in town,
Half his worth is at once down!
And, God forbid! that his own spouse
Should lodge him in her father's house!
A beast of burden, loaded at will:
To this sad lot, he's condemned still!

Widows

There is no prohibition against the re-marriage of the widows. They can marry any person they like. Widow remarriage is known as *Natra.* The bride-price in case of widows is generally very low. The common practice is for the widow to marry her *devar* (husband's younger brother) if he is unmarried. This is known as *devar-batta* (Levirate). The widows are, as a rule, not permitted to take the children along with them to the house of the new husband.

Divorce

Divorce is common among the Bhils. There is no formal procedure gone through for effecting a divorce. The woman just leaves the husband and enters the house-hold of a man with whom she has had a prior understanding. This would be simply *Aa bharana.* In such an event the former husband will demand the refund of bride-price and the expenses he had incurred over the present woman. A *jhagra-todna* panchayat would be held and the sum settled. Sometimes the divorce is settled through the Panchayat, in which case the break of the relationship is signified by breaking a twig or tearing a piece of cloth.

In cases of the existence of bad blood between the former and the new husbands, or a refusal by the new husband to pay the damages, a bloody feud ensues, resulting in murders and arosen running a long course of destruction in the families concerned and passing on from one generation to another as a sacred behest!

Polygamy

It is prevalent in the tribe. But the practice is not very common. The reason is largely economic. As we have seen, the Bhil marriage is a costly affair and those who can afford it are few. The explanation generally given by a Bhil for taking another wife is invariably economic. "She would share the work in the field and the house".

Polyandry is altogether unknown.

Death

The Bhils cremate their dead. Only young babies and victims of leprosy and small pox and snake-bite are buried. The corpse is laid on a bier, feet pointing south and head towards the north. After the body is consumed the unburnt bones are collected and placed in an earthern vessel and buried near the house. Sometimes the bones are deposited in some stream nearby. On the twelfth day at the spot of burial of the ashes a ceremony is held.

Bhils give expensive feasts to pacify the dead. These feasts are known as *Nukta*. Mutton, liquor, rice, *makki roti* and *gur*, etc. are served in these feasts. This feast is an celeberate affair and several villages join these feasts for which no formal invitation is deemed essential. If the deceased came of a poor family and his family was not in a position to bear the expenses, the friends and relatives coming for the *nukta* bring goats, grains, *gur*, etc. with them as presents.

Religion

The religion of the Bhil is generally described as animism. But a long contact with Hindus has resulted in the adoption of many of the Hindu gods and goddesses by them. The feeling of caste, also a result of Hindu contact, spurs their desire to be considered high in the social esteem. And, as a result, the Bhils living in contact with Hindus like to be regarded as Hindus. Particularly Mahadeva, Ganesh and Kali Mata, they have made their own. Instances are not rare where they worship Vishnu (Rama and Krishna *avataras)*. As a matter of fact, Hindu religion itself is not a religion in the strike sense of the term but an agglomeration of religions not infrequently widely divergent and markedly antithetical to each other. It has been described by some as a vast canopy under which are collected all sort of gods and goddesses. Many practices of caste Hindus are purely animistic in origin, concept and observance. To describe animism purely as that category of faith which includes all "pre-Hindu religions of India", would not be quite accurate in the light of the modern theories and views. Hinduism not only absorbed all faiths existing in India before the Aryans came, but also developed and evolved them in higher forms. Mahadeva, for instance, definitely a god of the Austric Proto-Australoids, in the post-Aryan era, became altogether different.

The most important of the Bhil gods is the *Baba deo* or *Bara deo* who is the village tutelary deity. Every village has a separate piece of land allotted to *Baba deo*. It is marked either by a tree or pegs of *sagi* wood. The piece of land is held sacred and the forest on the land is never cut. Offerings of earthen wares, clay horses and toy swings are made to *Baba deo*. He is specially worshiped in the month of *Shravan* (July-August). On the day fixed for worship the whole of the Bhil village collects round the '*Baba deo*' and after making offerings spends the day in drinking and singing. In cases of ailments *Baba deo* is offered goats, cocks and other things to pacify his wrath.

BHILALAS

Bhilalas are included in the Bhil group and are quite numerous, next only to the Bhils.

Bhilalas claim to be Rajputs and do not inter-marry and inter-dine with the Bhils whom they consider to be of low status. Luard suggests that they are a mixed caste as a result of Rajput men marrying Bhil women of Central India. Russel confirms this view and further suggests that Bhilala is a corruption of Bhilwala, a term that might have been applied to those Rajput immigrants who came to Central India and in order to acquire estates here took the short cut of marrying the daughters of Bhil chieftains who then possessed these lands. Luard suggests a different origin of the term. He is of the opinion that the term Bhilala is derived from Bhilara meaning a Bhil by mistake (ara). Fuchs, who conducted anthropometric measurements of Bhils and Bhilaias, however, holds a very different view. He regards them, "racially more or less pure Bhils", and suggests, that "having acquired a better social and economic status, they have segregated from the ordinary Bhil tribal."

The Bhilaias consists of two main groups, the *Bade* and the *Chhote.* There is no inter-marriage between these groups. But there is no prohibition of a Bhilala of *Bade* (superior) caste taking water from the hands of another of the *chhote* (inferior) caste. Both these castes are further split up into numerous exogamous septs. In their customs and beliefs Bhilaias are hardly distinguishable from Bhils. Perhaps the most important distinction lies in the fact that Bhilaias do not eat beef, whereas the Bhils do.

Malcolm has written very contemptuously of the Bhilaias. He has reflected the turbulent and unsettled condition then prevailing in Central India. And, none was more actively taking advantage of the existing chaos and anarchy than the Bhilala chiefs of Nimar and Rath. A very notable example of this type was the Bhilala, Nadirshah, who had his capital in the small village of Jamnia near Mandu. At one time he had 200 horses and 700 soldiers. He was subsequently captured by the English and banished to Allahabad.

Their religious beliefs and social customs are like those of the Bhils with the only difference that the degree of acculturation due to Hindu influence is greater. Because of their historical association with the Rajputs they have better land and economically they are better off.

Language

Hutton regards Bhili as an Indo-Aryan tongue and suggests that it probably replaced an old Dravidian tongue and perhaps a Kolarian language before that. At present it is found overladen with Gujarati and to some extent Marathi.

Social Customs

Bhils are very fond of tattooing, and get various designs made on the cheeks, forehead, arms, chest and legs. In inaccessible areas the tattooting is done by the village people with *Babul* thorns and colour obtained from *Balor* and *Bijan.* Since the opening up of the areas we can see the tattooing machine in operation in the village *hats* in the tribal areas. The tattoo operator has a very busy time, particularly, with the tribal belles who flock to his shop in great numbers.

Ornaments

Bhils are equally fond of ornaments and spend a good deal of money on this form of decoration. Even men like to wear ornaments in their ears and neck. The ornaments are generally made of silver and *Kansa.*

Clothes

Men generally wear a *langoti* (loincloth) which just covers the organs leaving the major parts of the buttocks exposed. Even the most sophisticated Bhil prefers this *langoti* when at home or working in the fields and forests. It is only when he visits the market that he wraps a *picholi* (a piece of long cloth) round his waist, and sometimes puts on a colourful waistcoat known as *jhuldi* and a short turban known as *pagdi.* The *pagdi* inveriably carries a short comb tucked inside.

Women wear a skirt known as *ghagra* with red or black prints. The ghagra is not strictly a skirt for it is not stitched round. It is more like a long piece of cloth with the top carrying a *nara* to tie it round the waist. The *ghagra* is folded in front and passed between the legs and fixed at the back in the fashion male dhotis, leaving a major part of the thighs exposed. The breasts are covered with a short *kanchli* with open back. An *orhni* on the head, also of a red or black print, completes the female dress. The *orhni* is generally worn by married girls. The children up to the age of 5-6 years go about naked. All their clothes are sold ready-made at the villages hats. The art of the needle is almost unknown.

Men sometimes wear shoes which are called *khadha* in the Bhili. Women generally go bare-footed.

Food

The staple food of the Bhails in *makka* (zea mays) and *jowar* (sorghum vulgate) and *bajra* (Pencillaria spicata) and other small millets. Makki is used for bread (finely ground) and *thuli* (coarsely ground) which they call as *rabdi*. The bread or *roti* is taken with salt and chillies. Chutney of *kaitha* (Feronia elephantum) and other fruits are also used with *roti*. Among the dals their preference is for *urd* (phaseolus radiatus) and *tuar* (cajanus indicus), specially the latter. *Rabdi* is commonly taken with butter-milk. Generally vegetables are not used except those that grow wild. A very popular dish is thick and small makki bread covered with *palas*, leaves and baked in slow fire. This is known as *pania*. Gur is highly relished. Rice is rarely eaten.

The cooking is done in earthen wares and not more than a *karhai* (deep frying pan made of iron) or *lota* (of brass or copper) and a *thali* (copper plate) would be found in most of the Bhil houses. For drinking water they use dried and hollowed gourds. Oil (sesamum and ground-nut) is commonly used for cooking. Milk and ghee are not used by the householders. They are reserved for the weekly markets where they are sold for purchasing weekly provisions of oil, chillies *haldi*, salt, *gur* and kerosene, etc. They take meat whenever they can get it.

In times of distress they boil leaves, roots and wild tubers and eat them.

House

Bhils live in thatched huts. Each hut is situated on a high point separated from other huts. The hut is a simple and temporary affair. For long Bhils were a wandering tribe, going from one place to another in search of land and food. It is only in the last fifty years that they have settled down. The temporary nature of their hamlets is partly explained by this upsettled past and partly the explanation lies in their superstitions beliefs. If there is a sudden death in the family, they change their residence in the hope, perhaps, of throwing off the bad spirits.

The house is a *katcha* affair. The walls are generally made of mud and stones or bamboo or wattle and daub. The roof is thatched with grass, leaves or tiles. Generally *khajur* (phoenix sysvestria) trees are used to serve as beams. *Sag* (tectona grandis), *Anjan* (Hardwickia binata), *Sarali* or *Harsinga* or *Seharo* (nyctanthes arbortritus), *Salai* (boswelia serrate), etc., are used for various constructions in the hut.

The hut is erected by the tribals themselves with the help of their friends, relatives and neighbours.

SAHARIAS

Saharias are the third most numerous tribe of Madhya Bharat, numbering more than a lakh and concentrated in the Northern hilly regions of the State.

Saharias are the member of a very widespread kolarian tribe extending from North Madhya Bharat in the Centre to Andhra and Orissa on the Eastern coast of India. In different parts of the country they are known by different names such as sawara, savar, sora, saora, etc.

Saharias find mention in the vedic literature. *Aitreva Brahman* mentions 'sahara' as a well defined tribe. The later day historians have also mentioned this tribe. Pliny and Ptolemy mention them by the name Sahara, saying very little about their geographical distribution. Mahabharat *(santiparva)* makes a vague mention of the tribe. In Ramayana we find a more well defined and pointed reference of the tribe. In the *Aranyakanda* there is a description of Rama visiting the Sahara region, and his meeting with a pious Sahara lady. Mazumdar considers this area to be a "portion of the modern Chhattisgarh which is in the neighbourhood of the upper stream of the Mahanadi". Mazumdar further says that as late as the 8th century A.D. Pallava Malla of South India, in his record of his military expedition describes this area as the land of the Sabaras (Sabhor). Puranas speak of Sabaras as 'Vindhya mauliks', meaning thereby, the original inhabitants of the Vindhyas. Howsoever, uncertain be the evidence of the Puranas, there can be no doubt as to the presence at one time of the Saharias in the highlands of central India. Banabhatta and Dandin (7th Century A.D.) refer to the stronghold of this tribe in the Vindhyas. Poet Vakapati (also 7th Century A.D.) has described Vindhyachal as a shrine of the goddess of the Sabaras where leaf-wearing Sabaras offer human sacrifice. The Hindu hero of this poem of Vakapati worshipped this Sabar goddess as 'Kali Vindhyawasini'. General Cunningham has written of a principality of Sabaras known as 'Suiriki raj' near Gazipur. As a further proof of the extensive sway of the Sabaras may be cited the legend that the famous shrine of Jagannath Puri was originally in the custody of the Sabaras. Even today the priests and servants of the shrine belong to a sub-caste of the Sabaras. On the basis of the above evidence Mazumdar rightly infers that the "Sabaras have been in the forest tract of mid-India from pre-historic days".

At present the Sabaras are not found in large numbers in the Satpuras, the Maikal range and the Mahadeo hills where they were numerically very strong in the sixth and seventh ceuturies A.D. They are mostly found in Orissa and Andhra. Their disappearance from the central India (eastern) is generally attributed to the rise of the Gonds who replaced them. By the Ninth Century the Sahara region came to be known as Gondwana This replacement of a Kolarian tribe by the Gonds has not been explained.

In central India the Sabaras, or Saharias as they are known here, were probably dispossessed and displaced by Rajput clans as a result of the pressure exerted on the latter by the Muslim invasion. The various rulers including Mauryas and the Guptas who held sway over these areas in various periods, more or less, did not interfere with the Saharias much. When these rulers showed signs of weakness the Saharias strengthened their rule. This waxing and wanting of the tribal influence continued for centuries till the rise of various Rajput clans. Venktachar says, "We should rather look to the period of Rajput settlement for the disintegration of tribal areas, for the disappearance of certain aboriginal tribes and for the formation of Hinduized aboriginal castes". For the displacement of the Saharias we should look to the fortunes of the Kachhwahas who held Gwalior and Narwar and Parihars who held Bundelkhand before the Chandels. Subsequently, in the 15th century the Bundelas held sway over this region having successfully defeated the Parihars and the Chandels. The Kachhwahas and Parihars must have carved out new States for themselves after dispossessing the Saharias.

The dispossession of the Saharia and the inundation of his language and culture by the immigrating Rajputs was facilitated by the easy terrain and topography of the northern lowlands. Venktachar rightly says, "The nature of the north-Gwalior country could afford them no shelter as the Vindhyas have done for the other tribes".

Anthropologically, the Saharias are a Kolarian (or Munda) tribe. In central India they have been so thoroughly submerged by the successive waves of Hindu migrations that they have now lost their language and speak the language of the area they inhabit. Even in Andhra where the Savaras are in large number their language has been heavily influenced by Telugu. But even then the Austric elements are clearly discernable.

Marriage

Marriage among the Saharias is a very simple affair as compared to the Bhils and Bhilalas. The marriage is generally very early—10 to 14 years. As it usually happens in early marriages, the selection of the bride or the bridegroom is made by the parents. The selection of the partners is a very casual affairs. Sometimes unknown persons happen to meet on some road. They get acquainted and start talking. One has a marriageable girl and the other a marriageable boy. If they like each other and approve the details of their domestic circumstances the marriage is fixed. Later, the details are settled and the marriage is performed.

Dowry

Among the Saharias the *dahej* is not an important consideration. It is the bride's father here who gives the *dahej* which is known as *vardhan* or bridegroom's price. Poor people who are unable to give any *dahej* generally present their daughters with certain forests. The forest does not belong to him, what he endows is only the right of use of that forest. The father henceforth does not go to that forest for collecting minor produce.

Marriage Ceremony

More well to do Saharias use *palki* (palanquin) to carry the bridegroom to the bride's place. Ordinary people go on foot or in bullock carts. The *barat* stays for a day and a night at the bride's place and after the ceremony is over, the party returns home the next day. Generally no band is employed for the marriage ceremonies. The usual custom is to beat copper plates *(thalis)* which make a sing song noise.

The *purohit* or Hindu priest is called far performing the marriage. The marriage is largely Hinduized with usual fire as witness and 7 circles round the nuptial fire.

Marriage is quite cheap. In case of the poverty of the bride's father the whole village donates *rotis* or breads for feeding the bridegroom's party. The usual menu at marriage parties consists *of jowar roti* and *jowar karhi.*

Widow remarriage is common. Divorce is also prevalent.

Birth

The Saharia mother continues to work till the day of delivery. Delivery sometimes takes place in the forest where she had gone to collect forest produce for barter, or dead-fuel for domestic use. The other women attend to the delivery and bring the mother home. She takes rest for a day or two after which she resume her old routine.

The birth of a male child is heralded by the firing of guns and much merry-making. Village women collect round the mother, sing songs and do the *tona-tutka* to drive the evil spirits away.

During the maternity period the mother is fed on *gur* and *sonth,* mahua-water and *jowar* dalia.

The naming of the child is done by some old relative in the presence of friends and relatives. After the ceremony *gur* is distributed to the invitees.

Death

The Saharias cremate their dead. The males are carried for cremation with the accompaniment of music. Women are cremated together with their ornaments. But if the ornaments are made of gold or silver they are taken off before cremation.

No food is cooked in the house of the bereaved family for three days. This period is regarded as impure. The friends of the bereaved family bring food for the bereaved from their homes. On the fourth day there is bathing and washing of the house. Those who can afford it have a simple feast on this occasion.

Houses

The Saharias live in compact villages unlike the Bhils. The houses are arranged in a circular pattern with the common cattle-sheds forming the centre of the circle.

The houses are generally made of stone and mud, with thatched roofs. The Saharia house is neat and well kept. In wild areas the Saharias build watch towers known as *Ghopna* or *Korua* which are used for sleeping purposes. The Ghopna is a simply thatched tiny hut supported on four high poles. The Ghopna has no walls, the roof extends to the floor level. This Korua or Ghopna puts the Saharias out of reach of the prowling tigers.

Life and Living

Saharias live a very simple life, eating frugally and wearing coarsest clothes. The males put on a *dhoti* tucked back and wears a shirt or *phatuhi* to cover the torso. The headgear consists of *safa* or turban. The women wear *ghangra* or *dhoti, saluka* (blouse) and *orhni* with *ghangra.* The children go about naked.

They are fond of music and folk tales. In winters they sit round bon-fires and gossip for hours, recounting their experiences of the days of axe cultivation.

KORKU

Korku is a Munda or Kolarian tribe numbering nearly thousand and confined to the district Dewas of the Plateau division.

The appellation Korkus is derived from the Kolarian language meaning 'men' or 'tribes men'. 'Koru' in this language means a man and 'Ku' is a plural termination. Korkus are commonly held to be racially akin to the Kols and Korwas of Chhotanagpur. While present day ethnologists consider them to be closely related with the Sabaras despite some superficial changes that have been brought about by acculturation. Mazumdar has taken great pains to prove that the Mahadeo and Maikal Hills and the Satpuras in the middle India were once populated with Korkus and Sabaras and when the Gonds came into power in these areas during the rule of the Hindus they replaced the Korkus and Sabaras altogether. Venkatachar, writing of the Korkus of the Central India Agency in 1932 says, "In these parts they appear to have been ousted by the Gonds who held the Narbada valley till they in turn were subdued by the Muslims and the Marathas". As a matter of fact Korkus are the only tribe speaking the Austro-Asiatic language in the Madhya Bharat. During the census of 1931 the number speaking the Korku language was very small and "indigenous to central India and merely a spill-over from the Satpuras".

Korkus, like Bhils and Gonds trace their origin to the Mahadeva. Russell and Hiralal have quoted at length a legend of their genesis as recorded by Crosthwaite. This legend tells us that Ravan the Asura king of *Lanka* found the Vindhya and Satpura ranges to be uninhabited. He requested Mahadeo to populate them. Mahadeo discovered the suitable soil to make images of a man and a woman, and as soon as he tried to put life into them, Indra sent two fiery horses to trample the images to dust. Then Mahadeo made the image of a dog and succeeded in putting life into it. This dog kept the horses away and allowed Mahadeo to put life into the images of a man and a woman. These two became the ancestors of the Korku tribe. Korkus tell another tale of their origin which speaks of Dharanagar (modern Dhar) as being the seat of their forefathers. The tale runs like this: Once these forefathers went out hunting and followed a *sambhar* which ran on and on ultimately entering a cave in the Mahadeo or Panchmarhi hills. There Mahadeo appeared before them in the form of a hermit and revealed that he had lured them there to settle in that region and worship him. A Korku Zamindar continues to be the hereditary guardian of Mahadeo's shrine at Panchmarhi. The tale as such is regarded as merely an effort to connect the ancestry of the tribe with the Rajputs.

Funeral Rites

Korkus generally bury their dead. The body is laid in the grave, face upwards with head pointing to the south.

GOND

Gonds are the least numerous of the tribes of Madhya Bharat.

Russell and Hiralal have described Gonds as the principal tribe of the Dravidian family. This classification seems to be based on the linguistic similarities between the language of the Gonds and the Dravidian languages. Venkatachar probes deeper and says, "the Gonds may be the pre-Dravidians of the South on whom the Dravidians imposed their language, and due to some causes in the regions of North-east Madras, there must have been a large-scale displacement of the tribes into the interior of the Central regions". If we accept this view, the Gonds must have been living in the South long before the Dravidians entered the scene. This view is further supported by the fact that 'Gond' is not a tribal appelation. The name by which they designate their tribe is 'Koitur', or 'Koi'. The word Gond is an imposition of the Hindus and the Mohamedans. Hislop's view that Gond was a form of 'Kond' (Khond) tribe, and K and G being interchangeable the Kond became Gond. He further states that the Telugu people call the Khonds, Gond or Kod (kor). Thus, the two names Gond as Kod, by which the Telugu people know the Khonds, are practically the same as the names Gond and Gad of the Gonds in the Central Provinces. And Russell admits that "it seems highly probable that the designation Gond was given to the tribe by the Telugu and it is likely that they came from the South into the Central Provinces". Language not being the same as a race it leaves open the question of the racial origin and history of the Gonds. The guess may be hazarded that they are probably Proto-Australoids, the race with which is associated the culture of the Mohanjodaro and Harappa. Their old custom of burying the dead also points to a similarity with the people of the Mohanjodaro.

In the C.P. the Gonds destroyed the Hindu dynasties by subversion and by 14th century established their own kingdom and ruled well Rani Durgawati of Garhmandla was perhaps the greatest figure that sprang from the Gond tribe. She occupies a high place in the history of India because of her good governance and bravery in face of the Mughal repressions. But, what they had gained from the Hindus they had to lose to the Marathas. In the eighteenth century they fell before the onslaught of the Marathas and took refuge in the hills. This dispossession they tried to avenge by indiscriminate murder and loot. From gentle and suave plainsman only a couple of centuries back, he had to become a forester and crude cultivator, tilling bad land and raising crude grains.

The Gond marriage is performed in several ways. The Raj Gonds are more Hinduised and they have more elaborate marriage ceremonies. The *dahej* is not an important feature of Gond marriage. The Gond marriage ceremony is marked by a special feature. The marriage procession starts from the place of the bride and the marriage ceremony is performed at the place of the bridegroom. The bridegroom's father gives a feast after the marriage. Poor Gonds, who cannot afford a feast, generally distribute a piece of bread to each member of the party, who eat it with some water and the feast is over. This is known as *'pani torna'*. Divorce and widow remarriage are allowed.

The most notable custom of the Gonds relates to their practice of death ceremony. The Gonds bury their dead, head lying to the north.

The Gonds speak Gondi which is a Dravidian language.

Tribes in Eastern India

NIRMAL KUMAR BOSE

When one reviews the position of tribal communities in Eastern India one is at once struck by the variety of ways in which they make their living. I believe that what is of primary importance to a tribe is the way in which it makes its living; although this is unfortunately an aspect of its life and culture to which less attention is paid by anthropologists in general than to the peculiarities of artistic products, social organisation and so on. Perhaps it is necessary for anthropologists to fall in line with the idea dominant in army circles, namely, that an army marches upon its belly. This is also true of every tribal.

There is a fairly wide range of activities by means of which tribal communities in eastern India earn their living. Tribes like the Adi or Naga of north-eastern India depend mainly upon cultivation without the plough. The Juang or some of the hill tribes of Orissa also live by shifting cultivation in which the plough is not used. It is interesting, however, to note that the Orissan or Central Indian tribes are surrounded on all sides by people who practise wet cultivation by means of the plough. In contrast, the hill tribes of Assam may be said to be comparatively isolated.

Isolation is never complete, for even such tribes have to gather necessary articles such as iron, salt, etc., by means of trade.

In the case of the Orissan or Central Indian tribes, however, the degree of dependence upon neighbouring peasant communities or on traders who do not belong to the tribe is greater than in the case of the tribes of north-eastern India. So much so that in some parts of Orissa and northern Andhra, the tribal communities produce crops by shifting cultivation which are not consumed at home, but are meant for sale. Thus, in the first year of this kind of slash-and-burn type of cultivation, the Juang produce *til* or sesamum meant for sale. It is only in the second year, when the fertility of the unploughed soil is partially reduced that rice is grown in the same field for domestic consumption. In any case, shifting cultivation does not necessarily mean economic isolation. It may bring about a closer interrelationsip with neighbouring communities in an organisation in which the shifting cultivators produce certain specialised crops and exchange them for goods which they require from other people.

For example, some of the Saoras who live in the neighbourhood in Parlakimidi in the south of Orissa were found to produce crops for sale in the valley below, while some of them were actually employed as sweepers in the municipal town of Parlakimidi. Occasionally, the plains' people employ these tribal communities to continue the process of slash-and-burn type of cultivation on the hill-slopes so that some for the soil and ashes may be washed down during the next rains to their fields at the base of the hill. The isolation of communities practising primitive forms of production is not necessarily proportional to the primitiveness of their methods of production.

Another interesting case might be cited here by way of illustration. A section of the Mundari people, namely, the Birhor, live in the jungles or southern Bihar and northern Orissa. One branch among them is nomadic. It shifts its camp three times in a year according to the seasons and two very competent anthropologists imagine that its way of life is a 'survival' from the past, in the Tylonan sense of the term. But an enquiry into the history of several of these communities in Hazaribagh leads one instead to the hypothesis that they are not as isolated as they appear to be on first view. These Birhors are specialised in the manufacture of a particular kind of rope from jungle creepers, which is exchanged for paddy with the neighbouring Bihari farmers. Small game killed and captured is not consumed but sold instead to the nearby villagers for cash. The settlement of the Birhors, nowadays, is never very far but actually within easy reach of the villages of those who need goods produced by the Birhors. The hypothesis referred to is that the extreme specialisation of the Birhors, is a product of their own unfriendly contact with the neighbouring farming communities rather than an unchanged 'survival' from the past.

A large number of tribal communities in eastern India, particularly in the plains, have taken to wet cultivation already. In this cultivation with the plough and bullock, they hardly differ from other farmers. Many Santals, Oraons, Mundas and Khanas have also found employment in the tea plantations of Assam or as farm labourers in the villages of western and northern Bengal. They retain their own language, live separately from their neighbours in settlements of their own and 'thus' try to preserve their cultural integrity; but in economic affairs, they do not differ from other agricultural labourers who have nothing else for sale except their labour.

Some members of these tribal communities have succeeded in becoming owners of land. The money earned in tea plantations come in handy for this purpose. Quite often, prosperous families among such tribal peasantry try to rise higher in the social estimation of their Hindu neighbours. The Hindus worship various gods and goddesses and have certain practices which are absent in the culture of the tribes. And the tribal communities identify, perhaps unconsciously, these points of difference as the sources of power of the Hindu community. Consequently, they are attracted towards the imitation of the Hindus in worship as well as in certain social and ritual practices. Beef-eating is given up, the drinking and use of wine at social ceremonies and rituals is forsaken, and gods belonging to the Hindus are worshipped occasionally in their own tribal way.

Such a slow movement of economic change, spread over at least a hundred years or more, has led to the gradual absorption of some sections of tribal people into the Hindu fold. The Raj Gonds of Madhya Pradesh or the Tana Bhagat movements of Chhota Nagpur are cases in point. One thing, however, has happened during this process of slow Hinduisation. Those who became absorbed within the caste system were generally given a very low place in the system. Inwardly there was resentment, and consequently, the absorbed people, even after becoming a caste tried to preserve their dignity and self-respect by remaining apart from their Hindu neighbours in social matters. There was economic integration, but, none or very little at the social level.

Christian missionaries have operated for more than a century among these tribals. A human dignity was accorded to Christian converts which the tribals never received under Hinduism. But dignity apart, the education given by missionaries in the arts and crafts and the help which was rendered to exploited tribal communities through the influence exercised by the missionaries among the rulers during British days, led to a fairly large-scale conversion to Christianity.

After Independence, a new situation has arisen. The Republic of India has decided to do justice to the hitherto exploited Scheduled Tribes and Scheduled Castes. There is an earnestness and, sometimes, even an overwhelming haste in the attempt to help such people. Sometimes, unfortunately, programmes are drawn, not so much on the basis of firm and accurate knowledge, but because of the stirrings of a retarded conscience. Money has been pouring in for the uplift of the tribal people, apart from the establishment of schools, ashrams, and through the extension of medical and agricultural services in areas predominantly inhabited by the tribal people. One of the results which has become increasingly evident is that some tribes are trying to take greater advantage of these benefits than the others. The result is that field which need more water are left unirrigated, while those which have enough, receive more. This, of course, does not represent a universal truth.

Formerly, the tribal people exercised hardly any political power, but after the introduction of adult franchise, they are courted by political parties from all directions, particularly when the time of election comes. The result has been that this new factor has begun to play a fairly important part in the changes to which tribes are being subjected today. There is nothing inherently wrong in this. As a matter of fact, every unit in India, tribal or non-tribal, should in fact share in political authority. But what is happening today under the exigency of present circumstances is that, among tribal communities, power tends to gravitate into small pockets, instead of being more uniformly distributed. For instance, the Santals of northern Orissa, who are a fairly advanced peasant community today, and among whom some have had the benefit of education in schools and colleges and of employment in the professions, are gradually assuming leadership in the hegemony of several tribes who speak allied languages. So much so, that a new script has been invented by a Santal author for printing books either in the Santali or Ho or Mundari language. The Roman script or Hindi or Bengali are being banned by the authors of this movement.

This new situation in which political power has become an important variable has led, thus, not to a progressive isolation of tribes from the Hindus alone, but towards the formation among them of the nucleus of a dominant middle class. This might lead to a situation similar to the one which existed in rural Bengal in the past. There was the rise of a new middle class in place of the old one based on caste. And under the exigencies of modern economic development, this comparatively recent and almost purely economic middle class is being shifted once more so that some sections might rise to the rank of propertied rulers and others be merged with the proletariat.

Is it necessary for the tribes to go through a similar process before a better type of social and economic integration takes place? India has set her mind upon a socialistic pattern of economy. In it there shall be diversity under a general frame of unity. Could this pattern of life not be built among the tribal people without the bitter experience through which the general population of eastern India has been passing? Perhaps the solution lies in breaking the comparative isolation of the tribal people through the development of a reciprocal interest among the tribals and non-tribals alike regarding the language and the ways of life of each other. This would, hopefully, result in a harmonious development of all concerned through a beneficent exchange of creativity.

Forest and Tribal Life

L.M. SHRIKANT*

The life of the forest dwellers is so much linked and intertwined with the Forest that the problems of Forest development cannot be considered without this aspect of the question and hence I have taken the liberty of giving precedence of Forest Dwellers over the Forest Development. The Minister of Irrigation and Forests of Irrigation and Forests of Gujarat, Shri Chaudhary has rightly stretched the importance of this problem by stating that "the Forests are the life streams of Adivasis" (Forest Dwellers). As a voluntary advocate and a life long friend of the tribals, I may be excused in emphasising this particular aspect of the question by assigning the heading of this paper placing "Forest Dwellers" before the Forest Development.

Forest has attracted of all the various sections of society not of India but the world over as the world renowned forest lover Dr. Richard Barbe Baker has said, "Tree is Life" and some one has said that forest precedes mankind.

The recent radio talk I had the opportunity of noting that some Tribe or Race in America was recorded as extinct because there were no trees in the area inhabited by them, and I believe

*Bhil Seva Mandal, Dahod, District Panch Mahals.

the news as reliable. This justifies to some extent the movement of "CHIPKO" started in Tehri Garhwal by the eminent and well-known selfless social worker Shri Sunder Lal Bahuguna and surprisingly ladies of the area joined in the movement in very good number and it seems to have succeeded so far.

In spite of this I am aggrieved to find today from newspapers that a good number of trees have been uprooted for arrangement to be made for holding in the month of November the International Asiatic Sports and Games Festival to be held at Delhi involving a expenditure of Rs. 55 Crores and an income of Rs. 5 Crores only. Similarly, some years back good number of trees and a good portion of forest area was destroyed for settlement of Bengali refugees in the Bastar District, Danakia Aryan Forest area in Madhya Pradesh. I try to understand the various projects of irrigation and for construction of dams and other such schemes of national benefit and importance for which the deforestation is undertaken. Prevention is better than cure. Let us put a stop to auctioning forest to selfish and of vested interests contractors who have been known to cut down trees randomly with the connivance of Forest Officers and to make huge profits.

The illicit cutting of trees through contractors is much more damaging than by the Forest Dwellers. Tribals who resort to it for earning their daily bread by toiling hard from early morning till late in the evening I am stating this with a due sense of responsibility as I am in possession of facts for this. I admit the charge made against the Tribals without any hesitation or reservation for this process of illicit cutting of trees, but I want to present very briefly the picture of their life which is below poverty line.

Forests are more dear and valuable to them than to others, but the tragic fact is that they have to take this practice of illicit cutting, being compelled by dire economic necessity. Before the advent of Independence the Indian States whole merger was tactfully brought about by the strong statesman and great political leader Sardar Patel had contracted to part with their private forests to contractors who earned money by cutting down valuable trees. Thus, the area become rapidly deforested.

May I remind friends that in the memorable year 1930 of Mahatma Gandhi's Salt Satyagrah, I had undertaken Jungle Forest Satyagrah in a village of Kalol Taluka (Malav) of Panch Mahals

District of Gujarat. I was inspired to do so being permitted by Mahatmaji because the Tribals of the Panch Mahals District, Bhils were debarred from carrying head-loads of dead wood, which they had traditionally enjoyed so far. As a result of this Satyagrah, the demand was conceded and the Bhils even today are allowed to sell such head-loads in cities and towns where intelligent public is becoming a abtar by purchasing it for fuel, etc., as it is cheaper. In the absence of any other occupation for honest earning of daily bread the Tribals are still following this practice of carrying head loads of wood dead or live even coming from adjoining areas of other States. The proverb "Buy, Borrow or Steal" is literally true in the case of Tribals who are even today half starved and ill clothed.

The Forest provides fuel, food, fodder and fibre and timber for housing, ploughing and such useful materials. But as the Tribals fail to get daily bread, they take recourse to this damaging practice of illicit cutting of trees and as the traditional practice of Shifting cultivation in Nagaland. Mizoram and other areas is still persisting and can be stopped by pursuation and not by prosecution. Similar efforts should be made to make the Tribals understand the immense value of trees and forest not only for them at present but for their future generation also.

It is universally recognised that Forest is a dire necessity for human beings for the following main reasons among others:

1. 80 per cent of the rural population depends on wood (fire wood) for domestic energy as it is most readily available and cheapest of all energy resources. Wood is an alternative to fossil fuel.
2. Technically, it is the simplest to develop. It can be raised with a minimum of financial investment.
3. It can store energy for use at will.
4. Energy supply for plantation and for biomass.
5. It supplies food fodder fuel fibre besides grass and minor forest produce like Honey, Lac, Timber, Charcoal, Bamboo bark and Flowers.
6. It prevents erosion floods drought and it is helpful in conservation of water and prevents population.
7. Great contribution for atmosphere purity.

Forest is a national necessity. This was well expressed at the National Seminar (The people and the Forest) held at Rajghat, New Delhi in the year 1977 organised by Himalaya Siva Sangh which is rendering yeoman service in this respect.

The Sixth Conference of Food Agricultural Organisation of the United Nations held at Rome in the year 1951 has laid down guiding principles for the countries to follow for the development of forests. The salient ones are as follows:

1. Each country should determine and set aside areas to be dedicated to forests, whether at present forested or not;
2. Each country should apply the best practicable techniques in seeking to derive, in perpetuity, for the great number of its people the maximum benefits available from the protective productive and necessary values of its forests;
3. Adequate knowledge of all aspects of forest resources and forest management including consumption and utilisation of forest products were indispensable; and
4. Public consciousness of forest values should be developed by all means possible.

The workshop organised by the Xavier Labour Relations Institute at Jamshedpur held in 1978 has made 9 recommendations, some of which are as follows:

> The development of Forestry has to be linked with the improvement of the standard of living of forest-dwellers M.R. Chakravarti, Deputy Chief Conservator of Madhya Pradesh observed, "for over a Century the Forest Department had been made to be a *quasi*-commercial department but never a *quasi*-social or *quasi*-welfare. The use and out-side sale of fuel should be regulated subject to the availability of other sources of income to the villagers."

Bombay State (then corporate consisting of Maharashtra, Gujarat and Karnataka) under the able Chief Ministership of Shri Bala Saheb Kher associated by Shri Morarji Desai was the first pioneer State to abolish contractor system for auctioning forest coupes to selfish and interested contractors who made a common cause with Forest Officers for piling up profits even by illicit cutting and other doubtful methods. They were replaced by organising Co-operative Forest Societies which were mainly composed of Forest Dwellers Tribals and were offered coupes at upset prices. These societies are successfully doing their work in partnership with Government Department much more in Gujarat as I am in know.

This is right step in the direction of prevention of illicit cutting of trees and deforestration. The Tribal labourers-share holders of such co-operative Forest Society feel for the protection of the Forest as they allowed some previleges for fire wood and timber. I had been able to get organised for the collection and sale of Forest minor produce which is worth a good amount in the State of Orissa, a Finance Department corporation by getting financial aid for godown construction and transport when I was the Commissioner for Scheduled Castes and Scheduled Tribes. The corporations were started in other States also. The Tribals inhabiting the forest area were able to get good wages for collection of minor forest produce and other such labour. This instigated me to announce at the Tribal Co-operative Forest Workers' Conference at Devgarh Baria in the district of Panch Mahals (Gujarat) that the Tribals were really the owners of the forest, as they alone can be able to protect the forest as they are doing forest labour works drawing firelines, sowing weeding, etc. being employed by the Forest Department:

> "The traditional rights of the Tribals no longer recognised and emphasis was laid on realisation of maximum annual revenue resulting in the system of monopoly of contractors."

The Backward Class Commission in its report published in 1960-61 has further to state, "Due sense of identity with forest of the Tribals from times memorial. The Tribals have enjoyed freedom to use the forest and this has given a conviction that the forest belong to them till the middle of 19th Century when it disturbed the Tribal economy and introduced a psychological conflict. It has resulted in creating delicate and strained relation between the Tribals and the Forest Department.

This is how I will state the difference in the forest policy of the Government of India laid down in 1952 by modifying the former one of 1894. To put it with more brevity the rights and previleges of the forest dwellers were converted into concession. Even the Hari Singh Committee appointed for Tribal economy and Forest Area did not recommend any change in the forest policy of 1952 and it continues even today.

Now in conclusion I would like to mention briefly the various schemes and projects undertaken and implemented satisfactorily during last three or four years after the deliberation of Gujarat Forest Officers' Conference held at Sachivalaya, Gandhinagar on 4th November, 1981 after which a massive programme has been launched by the Gujarat Government for expansion of Forests in Gujarat so as to attain the target of 30 per cent which is now only 10 per cent of the total land.

This extension programme was tried in four Talukas of Panch Mahals District, e.g., Dahod, Jhalod, Limkheda and Santrampur populated mainly by tribals where they were involved under system of partnership and ownership in the long-run with and under Forest Department.

The Scheme of such a system are as follows:

1. Strip Plantations on

(a) Roadsides	31,609 HC.
(b) Canal Banks	3,400 HC.
(c) Railway Lines	2,000 HC.
Thus the target reached is	37,000 HC.

2. Large forest areas are without tree and are so called forests to be converted into productive forests.
3. Village forests irrigated as well as unirrigated village Panchayats to be involved in this.
4. Private forests under the guidance and supervision of the Department.
5. Farm Forests if fields of agriculture.
6. And lastly, most important and useful projects of family social forest which can be briefly described as mentioned below:

The world bank has promised financial help to the tune of Rs. 31.82 crores during a period of five years for the Forest Dwellers' partnership in this project.

A Tribal family residing near the forest area is given monetary help of Rs. 250 per year if the result of afforestration is 70 per cent. This Scheme is called Sanjay Van (Forest).

A Tribal who has less acre of agricultural land and whose annual income is less than 1000 should be given 2 to 2.5 hectare of land for afforestration so that at the end of 15 years 30 hectares of land will be afforested and financial help of Rs. 200 for eracting a cottage nearby such seven or eight families will have to stay together; additional amount Rs. 250 will be given for afforestration work with free gift of any material necessary for this purpose. After the period of 15 years when the trees are to be cut down, fifty per cent of the profit will be given to the family and will be allowed together minor forest produce freely. This practical training will ensure the protection of the forest and instil in the tribals a feeling that illicit cutting is damaging to him and the State and the country. I welcome this scheme of small beginning of partnership and ownership and I would request other States to study these areas and then try to emulate them with any modification necessary in their own States.

BACKGROUND

The tribal communities in India largely occupy the forest regions where, for a long period in their history, they have lived in comparative isolation. These communities have had symbiotic relationship with the forests as was the case in the early history of the entire human society itself. They drew their sustenance largely from the forests, a relationship which continues undisturbed in the remoter tribal areas even now. In the more advanced regions, however, many tribal groups have got transformed into agricultural communities. Another qualitative change in the life of people in these areas occurred with the immigration of more advanced agricultural groups. These communities had their base in agriculture but they depended on forests only for limited purposes like grazing of their cattle or meeting their fuelwood needs. This relationship was entirely different from that of the original tribal communities with the forests. As pressure of population increased, they became competitors for use of limited resources thereby adversely affecting the tribal economy in many areas.

The forest resources came under systematic management of the State gradually from about middle of nineteenth century. The State was concerned for the preservation of forests from the wider angle of ecological balance as also maintenance of natural resource-base for economic use and sustained income. Some conflict of interest arose regarding the traditional use of the forest by the local community and the States long-term interest. Further, the difference between the symbiotic relationship of the tribal communities with the forests and its limited use for nistar by migrant agricultural community was not adequately appreciated. The result was that the growing population in many areas resulted in continuously dwindling forest base adversely affecting the tribal economy. There was considerable gap between the States' forest policy as enunciated and its actual implementation in the field depending on the local situation and changing emphasis from time to time.

NATIONAL FOREST POLICY

The first national forest policy was enunciated in 1894 which accepted administration of the State forests in the public interest as the sole object. The idea of regulation of rights and restriction of privileges of the user in the forest by the neighbouring population was introduced as a measure for preservation of forests. Forests were still plentiful and the pressure of population was not large. Therefore, subject to the preservation of natural forests on the hill slopes and commercially valuable timber, the policy envisaged even clearing of forests without honey-combing it for cultivation wherever such a need arose, with the growth of population. A fourway classification of the forest was introduced keeping in view these objectives.

The national economic scene remained near static during the early part of the twentieth century. However, the pressure of population was gradually increasing and by the mid-twentieth century the increase was more than 40 per cent. War affected the economy in many important ways and under scored the value of forest-resource-base for the industrial system and even for defence. The national leadership decided to make a determined effort for fast economic development soon after Independence which necessitated a second look at the forest policy. The forest policy, therefore, was revised in 1952. The new policy accepted as its primary goal the need for evolving a system of balanced and complementary land use under which each type of land is allotted to that form of use under which it would produce most and deteriorate the least. The policy also took note of the needs for checking of denudation etc., establishing tree-lands, providing *nister* facilities, defence and industrial use and maximum revenue consistent with its primary goal. The tribal communities were granted certain concessions under this policy including collection of minor forest produce grazing of cattle, etc.

Another important element in the context of overall forest resource in the country was added soon after Independence with abolition of princely states and Jagirs and Zamindars. The forests in these areas were generally personal property of the chieftains. They were also the main source of revenue for many a 'Jungle-State'. Therefore, they were carefully protected and jealously guarded. Many states promoted forestry on a substantial scale. The taking over of these forests by the State resulted in a period of uncertainty which caused substantial damage to the forest. It took considerable effort before the new area was put under systematic administration and control, and covered by the general State policy on forests. Even now there are major gaps in the forest lands in many States. There are substantial areas which are privately owned or even where these are taken over by the government, their management remains to be systematised.

In the post-independence era, the pressure of population in some of the tribal regions began to rise very fast with their getting opened up. These regions also provided a rich resource-base for new developmental activities which had resulted in considerable in-migration. The demand for timber, fuelwood and other commercial uses of forests continued to rise substantially during this period. Further, the forests provide a good source of augmenting state income. The unsatiable need of fuel in growing centres in and around the forest regions resulted in vast areas being cleared legitimately under the prevalent rules which have become incongrous or many a time illegally. This new configuration of forces has been carefully studied by two Commissions in the recent years—the Scheduled Areas and Scheduled Tribes Commission (Dhebar Commission) so far as it related to the tribal economy and the National Commission on

Agriculture subsequently in the broader national context. The Dhebar Commission observed that the full control of tribal communities over forest resources was changed into merely some rights by the 1894 Forest Policy. Even these rights were reluctantly accepted merely as concession by the 1952 policies which did not mean much in concrete terms. They urged a basic change in the forest policy so that the tribal communities can regain the control of this resource-base and the earlier balance in their economy was restored. On the other hand, the National Commission on Agriculture accepted inter-relationship of forest economy with rural and tribal economy and urged for a better rationality in the forestry operations and their utilisation. The two could not work in isolation and the inter-relationship between them had to be considered in terms of employment, rights of user and involvement of the local people. Employment itself could be treated as an alternative to 'the right of the user' if the forests had to be properly organised. The forestry base itself needed strengthening by larger investments and use of new technology so that it could yield a greater surplus to be shared locally, regionally and nationally.

SUB-PLANS AND FORESTRY PROGRAMMES

Even though the need for a change in the forest policy and their implementation had been increasingly felt throughout this period, the forestry schemes and other State Plans functioned in relative isolation. A comprehensive plan frame in the tribal regions with the possibility of all aspects of area development with focus on the tribal communities became available after the tribal sub-plans were prepared during the Fifth Plan. The Working Group on Tribal Development (1978-83) reviewed the programme and urged that comprehensive plans for all those projects which have sizeable forest areas may be prepared in which tribal development and forestry development would become two co-equal goals. In the forest rich regions, forestry-based programmes may be assigned the central position while agriculture may have a secondary and supplementary role. The Working Group also recommended that the forestry plans may be prepared in two parts. The basic needs of tribal economy should be provided on a priority basis as part one in all forestry schemes whether conventional, intensive or commercial. In case commercial forestry and intensive utilisation of forest resources is planned for an area, it should have a counter-part plan for development of the tribal communities living in the area so that balanced development of the region and the people is ensured. The Working Group recommended a large programme of horticulture, fuelwood species, etc. with the help of tribal community themselves giving the community or the individual, as may be suitable in each case, the right on the trees planted and their usufruct. Mixed fruit trees and other useful species should invariably be planted as part of all plantation programme. They recommended recognition of full rights of the tribal on minor forest produce and arrangements for their marketing through co-operatives eliminating the middle man. All major forestry programmes should be organised through co-operatives.

A Conference of State Ministers of Forests and Tribal Welfare was convened in 1978 which considered the various issues relating to forests and tribal development. The Conference concurred broadly with the approach outlined by the Working Group. The Conference recommended that forestry development, instead of being planned in isolation, should become an integral part of comprehensive plan for that area in which the needs of the local economy should get the highest priority and consequently influence the choice of the species for each area. The Conference accepted the need for associating the tribal in a high plantation programme giving the individual right on the trees and their usufruct. In the intensive forestry programme the socio-economic constraints have to be kept in mind and the tribal community should be enabled to become partners in benefit accruing to those areas. The Conference underlined the need for establishing a strong co-operative base for the Tribal Welfare Department in conjunction with the Forest Departments. Till such time as these arrangements are made responsibility for a fair deal to the tribal must rest with the Forest Department.

A RESUME OF STATES SCENE

The various State Governments have taken a number of measures in pursuance of the guidelines and suggestions made from time to time particularly after the sub-Plans become operational. Our review shows that there is consensus about rights of land being given to the tribals living in the forest villages. In Maharashtra, Gujarat and Orissa forest villages have already been converted into revenue villages. In Madhya Pradesh 15 year lease of land has been given to the forest dwellers. In West Bengal, however, the traditional forest villages continue. Large sized Multi-purpose Cooperative Societies (LAMPS) have been organised in all the States. One of the important functions of the LAMPS is the purchase of minor forest produce. In some States particularly Andhra Pradesh, Maharashtra and West Bengal monopoly rights have been given to the LAMPS. The position in other States remains uncertain. There is a general reluctance on the part of the States to link the price of minor forest produce with their market price and even where nationalisation has been done, the middlemen operates in a new form. The principle that the first processing of M.F.P. should be through the cooperatives of primary collectors of M.F.P. does not appear to have been very favourably received and the tribal has to be satisfied with what he can get as gatherer of forest produce. The co-operativisation of forest labour is limited to the States of Maharashtra and Gujarat and no significant advance has been made anywhere else which is indicative of almost instinctive acceptance of the fate of a tribal as a casual wage earner without any concern. Forest corporations have been established in most of the States. Institutional finance is now gradually becoming available through them. Some corporations have taken up the task of training tribal youth in new techniques. However, the broader questions of the role and place of forestry labour in the new institutional set-up remain to be defined.

POLICY FRAME

The above review shows that although a number of steps have been taken, one by one, in the past few years, a comprehensive frame to which all aspects of forestry and tribal economy are fully reconciled has not yet emerged. There is a search for such an approach both amongst foresters and planners for tribal development. It is clear that the overall national interests, particularly ensuring ecological balance must be paramount. Yet, within the parameters, as defined by national considerations, there are many alternative action plans possible which may have varying implications for the local tribal economy. An extreme view can be taken that the tribal economy could be left to adjust to itself to the new situation. At the other extreme tribal interests could be accepted as an important objective and a middle path chosen.

It is clear that rights on the forests as were envisaged in the early days cannot be sustained in the same form. The situation has considerably changed and any effort to go back to the old form will be disastrous. The rights in forests can be sustained only if there is a comprehensive frame for the protection, use and development of forests in which the community and the individual must assume the responsibility for creation of new forestry wealth and its protection. We do not agree with the approach of Dhebar Commission since they ignored these aspects and emphasised only the rights. The broad approach outlined by the National Commission on Agriculture will have to be followed.

Thus, the local tribal community, which has symbolic relationship with the forests, should be accepted as partners in the local forestry development efforts in each area. Unless this premises is accepted and built into the system, it may not be possible to avoid conflicting situations at the local level. The best protective device for the existing forests and the new additions is to create an interest of the local community in the forest wealth.

We may point out that there is a tendency to treat all persons living in the tribal areas alike in the programmes and policies for the use and working of forests resources. It is necessary to distinguish between the tribal communities who have a long tradition of symbolic relationship and other agricultural groups for whom the forest is just a source for satisfying some of their needs. The relationship of the two is qualitatively different which should get reflected in the policy frame and developmental programme for these areas.

We consider that the potential of tribal areas which have even moderate forest resources, is so good that a mere linkage of the individual with the process of comprehensive development in that area can provide a satisfactory solution to problem of economic development of the people. It is the tendency to disregard this important aspect in the forestry programmes as also in the tribal development schemes which is resulting in conflicting situations and disharmony. The symbiosis between the tribal community and the forests should be re-established through suitable plans of development of these regions.

Tapping New Technology for Development of Tribals and other Weaker Sections

Social forestry is an important step forward in associating the local community with the creation of new tree-wealth. However, the maximum potential which can be developed under this programme is small compared to the total potential which can be achieved by the use of new technology now available for tree-culture. We are on the threshold of technological revolution in agriculture and land-use whose significance is not quite appreciated as yet. The new agricultural technology is inevitably loading toward higher specialisation in land-use. Now comparatively smaller areas can support bigger populations so for as foodgrains are concerned. The sub-marginal lands, which are being used for raising poorer grains or where cultivator has to remain satisfied with poor yields can be put to many better alternative uses which incidentally also help in resorting the ecological balance. The energy crisis is also pointing in the direction of tapping biosources for energy. Today it is possible for choice of a suitable technology and production pattern that any piece of land, about a hectare or so, can make a family economically viable. The choice can be as wide ranging as the capital intensive coffee plantation on one hand through plantation of fruit-bearing trees, host plants for tassar to plantation of fodder trees linked to the animal husbandry and fuelwood plantation on the other. Tassar cultivation with plantation of host trees is important area of food potential for some regions. These programmes may be taken up on private lands or government lands, particularly those recently excised from forests and also in the large blanks within the forest areas which, in quite a few cases, are still under State control.

The weaker sections of the community can provide necessary manpower to create tree-wealth on marginal lands which, in quite a few cases, are still under State control. The traditional programme of forest plantations are too costly since heavy investment is required for their protection and for administrative infrastructure. All these elements in the cost of plantations are reduced with the individual beneficiary coming on the scheme.

The experience of horticulture programme in Orissa shows that the cost of programme with individual ownership is likely to be moderate. The problem with an average person may be of sustenance for the period of his engagement in this activity. Methods can be found to provide financial support to the landless labourer or marginal cultivator for a limited period till he acquires the new resource-base and becomes viable. A large programme of coffee plantation has been taken up in Andhra Pradesh with financial support from A.R.D.C. Each individual tribal is assigned a piece of land for plantation and he is provided technical and financial assistance. He has a right on the trees and their usufruct but he does not have the right of alienation. It is such groups of individuals interested in creation of new tree-wealth as a part of their individual development plans that will get vitally interested in the development and protection of the forest. The planning for creation of this new tree-wealth may also keep in view the requirements of the community of the region and of the national economy. It will thus, be possible to have a frame in which the local needs, national priorities and economic well-being of individual tribal living in these areas are fully harmonised.

The above programme envisages pre-option of the growth-potential of sub-marginal lands in favour of the landless and the marginal cultivator particularly the members of tribal communities. If due caution is not exercised a new interest may emerge and make a bid to acquire control over the new resource potential with the backing of financial resources. The results of some of the earlier programmes basically designed for the weak but missing the target group is an indicator of this tendency. We are at a point where full implication of new technology have not yet been appreciated and there is time when the landless and the weaker sections of the community particularly the tribals can be given a resource-base. It may be necessary that a strong organisation is created for this programme which may provide necessary technical support as also the financial resource for this programme which has a comparatively longer gestation period. The organisation may also organise in due course marketing with a view that the primary producer gets the maximum benefit. It will be necessary that the personal and social needs of the tribal producer are also fully provided for by this organisation so that the individual is not required to go to a money lender which may mean symphoning off the benefit of new development through indebtedness.

All these aspects require a very careful consideration at the stage of planning of each programme and preparation of area-development schemes for each area. Even though the tribal sub-plan and Integrated Tribal Development Project envisage a comprehensive frame in which forestry programme should be fully reflected so that the inter-dependence between the forests and the tribals is clearly brought out and policies and programmes are suitably adapted on either side, adequate attention has not been paid to this aspect in planning so far. The plans of Integrated Tribal Development Projects and the Working Plans of forests should be reviewed and suitably reformulated for achieving the balance in the development of the people and the forest.

Minor Forest Produce

Minor forest produce provides substantial sustenance to the tribal communities particularly in the backward regions. In some cases they are the main source of their cash incomes. New uses of some forest produce have added to the list of collected items and has also increased their value. However, no special attention has been paid to this aspect in the management of forests. Consequently, collection of minor forest produce continues to be incidental to or at best a minor activity in the general forestry operations. It is only recently that a small beginning has been made in some States for regeneration of tree yielding minor forest produce. The collection of minor forest produce by the tribal in the earlier days was primarily for meeting their personal requirements. As a few commodities acquired commercial value, some trade also developed and they become source of cash income to the tribals. The forest departments started the practice of assigning collection of minor forest produce to traders on payment of a lumpsum amount of royalty based on the quantity collected. They got the minor forest produce collected through the tribals and the charges for collection were fixed by the trader or by the department. The collection charges usually are very low and the State also gets only a small royalty. Many malpractices also developed in the trade of minor forest produce. Therefore, the trade in some of the minor forest produce was nationalised in some States. The States acquired, through suitable legislations, monopoly rights to purchase the items nationalised. They also fixed the charged for collection of minor forest produce. However, the situation did not improve substantially even in nationalised commodities. The States started the practice of advance sale of future collection to the contractors and entered into agreements with them accordingly. Since under the law only State can purchase the nationalised commodities, the collection in some cases is from the tribals directly by the department but in most cases it is done through agents formally or informally. The agents appointed by the State are generally men of the final purchaser because it solves the problems of quality of collection and handling, storage, finances etc., which otherwise would be the responsibility of the Department. The agents purchase the produce formally on behalf of the department but the collection is simultaneously deemed to be handed over to the final purchaser. The State in this arrangement becomes entitled to the margin between the final sale price and the collection charges which may be naturally agreed to. In this arrangement the primary objective of removing the middlemen and passing on the maximum benefit to the primary collector is lost. In many cases, there has been a reversal of the policy of nationalisation and the old system of working through the contractors has been resumed. In some States the collection of some of the minor forest produce under the nationalised scheme and even otherwise is being undertaken through cooperatives of tribals on a monopoly basis. In this way three different practices are in vogue for the collection of minor forest produce viz., through the contractors, cooperatives and departmental agency.

The other important question is about the policy of fixing the purchase price of the minor forest produce from the primary collectors which is a vexed one. The minor forest produce acquires economic value only when it is picked up by the tribal and brought to the market. Moreover, it also provides for a substantial part of the cash need of an average tribal. Therefore, his right to collect minor forest produce was formally recognised. After the collection has been organised by the Forest Department, there is a tendency to determine the purchase price of minor forest produce from the tribal with reference to the national labour inputs in its collection. This cannot be realistically assessed since the collection of minor forest produce is done by the whole family sometimes during odd hours in different seasons. The place of purchase is also a very important factor particularly in the case of bulky commodities. In this case collection from the more inaccessible areas will be taken up only if it is worthwhile for the tribal to undertake collection and bring out the commodity from the deep forest. The law of average in fixing of collection charges makes the wage unremunerative in the more inaccessible areas which are very large in some cases. Therefore, the total collection of minor forest produce is considerably reduced compared to its total potential.

The only rational consideration in fixing the collection price of minor forest produce can be to ensure maximisation of return for the labour input of the primary collector and, thus, enable him to make maximum collection of the minor forest produce which otherwise would be lost to the national economy. Therefore, the purchase price should be fixed with reference to what the market can bear. In some cases, it may be necessary even to subsidise the collection price. There is no case for fixing a lower collection price on considerations like encouragement to setting up of industries in an area. The economy of industrial units must be worked out with reference to the value added by processing and other services which they can perform. The hidden subsidy by supply of raw material at lower price to the industrial units is not in the interest of the national economy. This practice clearly deprives the tribal of due share in the benefits of economic growth in the area.

A large differential between the market price and the collection price also leads to certain other malpractices. It has to be conceded that a lower price will inevitably result in lower overall collection. When the collection prices are low, the traders do not bring into their formal accounts the entire collection. Sometimes they may even pay penalty for shortfalls in collections in case there are conditions stipulating a minimum collection. The benefit which they got by mopping up the large margin in unrecorded transaction is much more than the penalty. This also leads to corrupt practices. Even when collection may be through cooperatives, in case the rates are low, the tribal may be tempted by even a slightly higher price to sell the produce to unauthorised private parties. Officials of the cooperatives themselves may get involved in malpractices. In such a situation the collection of minor forest produce does not get properly organised and even though the State may get some royalty, there is heavy leakage and bulk of the benefit accrues to the trader. The collection of minor forest produce, therefore, has to be organised as an economic operation taking into account the market forces. It is only when the collection prices and the market prices are almost equal that the temptation for bye-passing the normal system can be curbed. There may be a national reduction in the royalty of the State but it will be more than fully compensated by many other gains to the State by the fact that the total collection will be duly accounted for.

The trader and the contractor are primarily interested in maximising their profits from the operations during the period of their lease. This generally leads to over-exploitation of minor forest produce which may even be detrimental to the forest itself. This is particularly relevant in the case of collection of resins. When the workers are brought from outside, as happened in the case of tapping of forests in the U.P. hills, the damage was very serious. Sometimes, even the tribal himself may be tempted to over-exploit if he gets an abnormally high price. The *kosa cacoons* in Baster were over-exploited with the result that sufficient cacoons were not left even for regeneration and there was a serious shortfall in the total production. Introduction of a system of rotation, closing each area for one year in four years has restored the normal production.

One of the important basic premises in any forest programme is to strengthen the resource-base and establish linkages with the long-term interest of the local economy. This applies equally in the case of minor forest produce. It is, therefore, necessary that a systematic plan of action is worked out for minor forest produce. The middleman in all forms, whether contractor, trader or agent must be removed from the scene. Minor forest produce should not be treated as a source of revenue to the State. It should provide maximum return to the tribal so that economic interest is created in the maintenance of forests with the possibility of substantial incomes accruing to the individual regularly from its collection. The price of minor forest produce be remunerative and linked to the market price. All leases for collection of minor forest produce should be given exclusively to cooperatives of tribals. The large-sized Multi-purpose Cooperative Societies (LAMPS) have been set-up in the tribal area at a considerable cost primarily for organising marketing of minor forest produce in the first phase.

Already much time has been lost even after repeated policy decisions at the highest level. The Ministries of Agriculture and Home Affairs together should ensure that the entire trade in minor forest produce is organised through the cooperatives on monopoly basis and this new system is introduced with effect from the next working season. The necessary regulations or other legal support should be provided to make it effective.

With the collection of minor forest produce though the cooperative system, it should be possible to avoid abnormal low prices usually contrived by the middleman. Nevertheless, there may be some occasions where the national or international market may not behave. A system of announcing support price for minor forest produce, should be introduced so that the tribal may not be suddenly faced with the possibility of erosion of his income in some areas. The purchase of minor forest produce should be taken up by a State level or regional organisation through LAMPS. A risk fund should be built up for meeting the contingency of a sudden slump in the market in one or more commodities. Since the size of operations in each State will be large, this should not create a serious problem. A contribution could also be made from tribal welfare fund for this purpose. If the trend in relation to some minor forest produce is a long-term one, it should be possible to plan a gradual shift. The concerned Ministries in the Central Government may support these operations through the net work of LAMPS wherever necessary. The Ministry of Home Affairs should assume the nodal role in guiding the policies and monitoring the progress.

The tribal should not merely remain a collector of forest produce without any role in the maintenance or augmentation of resources. The extension programme for training of tribals collectors of minor forest produce particularly those engaged in tapping the trees should be taken up. The LAMPS should assume a central role even in the maintenance of forest base. The training programme for maintenance and scientific working of minor forest produce should be organised through the LAMPS. The programme should aim at making the collector aware the role of the minor forest produce in his economy and about the long-term adverse effects of wrong practices. He should also be given training for acquiring necessary skills so that there is larger income without detriment to the forest base. In case of some forest produce the individual tribals may be given the right to collect from specified areas or trees so that their proper upkeep is ensured and the individual gets interested in their continued maintenance. This practice has been started in Andhra Pradesh for collection of gums from the reserved forests. Similarly, the hosts plants are assigned to individuals under tassar programme in some States. This approach should be adopted whenever feasible.

No significant work has been done for assessing the potential of minor forest produce so far with the result that an item may acquire economic value only by chance discovery. Even use of forest produce by the local tribal communities has not been systematically studied which could give a lead to the possible lines of research and development. For example, the tribals have been using the *sal* seed for extracting oil and also for augmenting their food supply during periods of scarcity. However, *sal* seed acquired economic value only after there was shortage of oils and non-traditional sources were searched by the industry. A comprehensive programme of identifying the various forest produce, assessing their potential and also feasibility of marketing and their alternative use etc. should be formulated. The Forest Research Institute should take a lead in this matter and direct suitably its research programme. It should provide guidance to the States in this matter on a continuing basis.

The minor forest produce provides raw material for a number of important industries. However, since most of these industries are generally located outside the tribal regions, tribal areas are merely suppliers of raw materials. We have already seen that the primary collector or minor forest produce does not get even a reasonable wage. The raw materials are also subject to uncertainty of Market. The cost of transportation of heavy materials over long distances before they are processed ultimately results in lower collection price. In this arrangement it is the processing unit which gets maximum advantage from value-added as also of the difference between the market price and the collection price. Once a raw materials is processed, the industrial unit acquires added strength and is able to organise the marketing of semi-processed or final product to their best advantage. It is necessary that the first processing of minor forest produce is organised within the tribal area and through the cooperative system. The main objective should be to retain maximum benefit from this activity within the local economy which should accrue to the primary collector.

The above approach has been accepted at the highest policy level for quite some time. Nevertheless, not much progress has been made so far since the profits accruing to the private sector are very large for the reasons which we have discussed above. For the same reason, cooperativisation of minor forest produce should be accorded a very high priority since this will give immediate additional income to the average tribal and will also be in the interest of development of the forests themselves. A time bound programme of 2 to 3 years should be prepared for establishing processing units for minor forest produce in the cooperative sector within the tribal area.

Forest Plantation and Choice of Species

When the natural forests were taken up for scientific management, plantation of selected species like teak, pines etc., was also started in suitable areas. The main consideration was the economic utility of those species as could be established at that time. The Working Plans of forests have continued to be prepared following the principles laid down in the National Forest Policies referred to earlier in the chapter. So long as the forest resources were plentiful and the pressure of population was low or even moderate, this did not create problem for the local economy. However, as the areas under economic plantation increased while the area under forest decreased and the pressure of population grew, serious imbalances appeared in many areas. Even though the rights of tribal communities have been recognised for "nistar" as also for collection of minor forest produce and their utilisation, in many areas they were no longer significant with the depletion of the forest resource-base. The National Commission on Agriculture reviewed the situation in considerable detail and recommended a massive effort for afforestation and tree-culture keeping in view their relevance and utility to the local economy.

A substantial programme of social forestry bas been taken up recently which aims at providing for the needs of local community from the proposed tree-lands outside the reserve forests. These new 'social forests' may be managed by the community after they have got established. They are expected to cater the various needs of the community like fuelwood, timber for housing, agricultural implements, etc. The social forestry programme and the tree culture programme as recommended by us earlier will help substantially in restoring the balance. Nevertheless the social forestry programme is still in the early stages and its cost is comparatively high. The social forestry by itself may not fully meet the needs of the tribal economy since the relationship of the tribal economy with the forest is very intimate and far-reaching. It will be necessary to review the population policy in the forest area as well as in a larger frame.

The investment policy in the forestry programmes has tended to over-emphasise the exotic needs of the modern sector disregarding, sometimes even at the cost of the needs of the local economy. The plantation or single species has led to the disappearance of many useful trees which provided sustenance to the tribal community as also were a source of minor forest produce. In some cases the problem of availability of suitable grazing lands has also arisen. The programme of forestry, therefore, should make adequate provision for mixed plantations with the objective of providing the tribal community with their basic requirements and increasing production of minor forest produce which may help them to supplement their cash incomes. A minimum percentage of useful species in all plantations should be fixed for each area taking into account their potential and the needs of the local economy.

INTENSIVE FORESTRY MANAGEMENT

The National Commission on Agriculture had drawn attention to the need for substantial investment in the forestry sector. Forestry in our country has been conservation-oriented. Here is, however, a resource base which could be augmented and its utilisation planned on the basis of higher production per unit area. The gestation period for traditional forestry is quite long. The new technology, however, is available which makes financial investment in the sector possible giving a much larger income added from this under-utilised resource-base. A scheme of financing forestry programme, therefore, has been prepared which is supported by the ARDC. The Forestry Development Corporations have been established in many States which are expected to prepare bankable schemes and take up long-term plantation programmes with this new sources of financial assistance. The basic objective is that the additional financial investment in these areas should help in augmenting the forest-base in the depleted and under stocked areas over a period of time so that available land resources are optimally utilised.

Now that a new source of financing forestry programmes is available, it should be possible to prepare comprehensive programmes which may not necessarily be limited to single species for meeting the requirements of certain industries only. These programmes could be broad-based which may help in creating a better ecological balance as also keep the needs of the local community in view. The objective should be that the new plantation programme becomes self-sustaining in the long-run. The dividend that the region and the State economy will get in diverse forms will fully justify such investments which need not necessarily yield high financial profit.

Even though substantial financial resources are now available, the Forest Development Corporations have not as yet taken advantage of this source in a significant way. Our attention has also been drawn to the fact that in some cases large scale felling and plantation of single species have been taken up ignoring consideration of ecology and the needs of the local community. This has resulted in local resistance to this programme in some areas. In some cases the Forestry Corporation have adopted the easier alternative. They have picked up rich forest areas under the new programme. Clear felling of the rich forests yields high returns which has become an important source of additional revenue to the States. The investment on replantation is small compared to the total income from these areas. Consequently the Corporations in relation to the new forestry programmes are not able to take advantage of institutional finance. Even if they draw upon the institutional finance, it only improves the ways and means position of the State but does not serve the basic objective of marking additional investment in the forestry sector. The depleted and understocked forest areas are also avoided by the Corporations because many of them are encumbered and it will require considerable effort to convince the people before the plantation programme can be taken up. Thus, easy resource generation in comparably richer forest area and the absence of any encumbrances result in easy choice being made in favour of better areas. In such a situation the Forestry

Corporations just become a costlier model for working of forests without much additional benefit. It is, therefore, necessary that Forestry Corporations concentrate on the poorer areas and ensure investment of substantial additional funds from financial institutions in these areas.

FOREST LABOUR

Another important aspect of the forests and the tribal economy which needs urgent attention is the method of working of the forests. The tribal communities provide bulk of the manpower for forestry operations. In the sparsely populated areas, there is substantial immigration for meeting the demand of labour. The contractors recruit the labour in groups and bring them from outside. In the earlier days the Forest Department itself established forest villages to meet the need of labour for silvicultural operations and working of forests. However, the forest labour is entirely casual and is also largely seasonal. The employment of forest labourers is generally through contractors. Even where the working of forests is organised through the forest department itself, the working may be assigned to petty contractors who employ the labourers on piece-wage system. In the areas now brought under intensive forestry management scheme, there is comparatively a more sustained demand of labour in limited areas. Although the Forestry Corporations, to some extent, have introduced commercial concepts in the working of forests and also in their own organisational structure but so far as forest labour is concerned, the earlier arrangements continue.

The forestry operations are not covered in many States by the provisions of minimum wages for agricultural workers. In remote areas, the labourer is at the mercy of the forest contractors, his agents or the petty officials of the department. Even when a better wage employment may be available in some area, the local tribal may still be obliged to work on forestry programmes at the lower wages because he has to live in the area and maintain good relations with the forestry officials. The relationship of the forest labour and the employment agencies, therefore, are to a large extent exploitative, the advantage of which is taken by the middleman or it may get reflected in lower working expenses of the forest department. It is necessary that the forest labourer in these regions should be ensured a reasonable wage taking into account the factors like arduous nature of the job and its casual and seasonal character.

The need for giving a better deal to the forestry workers has been recognised and accepted at the highest level now for a pretty long time. It has been suggested that the working of forests should be organised through the cooperatives of forest labour. However, it is only in Maharashtra and Gujarat that a sustained movement of forest labourers cooperatives has been built up over the past four decades and a substantial part of forestry operations are now being organised through the cooperatives of forest labourers. In Maharashtra, there has been some set back in the recent years in areas which have come under the management of Forestry Development Corporation. In other States it appears that no serious effort has been made so far even though in principle it has been accepted that the entire working of forest should be planned through the cooperatives. Neglect of this aspect besides affecting the average tribal adversely, is against the long-term interests of the forests. So long as the individual tribal remains a casual wage earner, he is bound to seek a firm base in agriculture or other activities which may lead ultimately to the denudation of the forest.

There are two basic issues in relation to the forestry labourers. In the first instance it should be possible to make forestry operations as dependable a source of employment as possible with a remunerative wage. Secondly, the community should have a sense of participation and a stake in the growth of forestry resources through sharing of profit from the forestry activity in the area. In view of the fact that forestry operations have widely fluctuating labour requirements during different seasons, it may be possible to provide regular employment only to a small proportion of total labour force even under intensive forestry management scheme. This inherent problem can be resolved by organising the forestry work through the cooperatives. The working of forests could be so organised that each member of the cooperatives be provided wage employment for a minimum number of days. Once the working of forest has been organised keeping in view the local situation and through the cooperatives it will be possible for the members of the cooperatives themselves to plan their other economic activities to the extent possible with reference to the likely demands of labour in forestry in different seasons in each area. The cooperatives could organise labour teams for working even in the distant regions which may be outside the reach of an individual. This regularity and predictability of wage employment will help in establishing the local economy. The cooperatives should also be in a position to ensure a reasonable wage for their labour.

The other facet of the problem is the share of the forest labour in the net profit from the working of forests. In Gujarat and Maharashtra the Forest Labour Cooperative Societies are entitled to 20 per cent of the net profit from forestry operations which is arrived at after deducting the actual expenses according to the prescribed scales from the net sale proceeds. The same principle should be extended to all forestry operations in the country. Each member of a Forest Workers' Cooperative, who may put in qualifying number of mandays during a year, should be entitled to a share in the net profit. In this way the members of the tribal community will become a partner in the benefit from the developmental programmes in the area. Cooperatives thus, should become a viable alternative to the system of contractors, large and petty, which has become a part of our system. Even in those areas where working is being done through the department or where Forestry Corporations have been established, forestry works should be executed entirely through the Forest Labour Cooperative Societies. The change over to the working through the cooperatives should be completed within a period of 2 to 3 years. The forest department should assume the responsibility of organising the Forest Labour Cooperatives.

Although participation in the management of labour has been accepted in principle in all modern economic activities, no organisational form has been evolved for operationalising this concept in the forestry management. In this case it is not only the labourer who is interested in the forestry programme but the entire community has a vital interest in forestry operations. The organisation of forest labour in cooperatives will enable the Department to associate them in the management and working of the forest which will also help in moving towards a more balanced development in these regions. It will, thus, be possible to re-establish a symbiotic relationship between the forest and the tribal economy. This will help in ending the climate of distrust arising from the ignorance of the other's point of view and lead to harmonious functioning of the system for achieving a common goal.

FOREST VILLAGES

We have referred to the establishment of forest villages by the Forest Department during their early years primarily for meeting the labour needs of forestry operations. The obligation to provide labour even on payment of wage, as a condition for residence in the forest villages has been held *ultra vires* of the Constitution by the Kerala High Court. The Conference of State Ministers in charge of Welfare of Backward Classes held in 1972 had recommended that all the forest villages should be converted into revenue villages. In pursuance of their recommendation, the forest villages have now been declared as revenue villages in most of the States and the obligation of compulsory labour by members of the resident families in these villages has also been discontinued. In most of the States the tribals cultivating lands in the areas of forest village have been given full tenancy rights. However, in some States they still continue to hold lease for a limited period. It will be necessary that all these anomalies are removed without any further loss of time and a programme of development of forest villages is taken up systematically. The forest department will, however, continue to have in many cases a special role in the development of these villages in view of their physical location. Moreover, these villages will still provide them a major part of required labour force for forestry operations. The need for establishing the symbiotic relationship referred to earlier is most urgent in their case. Suitable programmes for development of erstwhile forest villages, therefore, should be prepared urgently and implemented, if necessary under the aegies of the forest department. They should particularly concentrate on tree-based economic activity.

FOREST-BASED INDUSTRY

Establishment of Forest-based Industries can play a crucial role in the development of tribal communities in many areas. As we have noted earlier the basic weakness of the primary producer is that he has no link with the organised market and the value-added is syphoned off by the trader and the industrial sector. If it is possible to have processing or at least semi-processing of all forestry products within the tribal area, much of the profit can be retained in the region. It will give considerable strength to the local economy. The tendency of the industrial units is to dig into the capital gains of forestry products by manipulating their pricing. But the forestry labour continues to work at subsistence level. If instead of exporting logs of wood, small saw mills are established in these regions it will help in diversifying the tribal economy. Moreover, if members of the tribal community are also suitably trained it will also help in upgrading the level of their skills. The industrial units should be set-up in the cooperative sector so that there is sharing of net benefit between the forest labour and the persons employed in the processing unit.

In the highly capital intensive industries like paper, while interests of the State, the entrepreneur and labourer in the organised sector are adequately taken care of, the forest labourer has to be satisfied with casual employment which is generally seasonal in character. Even in this case a fair deal can be given to the forest labourer if a programme for training them for higher skill jobs is taken up. The Forestry Operations in these industries also should be organised through the cooperatives as earlier recommended by us. The leases for supply of raw materials from the forest should be given to the labour cooperatives. This will help in establishing a better balance in favour of the fourth partner.

The organisation of the forestry activity on the lines suggested in the preceding sections will benefit the local economy in three stages. In the first instance, the labourer will become entitled to a fair wage through his participation in the cooperative system. Secondly, it will be possible to work out a system of sharing of net profit from the forestry operation so that the tribal community becomes a partner in the net addition which accrues to the national economy as a result of higher economic activity in the region. At the third level with the organisation of forest-base industries in the cooperative sector, assigning leases for supply of raw material to the cooperatives and training up of tribals for skilled jobs, it will be possible to diversify his economy and enable him to get a share from the organised industrial activity also in the region.

SHIFTING CULTIVATION

Shifting cultivation is a major problem in the States of Orissa and Andhra Pradesh besides the North-Eastern Region. We have considered this question in detail in our report on the development of hill areas. The approach suggested there should broadly be adopted for other areas as well. It may be mentioned here that the programme of agricultural development in the States having settled cultivation as well as shifting cultivation generally bye-passes the shifting cultivator groups, who comprise a sizeable population in the tribal communities in these States. The plans of Integrated Tribal Development Projects in these areas, therefore, are imbalanced and incomplete. Shifting cultivation practices have developed over thousands of years in which the labour input by the individual is meagre. He has learnt through long experiences the use of hardy varieties which can survive the vagaries of nature. Weeds glow in these areas but the local varieties are also able to survive notwithstanding scanty attention by the cultivator. The balance between the resources and the population has been maintained though at a low level of economy, which, however is now getting disturbed. There are signs of change even amongst the shifting cultivators, who are facing the problem of growing pressure of population and dwinding resources. In these areas if a viable alternative can be given to the tribal, it may be acceptable. The areas where the cycle of shifting cultivation has got reduced below the critical period of 10 years or so should be taken up for tackling this problem on a priority basis. Special comprehensive plans for the concerned regions with problem of shifting cultivators as their focus should be prepared.

The development of shifting cultivators should primarily be within the area of their traditional habitat. There should be a mixed programme of developing valley lands for permanent cultivation with provision of irrigation wherever possible, horticultural programmes on moderate slopes and forestry plantations on top lands. Animal husbandry, poultry and piggery should be provided as subsidiary occupations. The broad approach of family-based programme should be followed in those areas in which the aim should be to make each individual economically viable with a suitable mix of economic activities and choice of tree crops. Each shifting cultivator group may be accepted as a unit under this approach so that suitable leadership can emerge from within and the programme can become self-sustaining. It may not be possible that the entire group withdraws from shifting cultivation simultaneously but if substantial development programmes within the frames suggested here is taken up which provides wage-employment on a continuing basis as also builds up the resources base for a viable economy of the individual, it should be possible to wean away these groups one by one from shifting cultivation. Andhra Pradesh has already taken up programmes on these lines with encouraging results. The shifting cultivators are taking to fruit cultivation and growing of coffee in certain areas. It will have to be ensured that the lands set free from shifting cultivation are put under alternative use without any time lag so that the individuals in the group are not attracted to resume shifting cultivation at the slightest pretext. If the group itself is engaged in plantation programmes on the vacated lands and is also aware about the accrual of benefit therefrom to the community itself, it will help in the possibility of resumption of shifting cultivation being completely ruled out. Comprehensive micro-plan for each group of cultivators should be prepared by inter-disciplinary teams which may be constituted exclusively for this purpose. Necessary funds for implementation of this programme should be the first charge on the resources earmarked for these areas from the relevant sectors under the tribal sub-plans.

TRAINING AND PERSONNEL

An average tribal has a wealth of knowledge about the forests and their produce, wild life, etc. The forestry programme should be so organised that full advantage can be taken of these skills. In certain cases it may be necessary to upgrade these skills and give them an understanding of the broader frame so that they can appreciate their role in the new perspective. The base, however, in all these cases should be the native skill of the individual in each area. The programme should be to upgrade their skill rather than superimpose unfamiliar methods which may be difficult for them to master in a short period. The Orissa experiment of extension in horticulture has some useful lessons. Instead of creating a big organisation with a large number of lower functionaries, tribal youths from amongst the beneficiary groups were picked up who were trained in certain essentials about plants, their upkeep and plant protection. This approach has helped in building up these skills within the community. Similar experiment in Tassar cultivation, agriculture and animal husbandry programmes through training of tribal youths has also been quite successful. Creation of functional leadership through transfer of technology, therefore, should be an important aspect of forestry and allied sector activities in the tribal areas. This will help in reducing the cost of overhead in various schemes and solve the problem of managing big organisations in remote regions. Such a programme may perhaps mark the beginning of a new relationship developing between the administrative system and the local communities.

While these factors may be made administrative organisations have inherent limitations regarding the quality of personnel, their aptitude and sense of participation. A new climate of participation can be better engendered by voluntary organisations who can make a choice of persons for each area or task taking into account the precise requirements particularly on the human relation side. They are likely to adopt a problem-solving approach rather than being bound by rules and procedures. There is, however, considerable reluctance to associate voluntary organisations in many States though commendable work has been done in some pockets where the State and the voluntary organisations have joined as partners in certain programmes. The work done by Bharat Agro-Industries Foundation is particularly noteworthy which has become a pace-setter in fodder tree cultivation and improvement of cattle. Special effort should be made to encourage voluntary organisations in specific programmes in the remote forest regions.

The new approach in the forestry programme will require considerable reorientation of the officers and men of the forest department. These officers do acquire a good knowledge of the area through long association of officers of other departments including even tribal welfare may not have. However, their basic approach to the problems of the tribal people and their association in the forestry programmes is not in consonance with the changing times. A relationship of authority and subservience is underlined and even considered necessary for smooth and efficient functioning of the system. The interests of the tribal community tend to be disregarded. This is one of the important contributing factor for the climate of distrust between the administration and the people in the tribal areas. The reorienation of the forestry personnel is crucial and should be taken up urgently. All officers and men at all levels must appreciate the symbiotic relationship between the forest and the tribal community. One cannot develop at the cost of the other. Nor can the forest be saved against the people. Therefore, all officers and men in the forest department should be given a good idea about the tribal life and their economy and interdependence between the development of the tribals and the forest. All programmes of training, both at the point of entry and inservice should have Forests and Tribal Development as important item. In courses leading to formal examination, full papers should be introduced on this subject, in other cases capsule programmes, depending on the level and duration of each course may be prepared. A tribal development unit should be established in the Forest Research Institute which should have a full faculty of tribal development comprising disciplines of tribal sociology, tribal economy and tribal administration.

Forest and Tribal Economy

Tribal economy is intimately connected with the forest and their economy. This relationship has been recognised, but has not been articulated in terms of clear policies and programmes. The tribal economy and the forest economy, therefore, have tended to drift apart with adverse implications to both. In some cases, the forests have suffered tremendous loss, while in others, the tribal economy has been shattered. In some cases, the loss to the national economy has been sizeable and, to the extent it has adversely affected the weakest groups, the imbalance in the socio-economic structure has increased. A clear analysis of underlying processes in the changing socio-economic structure of the tribal communities and their implications to the forest economy, therefore, is urgently needed. It will help in evolving a viable policy for development of the forests and the tribal economy.

There is another aspect of the tribal-forest system in the context of the national economy. The forest regions are sparsely populated, generally inhabited by the tribal communities who are at one of the earlier stages of economic development compared to other communities in the country. These regions, therefore, are comparatively under-developed though they have rich natural resources. These dormant resources have to be activised for faster regional growth. Here we face a dilemma. It is possible to speed up regional development without any consideration for the local tribal economy by using a suitable combination of factors like in-migration of skilled man-power, using a better organizational structure and more capital-intensive working of forests. In this process, the tribal community would be left to adjust by itself. The impact of such a policy will be almost the same as the establishment of a big industrial complex in that area, the only difference being the new activity is not physically circumscribed to a small area like an industry and is much more pervasive in these regions. Unless clear linkages are established with the tribal economy and the absorption capacity of the tribal community itself is accepted as an important constraint in the development and exploitation of various natural resources, the results for the tribal economy are likely to be as disastrous as around an industrial complex. *They may, however, go unnoticed because the drama would have been enacted in more inaccessible regions and impact at any one point, in absolute terms in the national perspective, will not be large, although it may be decesive for the local economy.

MAN AND FOREST—THEIR CHANGING RELATIONSHIP

(i) The Beginning

The story of man can be narrated in terms of bis changing relationship with nature and forests. Man appeared in the world as a part of the 'nature-system' like other animals who either depend directly on the natural produce or on other animals who, in their turn, depend on the natural produce. As the early man advanced from this 'animal state', he became a food-gatherer and hunter. Even in this stage, he was entirely dependent on the forests and continued to be an integral part of its ecological system. Some tribal communities like Sentenalese, Jaravas and Onges of Andaman Islands and Birhors of Bihar even today are in this stage of development. The important feature of this stage is that man was not disturbing the ecology and was in the state of natural equilibrium. The nature, like mother, was fostering the human society with care and affection.

*For a detailed analysis see 'Industrial Complexes and their Tribal Hinterland—Occasion Papers on Tribal Development No. 16, Ministry of Home Affairs, New Delhi.

(ii) The Early Struggle

Man is a skillful animal. Therefore, gradually as man acquired greater skills in food-gathering and hunting his power of exploiting natural resources increased. In the course of time, his number began to increase faster than was possible for the nature of support. In terms of the food-gathering and hunting technology, therefore, the human society tended to outstrip the available resources. Therefore, man began to select useful plants, which would provide him food, with a view to preserve them and, in due course, to multiply them. He also began to discriminate between different animals and was able to domesticate some whose number he could increase by selective rearing. The human economy here branches off, in one direction, to agriculture for which clearing of forests became necessary. In the earlier forms of 'agricultural technology', he had to change the area of his cultivation regularly. He used ash of felled tree for augmenting the fertility of the soil so that the same area could be used for more than one year. There was another important development at this stage. He went out in search of pastures which would provide sustenance for the increasing herds of his domesticated animals. These new developments represent a break-through in the primitive technology because the carrying capacity of the natural resources, in terms of persons per unit area, became many-fold.

(iii) Primitive Cultivation

In the beginning shifting cultivation had no perceptible impact on the forest resources. It only meant felling of trees in the forest according to the need of the man, in place of their natural decay in an irregular cycle where older trees give way to the new ones at random according to their respective life cycles. Here was an unending series of land-parcels available for shifting cultivation. It continued till such time as one group of men touched the jurisdiction of another group and was obliged to turn back and follow a circular repetitive cycle. The population continued to grow with the changing technology. Its only implication, in the early days, was a comparatively shorter cycle for shifting cultivation.

A number of communities have continued in the pastoral or shifting cultivation stage of economy even till today, the notable examples being the tribals in the North-East, in Orissa and in the forest regions of Southern States. The pastoral communities are notably the Gujjars, Gaddis in the North-Western hills. In the case of shifting cultivators, the important distinguishing feature from their earlier stage is that instead of living from forests, as earlier, they now live on forests. As the cycle of shifting cultivation gets reduced, the forest resources decline in direct proportion to length of the cycle. Finally, the cycle became so short that soil gets fully eroded, leaving behind only stones and pebbles where once luxurious forest flourished. This is a common sight, for example, in Koraput, Orissa.

Not all tribal communities were caught in this 'technological trap' leading to complete denudation of forests through intensive shifting cultivation. At some stage early in his history, man learnt better use of limited land and moved ahead in agricultural technology with the utilisation of animal power for digging the soil deeper. The new practice, however, was confined to small enclaves in the vast forest areas. While the requirement of cereals was gradually met from the new settled cultivation, man continued to depend on forests for a variety of things for this sustenance. He would still take to food-gathering, hunting or even shifting cultivation in a limited sense depending on the level of technology of the community, availability of forest resources and the pressure of population. The earlier settled cultivator, thus, was largely dependent on forest resources though he was trying to have a foot-hold in settled cultivation.

(iv) Settled Cultivation

As the pressure of population further grew, agricultural technology advanced and the forests receded into the background. With larger land-mass coming under settled cultivation, it was possible to grow a variety of crops in different fields. With the development of communications, it became feasible for the settled communities even to specialise in agricultural production on a regional basis and satisfy all the need through mutual exchange, initially through barter and subsequently, through money. In relation to the forests, these communities can be said to be marginally located depending on them for grazing of cattle, fuel-wood and such other items which could be found only in forests. Even this dependence on forests gradually decreased as the settled cultivator learnt to plant useful trees near the village, or in their fields, or elsewhere. During this stage only a distant relationship was maintained with the forests.

(v) Small Number of Agricultural Groups

The next stage in human development is represented by semi-urban communities which gradually emerge from their rural hinterlands and take to some specialised functions or services. Their relationship with forests can be viewed as a hang-over from the previous era when the community depended on them to a much greater extent. They do not have any direct linkages with the forest, although, in some areas perhaps, they may still be getting their fire-wood from the forest. The direct dependence on forests, thus, continued to decrease.

(vi) The Industrial Man

In the last stage of this process are urban and industrial societies. These communities are entirely structured and have well defined functional specialisation. The forests in this system represent as specialised a sector as a big steel plant. Steel Plant produces finished steel while forests produce certain raw materials which are necessary for producing other finished goods for satisfying certain specialised needs. The forests are a part of a long 'assembly-line'. It would be immaterial to the Industrial Man whether the finished goods he uses are based on forests produce or on some other substitude. The forest resources themselves could be within the country or outside the country. The new Man may get concerned about the forests directly as an individual or as a group only when larger question of ecological balance for the human society as a whole arise. The forests may also provide him an outlet when he may have an urge to get out of his monotonous life and wonder into the woods, far or near, in the search of an age which the Man has left far behind.

The Two Phases

In the above analysis, as we proceed from the first stage to the last, the intimate relationship of the primitive man with forests gradually transforms into a distant and indirect relationship of forest with the city man. These six stages can be broadly divided into two phases, viz., the first three stages and the three as given in the schematic representation of Forest-Man Relationship. There is a qualitative change in the man's relationship with forests towards the end of the third stage. Broadly, it can be said that the first three stages of this forest-man relationship represent the tribal phase of his history. In the fourth stage as the 'tribal' character of human society undergoes an important change, the intimate relationship of man with the forest is irretrievably affected. The society enters the second phase the 'advanced' living, beginning with settled cultivation where the relation with the forest becomes marginal.

The Third and the Fourth stages overlap to some extent and no sharp dividing line can be drawn between them. The tribal communities, who generally represent the first phase, have already graduated in some areas into the second phase, (i.e., the fourth stage). On the other hand, some of the advanced non-tribal communities still have some characteristics of the first phase, (i.e., the third stage) economy. It may be noted here that in the last three stages comprising the second phase, mere physical proximity with forest resources does not define the relationship of the society with the forests. An industrial complex may be located deep in a forest area, yet the community may be entirely self-contained and the forests may be like a 'garden' to them with open space and fresh air. Similarly, on the other extreme, as the forest resources get depleted, the tribal communities may continue to draw sustenance from distant receding forests till becomes physically impossible. Finally, the early intimate relationship with forests may continue only in the folklore, rituals and ceremonies of the people for a long time after the forests have disappeared from their proximity.

Administrative-Legal Frame

One of the important aspects of man-forest system is the type of relationship between the two. As relationships in a modern society are defined in formal and mostly legal terms, it will be necessary to review the quality and characteristics of this relationship as the socio-economic system evolves though various stages noted earlier.

(i) Communal Ownership

In the early stages of human development, the local communities owned the land as well as the forest resources. When man was a part of the natural eco-system, the concept of 'ownership' was vague and its effectiveness depended on the man's natural superiority over other users of the forest. With the growing pressure of population, the forest areas got demarcated between different communities. The struggle for command over resources has continued till recent times in the more-backward areas. The concept of forests as communal property, developed over the millenia, has been recognised even under the law in some areas in the North-East.

With the emergence of the modern economies, forests became an important source of revenue and wealth to the State. Initially, the administration began to exploit forest resources for commercial purposes without challenging the rights of the local community or asserting State's exclusive rights. So long as there was no 'conflict of interests,' the tribal communities did not bother. For example, valuable *sal* trees continued to be extracted from the forests in different areas in Bastar, M.P., for supply to the Railways without any objection by the local communities. The tall *sal* tree was of no use of local community. Even today, the 'valuable' teak trees, worth thousands of rupees, may be used by the tribal in the more interior areas just for fencing his fields which may be producing commodities worth not even a hundred rupees. In the 'economics' of the tribal, a teak tree has not acquired a high 'value'. In this context, if the State, for that matter anyone else, were to take away the teak tree from his land or forest, it will not make much of a difference to the tribal and he will not be agitated over this extraction.

(ii) State Ownership

The situation, however changes when the administration begin to have an assessment of the forest resources in modern 'economic' terms in a longer time perspective. The local tribal practices are then viewed as 'destroying' this wealth which could be 'activised' at a future date. This State may begin to assert its right, while the tribal still believes that the forest 'belongs' to him. Here a conflict situation arises and the State assert its right through formal legal sanctions. These conflict situations have resulted in revolts in numerous tribal areas throughout the last two centuries. These 'rights' of tribal communities, which are numerically small, had ultimately to yield to the formal legal sanctions of the State. However, even when State asserted these formal rights, an element of compromise had to be accepted by it which can be seen in the procedures prescribed for reservation of forests. While undulated rights of the tribals on the forest, as in the North-East, were not recognised in the middle India, yet a tacit agreement was reached not to disturb his economy by unqualified assertion of the State's right and exploitation of forests purely from the angle of State revenues. Semi-judicial procedures were prescribed for assessing the conventional relationship of the tribal economy with the forest ecology. This relationship was expected to be honoured by treating them as 'rights' which had to be honoured by the State; and the working of the Forests had to be adapted to the basis needs of the local economy. The legal form to give expression to this central theme, however, varied. The continuance of these relationships was termed as 'concessions' in some cases and 'rights' in others.

(iii) Corporate Ownership

In the recent years a new concept of ownership is developing in the quest of attracting institutional finance for intensive exploitation of forest resources. Here we find the final formal frame of the western economies which are specialised to the core. The forest is viewed as a resources, owned by a corporate body, which is governed by purely the economics of plantations unconcerned with the local economy. For some time the tribal may be supplied, his requirements for a price, may be a concessional price, but all these considerations are irrelevant and irritants in the new systems in which relationship are recognised at formal level only.

In this way, there had been a steady and certain change from *de facto* ownership of forests by the tribal community, through economic exploitation by the State without asserting any right, economic exploitation by the State will *de jure* ownership but recognising the rights of the tribals for utilisation of forest at a particular level of intensity, non-recognition of the tribals' right but granting a few concessions, to finally a stage where forest resources acquire the action of corporate ownership, their working is governed by input-ouput considerations and tribal economies' needs are irrelevant and irritant to the system.

In this process, conflict situations arise where the administrative-legal form out-strips the appropriate stage of economy, for example, an industrial society is used to formal structures and, therefore, the idea of corporate ownership is as natural to it as the concept of community ownership to a primitive group.

Difference in Perception

The emergence of the concept of State ownership of forests made an important difference to the tribal economy. Instead of the community itself being the final arbiter of use of forest resources, it became entirely dependent on the State for use of the forest resource for subsistence. It may be useful at this stage to compare and contrast the concepts about the ownership of forests and ownership of land. In relation to the land, the early communal ownership concepts gradually gave way to individual ownership with an intermediate stage where landlords came in the picture who got ownership rights during the British days. After independence, the general pattern has been that the State has the final ownership right on the land whereas the individual has a right to till the land. In the case of forest dwellers, however, the change was not in the same direction. The tribal was the 'owner' of the forest, which came under the 'control' of the British or the land-lords/*rajas*. When the British rule came to an end, the tribal community did not regain it authority. On the contrary, the authority, of the State got consolidated. The basic reason for this unidirectional change is the general conceptual distortion about the tribal economy and its 'relationship' with forests. It is reinforced by the consolidation of the economic interests of the State and loosing of tribals' effective control under heavy odds.

The conceptual distortion arises from the fact that forest-based tribal economy, agricultural economy and urban economy represent three different stages in human development and each one of them has little appreciation of the other. In the early stages, man depended on the bounty of nature and his own effort was only in terms of wresting the fruits of nature in a state of raw struggle for life against other citizens. The *total effort* involved in hunting food-gathering and protecting the small produce from other wild animals was considerable and may compare favourably with the *total effort* involved in making a living through settled agriculture. There is, however, a qualitative difference. The direct effort involved in physically plucking the fruit or digging a root is not much. But this 'plucking' is to be viewed as the end-product of a prolonged struggle for existence involving precarious state of living in a difficult area. This struggle becomes more acute as population increases and the competition for limited resources accentuates. Thus, 'last act' of plucking in the 'production process appears to be very simple to a person belonging to another system but the entire 'drama of living' is extremely complex and hazardous. In contrast, in a settled agricultural economy, the physical effort in the actual agricultural production is comparatively much greater than the physical effort in 'plucking' of a fruit or digging of a root. But in this stage of economy the struggle for survival of the individual gets considerably reduced because of general advancement and organisation of a higher order. Thus, the community is saved the effort of the 'raw struggle for survival' necessary in the earlier stages. In fact, as we proceed further towards industrialised economic systems, the physical effort involved and the discipline required in the *'act of production'* is much more compared to the physical effort in agriculture. But there are compensations in other forms; the nature is completely 'trained', the organisation is of a much higher order and many of the individuals, other needs are automatically satisfied in a more organised society.

Another important qualitative change comes in the style of 'earning' a living as the capital base increases. The man begins to reap the fruits of his past effort. Thus, the direct effort-input in earning a living gradually becomes smaller because of capital intensity. On the other hand, the strong social organisation reduces the individual struggle against nature to almost 'negligible' quantum. In fact, here in its final form, the circle can be said to be complete. In the early stages, man was depending on bounty of nature whereas in the final stage he may be dependent entirely on *his past effort*. In this entire process, the struggle for existence at individual level continues to decrease and in the final form of a large organisation, the Man has only to fend against himself.

THE CONSEQUENCES

As the ownership of the State gets consolidated and formalised and the decision-making recedes farther away from the field, the special relationship of the tribal with the forest is not appreciated. Their rights are viewed as a 'burden' on the forests and an impediment in their scientific and economic exploitation. On the other hand, the socio-economic situation of the tribal communities itself is not static. As the pace of development in the country quickens, the tribal communities also begin to move faster in the direction of lesser reliances on forest, in some areas, in earlier relationship of the tribals with the forests is no longer valid; the traditional rights or concessions may be used by the community only to supplement marginally their incomes. However, the situation is not the same in all tribal areas throughout the country. The case of shifting cultivation will illustrate the point. There are tribal communities in Orissa and in the North-East who are entirely dependent on shifting cultivation. But there are also a number of communities, who have now taken to settled cultivation or even other modern vocations, yet they are continuing with shifting cultivation as well which merely supplements their incomes. It appears that while formulating the forest policy, the conditions in the more advanced areas are taken as typical and a uniform policy is sought to be implemented everywhere. The change in the policy may have only a marginal significance or no significance for the more advanced communities but may have far-reaching implications and may be crucial for the tribal economy in the more backward areas.

The forest resources are richer in the more backward areas since there is lower pressure of population and modern destructive elements have also not found their way to these areas. Therefore, these areas have the greatest potential for 'scientific' exploitation. It is an irony that it is here that the tribal depends to the maximum extent on the forests and is in the early stages of economic evolution. He is not prepared for a sudden change. He is not even in a position to accept the advanced technology of simple forestry operations. Thus, the conflict situation is most acute in the more backward areas.

We also find complete divergence in the perceptions about the forest resources as between the tribal communities in the more backward areas and the policy formulation levels in the country. The fact that a community in these areas can live with 'little effort' is highlighted. But the fact that the concept of 'little effort' is one sided and represents merely the perception of advanced communities is not appreciated. Their effort in the larger struggle for existence is disregarded. And a conclusion is reached that *no section of the community can be allowed to 'wastefully' use 'national' economic resources.* Since the forest produce is treated as nature's gift, State stakes its full claim over it. At the best, the tribal may be allowed a reasonable wage for the labour which he may put in for the collection of minor forest produce or extraction of major produce. Thus, the *de facto* and conventional command of the tribal over resources is completely denied in this perception and he is reduced to the status of merely a casual wage-earner.

II
DEVELOPMENT OF THE PEOPLE AND THE FOREST— A SYNTHESIS

The present scene in the forest regions, inhabited by the tribals, thus, is quite complex. There is divergence between the legal form and people's own frame of thinking, there are compulsions of the local economy and pressure for their optimal utilisation in a larger regional or national perspective; there is growing difference between conservationists and economic use protagonists; the people's development and the forestry continue as two non-intersecting segments. A clear policy frame taking all the diverse factors into account remains to be worked out. While all other factors in any scheme will be extraneous, the two elements are primodal, viz., the forest and its inhabitants. Therefore, there has to be a synthesis of these two interests. Two extreme models can be developed by treating either of them as a dependent factor. We may study the outlines of these two models with a view to build a model of synthesis.

(i) Forestry Development Model

In this model, the forest resources occupy the central position. Their contribution to the national economy becomes the primary consideration, taking, however, both the short-term and long-term interests into account. Such an extreme model is conceptually akin to forestry practices in the western nations where the man-forest relationship has entered the last stages of specialised differentiated economy. There are no special relationship between the local community and the neighbouring forest. Man-power is as good factor of production as capital, the two being interchangeable on 'input-output' considerations. Labour supply in this Regional Development Scheme is expected to got balanced according to the principles of demand and supply. The mix of the tree-growth in the forest itself is decided on the basis of economic returns. In this model, we may find a plan for replacement of the indigenous slow-growing species by fast-growing economic species needed for the larger national economy; there may be larger influx of labour in response to a higher demand of intensive economic activity; sophisticated capital-intensive process may be introduced even in the more backward sparsely populated areas; operations may be taken up in concentrated regions for better management and economies of scale, and so on. Thus, in terms of Regional Development we may find a large in-flow of capital, greater deployment of men and materials which, in association with the rich unexploited natural resources, give a quicker return. And, the level of regional economy rises fast contributing to the national economy in the same proportion.

Since man-power has been treated merely as an ordinary factor of production, it is expected that the local people will acquire a position in this process according to their capacity and inclination. This story of regional development becomes quite different if we look at the same process from the people's end. The tribal is still in the integrated non-specialised stage of economy. He depends on the forests for food and shelter. The conversion of the local forest-mix by fast-growing economic species may change the ecology. The fruit bearing trees, giving sustenance of the tribal, may disappear affecting adversely his economy. The new forest may have no utility for him. The new demand of labour may be qualitatively different from the earlier slow pace utilisation of labour which was adjusted to the agricultural cycle of the local community. The tribal may become unemployable since the operations are now designed with reference to the requirement of the new organisation and its operational viability. He, therefore, slides back, both in terms of supplementation of his income from collection of minor forest produce as also in terms of wage-labour.

The immigration of labour itself may force a conflict situation on the simple tribal community since they may have to compete with more advanced groups. The Forestry Development Model, in its extreme form, may become more akin to a large scale industry with the only difference that its operations are comparatively dispersed.

(ii) Peoples' Development Model

In this model, the peoples' development becomes primary while the forestry resources become one of the factors contributing to their development. We find an extreme form of this model in the primitive economy where the community was subsisting entirely on the forest resources. In the early stages, the two interests were in balance and harmony. But increasing pressure of population, without corresponding change in the technology or form of exploitation of the forests, sometimes resulted in the destruction of the very base of the economy. It is clear that to avoid such a situation, the method of utilisation of forest has to change. But it has to be ensured that the local community continues to have full command of the resources and their economy gets strengthen by inputs for forestry development. The command of the community can continue only if they acquire higher skills, both technical and organisational, needed in the new context. Therefore, the path of development has to be gradual and any external input of technology of entreprenurial skills has to be minimal and temporary. Some of the European countries, which have forestry as their main economic base, are a good example of this model. Such an economy, however, can be aimed only as a long-term objective, the local community gradually progressing in that direction with ever increasing utilisation of forests and other natural resources for continued development. This model of development will be a 'closed' one with minimal external inputs but having carefully planned links with other spheres of economy, with interests of the local economy as the primary focus.

The final stage in this model in terms of forestry development, may be the same in the first model. The difference, however, will be in its intermediate stages. The next stage in the development may not envisage optimal utilisation of local resources' their contribution to the regional and national economy may be considerably smaller than in the first model. The resources may remain under-utilised as a policy decision. But these are crucial factors for tribal development, *since tribal development is essentially a problem of the transition.* It is in these critical stages that it has to be ensured that the community does not get swept-off its feet by super-imposition of a faster pace of development than what it can easily assimilate.

In the absence of a clear policy frame, accommodating the two interests underlined in the two models above, the situation is rather confusing. The course of action in different areas depends on the relative strength of diverse forces. In some areas, the community may assert its right, notwithstanding the State's effort to consolidate its position. The growing pressure of population, in the absence of adaptation of technology may result in ultimate destruction of forests. On the other extreme, in the more backward areas the State may be able to consolidate its position. It may give a new shape to the forest economy. But in this process the tribal economic may get disrupted and the community may be forced into the substratum of the new socio-economic structure which may get established largely with migrant population. The results may be mixed in the intermediate areas.

REFORMULATION OF SOME BASIC CONCEPTS

If tribal development and forestry are accepted as two co-equal goals, the emergence of extreme situations of these two models can be avoided. In the first instance it will be necessary to clearly appreciate the various issues involved and, if necessary, have conceptual re-formulation on certain important matters. Some of the important points are discussed in the following paragraphs.

(i) Minor Forest Produce

The tribal economy has subsisted on the minor forest produce since time immemorial. In the early phase of forest management, the right of the tribal on the minor forest produce was recognised sometimes for *bonafide* domestic use and sometimes even for sale. In a subsistent economy cash requirement of the individual was little. The value of many a item of minor forest produce was hardly anything more than for limited local use. The opening up of forest areas has made a qualitative change in both these aspects.

The consumption pattern of the tribal has been undergoing some change, reducing the direct dependence on minor forest produce. But the minor forest produce has become an important source for meeting his cash requirement, which has been increasing with the diversification of his wants. Simultaneously, the value of minor forest produce has also got appreciated in the outside markets. In some cases, there are situations of competing end-use like that for *mahua* flower. On the other hand, minor forest produce has also come to be looked upon as a source of revenue to the state with the introduction of royalty, the right of the tribal is being questioned or is being circumscribed strictly to '*bonafide* domestic use'. In a situation of competing demands, the dividing line between the two is rather thin. The price payable to the tribal is computed in terms of his labour input, sometimes even ignoring the 'cost' of transportation because of variation in distance. This renders collection of minor forest produce in the far off areas uneconomical.

This situation is a direct result of non-appreciation of change in the tribal economy. It is presumed that the tribals continue to live in pre-monetised subsistence static state. The introduction of contractors in the working of forest has consolidated the ownership of the State on these resources; the tribals' right first came to be violated by these new elements, they were questioned subsequently and nullified finally. This situation has been corrected in some States by talcing a policy decision to ensure full return of the minor forest produce to the tribal removing the incidence of royalty and sometimes even the operational costs. There is a consensus at the national level on this issue but it remains to be operationalised in the field. This single step will help the tribal economy substantially since it will give direct benefit to the individual tribal who is himself engaged in that economic activity. It is, therefore, necessary that the minor forest produce is not viewed as a source of State income but as an element which can be utilised to provide a sound economic-base to the tribal economy, particularly during the period of transition.

Once this concept is accepted certain other aspects of minor forest produce will also need attention. So far the tribal has been a passive participant in the production of minor forest produce coming on the scene at the collection point. The existing potential of minor forest produce is sometimes over-exploited. It is also getting exhausted because of non-maintenance or inadequate care. There is no clearly defined place for these items is new forestry plantation programme. A positive policy should be evolved for this purpose with active participation of the tribal so that *he gradually becomes a grower of minor produce rather than remaining merely a collector.* This will help in bringing about a structural change in the economy over a period of time, harmonising the interests of tribal economy and the forest economy.

(ii) Limited Ownership and Right of Usufruct

This brings us to the next crucial issue of divergent claims and differing perception about the ownership of forest resources. The Forest Department tends to view the tribal as an intruder and encroacher; the tribal visualises the forest department and the contractor as competitors in the exploitation of forests, which he feels belong to him. The pressure on forest resources continues unabated, little effort being made to take the tribal into confidence and try to presuade him to become to tenderer of trees and to take to scientific exploitation. Even in those areas where some tribals suddenly found themselves as individual owners of sizable forest wealth, no attempt has been made to induce him to scientific management. In due course, he inevitably lost that valuable asset leaving the land without tree-cover.

It will be impossible to contain the pressure on the forest unless the tribal gets interested in plantation of trees and has a feeling that it will strengthen his economy. In this case, the objectives will have to be clearly defined. Today, conflict arises because there are only two mutually exclusive situations, viz., either there is a departmentally managed forest in which even the rights of *nistar* are considered as burden, or in the alternative, the tribal somehow gets hold of forest land, clear fells it and takes to cultivation irrespective of the quality of land or the yield which he may get. At the sub-subsistence level of his economy, he is satisfied with whatever he can get from it; and in his narrow arithmetical computation, he is a net gainer. It is clear that final objective of forest management has to be a better and extensive tree-cover notwithstanding the fact that considerations of revenue are becoming dominant with commercialisation of forestry operations. Can we simulate a situation where the tribal can also accept extensive and better tree-cover in his own interest? This is possible by given the individual or if unavoidable, the community a stake in the new trees-wealth. The sub-marginal lands, which should be brought under tree cover even for restoring the ecological balance, are extensive. No effort of whatever dimension is too big if this aim is to be achieved. Financial resources are not the only limiting factor. There has to be genuine involvement of the people. There is no reason why the tribal, who is lover of trees and who can easily take to plantation activity, should not be fully associated in this task. He can be brought into this programme by giving him limited ownership rights on the trees he helps to grow with the condition that he will accept necessary technical advice for their maintenance and future use. The experience of *tongia* cultivation in some States, where the lands finally got encroached, is not on all fours with this suggestion, since no cultivation at any stage is envisaged in the new scheme. The tribal, from the very beginning, has to take to plantation of trees. He is associated in the decision and should know that the new assets being created belong to him. Therefore, he can be expected to look forward to the groves getting established which would provide him substance in due course.

(iii) Casual Wage-Labour not Synonymous with Tribal Development

One of the important reasons for a comprehensive development programme, taking all aspects into consideration not emerging so far has been that mere provision of even casual wage employment in forestry operations has been treated as a measure of tribal development. This aspect needs to be analysed in some depth. It is true that bulk of the investment in forestry programmes goes towards wage-labour. But here employment is largely casual in character and ubiquitous in its distribution. The individual tribal is not sure either about the quantum of employment or its periodicity. Even accrual of additional income to the local community is subject to the overall labour position in the regions, in fact, it is just incidental to the forestry development programme. It has no element for strengthening the tribal economy in the long-run. What he gets today as wage is what he can look for. And even this may be termed as tribal development. Sometimes this approach is adopted even in plantation programmes taken up as a part of tribal development schemes;

the tribal gets the wage for the work done while the permanent asset becomes the property of the State!

The basic objective of a tribal development programme is to make each family economically viable with a clearly defined time-frame. Therefore, a programme can be deemed to be a tribal development programme only if it strengthens the tribal economy on a permanent basis. The financial support of the State to the tribal, in this case, has to be used for converting his labour into assets which are under his own command. *A plantation scheme with limited ownership of the tribal in the tree and its usufruct would qualify as a tribal development programme whereas a plantation scheme which uses the tribal as a wage-labour and adds to the capital assets of the State is a forestry development programme.*

(iv) Forest Labour

The net question is about the special position of forest labour in our national economic scene. Forestry is one of the few organised activities where labour is entirely casual and disorganised. It is an irony that a group of people, who consider themselves to be rightful owners of the entire resource-base in these areas, have almost no rights even when they are employed to work the same resources. This situation may be contrasted with the new concept of partnership in management in big industrial enterprises where the capital is provided by the national exchequer. The labour simply joins us individual participant in that economic activity, with or without skills. In fact, in the new context, labour in the organised sector with high capital investment tends to become a vested interest which may try to appropriate unto itself to major share in the value-added, which should rightfully belong to the nation as a whole. In the forestry sector, on the other hand, since the State has emerged as an unquestioned owner of the resource-base and the participant labour is backward and largely dispersed, it has no benefit either as participant in management or in getting a share in the value-added arising from the new economic activity. This position is inequitous and requires to be changed. In any scheme of working of forests, the local tribal community, which provides the labour, should be accepted as a partner in the management and sharing of profits. They should not be taken merely as casual wage-earners whose services can be dispensed with at will of the Department.

If this concept is accepted, a healthy partnership can develop in the working and management of forestry resources in the tribal areas, tribal development and forestry development programmes reinforcing each other.

PEOPLES' PARTICIPATION IN MANAGEMENT

The above discussion brings about a number of issues which need to be resolved first at the policy level. Let us take the question of participation in management. This will not be possible so long as the labour is entirely casual and seasonal. But the casual character of labour-force is dictated by the nature of the work itself. Therefore, participation in management can be brought about by organising this workforce in a different way, say, by forming forest labourers' co-operative societies. If the entire work in a region is entrusted to these societies, they can organise their man-power supply on a voluntary basis, the community adjusting its work-schedule to the forestry work-schedule. The tribal communities are used to this type of collective decision-making. In this arrangement the worker, as an individual, may remain a casual labour, yet as a member of the group, he would acquire continuing interest in the forestry operations in which he will also participate as a decision-maker so far as the labour policy is concerned. This will provide a sound base for continuing relationship between the management and the labour. The profit-sharing can also be worked out on certain mutually agreed principles as has already been done in some States.

The same principle can be extended to the other forest-based industries. Take any example, say, a Paper Mill. At the moment there are four identifiable interests here, viz.: (i) the forest administration (or the State Government), (ii) the management of the industry, (iii) industrial labourer, and (iv) forestry labour. Two of them, viz., the administration and the management generally negotiate the terms and labour supply—both industrial and forestry—is expected to be determined by market forces. The administration gets the royalty while the management earns the profit. The industrial labour, through collective bargaining, gradually acquires independent personality and can press its claim for share in the profit of the enterprise which, to some extent, may even influence the royalty element. The last element, viz., the forest labour, however, is completely dependent and passive. The local community may not be even sure of additional income generation since the management can opt to work with migrant labour claiming greater dependability and higher efficiency in their favour. The pattern of forestry operations, in this case, will depend on the administrative convenience of the management and other factors of economy.

If the local community is accepted as a partner in the new economic activity, the working arrangement could be differently defined. For example, in this case, the local community can be visualised as the suppliers of raw material to the industries based on national resources. If the lease for working of forest can be given to the community or cooperatives of labour, they can have an agreement with the management to supply the raw-material according to a stipulated schedule. In fact, this arrangement can be incorporated as integral part of the original project design itself. In that case, the community can organise the working plan for extraction of raw material according to their calendar of agricultural operations, adjusting it to the requirements of the industry where necessary. For example, in the case of a Paper Mill, the supply of bamboos would be organised from numerous small areas, each of which may have a four year cycle for bamboo plantation and its working. In the other model, where bamboo lease is with the Mill, the areas of working of bamboos would be much larger for each year because its size is determined on administrative considerations, even though working cycle will continue to be four yearly. The larger size of yearly operations has the effect of spurt in labour demand once in four years in each area which cannot be satisfied locally and in-migration becomes unavoidable. The local community may not get any benefit from this activity. But in the alternative arrangement, when the local community is associated in decision-making, it becomes an equal partner in the industrial activity and can expect to share in the benefits accruing to the area.

The above illustrations relate to participation by the labour or the community in specific tasks like the working of forests and functioning of a forest-based industrial unit. The forestry management itself is a much wider concept. The present forest management practices were developed in the early years of the present century when the people were treated as the subject and their interest was expected to be taken care of by the administration itself. Balancing of forces, therefore, was sought to be brought about by inter-departmental consultations, people's part being limited to placing their case before the higher authorities. In some cases now an element of consultation with the people's representatives has been introduced. In some cases, the district level advisory bodies may be consulted. But the growing functionalism in the administration has tended to make forestry management more exclusive. When even satisfaction of local needs is sought to be computed in money terms, *nistar* tends to be taken as a 'burden' on the forest. The concepts of the developed and differentiated modern economies are unwittingly superimposed. The result is that the community and the administration have tended to drift apart.

This process has to be reversed. It is through active participation of the community in the decision-making relating to the management of the forests that they can be expected to share the common goals set for the development of the region with forestry as an important element. Suitable institutional arrangement, therefore, should be made at the local level for this purpose. For example, a forestry management advisory committee may be constituted for each project area or for each district. It may: (a) broadly approve long-term forestry plan for the region and five-year and annual programme for forestry development; (b) oversee implementation of the programmes, particularly forest-labour-management relationship re-stocking of the forests, individual and communal plantation and all matters relating to marketing and processing of minor forest produce. Similar bodies also be constituted at the regional and State levels.

FORESTRY-BASED ECONOMY

We have referred to forestry-based economy at a number of places in our discussion. It will be useful if this concept is spelt out in some detail. Our approach in planning so far has been compartmentalised. We have schemes for conversation of forests economic plantation, agriculture development or industrial development. Once a scheme is prepared, assumpting any of these alternatives for a particular area, it becomes exclusive and self-contained. Sometimes two schemes may be taken up in the same area which may not be fully consistent. For example, an intensive agricultural development programme and an intensive forestry programmes would both require a larger labour force which may not be locally available in a sparsely populated area. A large migrant labour force in the long-run may go against the interests of the forests themselves besides changing the demographic structure of the area. These contradictions can be avoided if an integrated approach is adopted to development.

In the first instance, the present practice of thinking of agricultural economy and a State owned forest economy as mutually exclusive frames has to be discounted. An individual tribal today has only two alternatives, viz., either one acquires some land or he becomes a casual wage earner. Similarly, the forest administration also has two alternatives, *viz.*. either the land is within the forest or it is excised in favour of an individual for cultivation. A third alternative, which we have discussed earlier, is that the individual may have varying degree of interests in the forests and their produce. Here the concept of 'forest' itself will have to be somewhat wider than mere 'reserved' or 'protected' forest areas. The individual may have full rights in the minor forest produce and he should gradually become a grower of minor forest produce rather than a mere collector. The collection of minor forest produce will have to be put on a more scientific base so that balance can be struck between the long-term interests of the community and immediate interests of the individual. Elimination of contractor will help in harmonising these interests. In suitable areas, the individual could be allowed to have second storey cultivation of economic species in the forests under expert guidance. The depleted forest areas could be re-stocked by suitable species, part of the new stock may be entirely State property, but part may be community-owned or with limited rights in favour of the individual.

All the above activities essentially fall under forestry programme because they all add to the existing stock of forests. The association of the tribal, as an individual or a cooperative, will give him a stake in this activity. But this by itself will not be enough. Planning of all these programmes should have a clear linkage with other economic activities of the tribal. For example, pasture development should be linked with cattle development and plantation with processing and marketing. All these activities together should provide full time employment to the local community and the whole working schedule of the community may be decided keeping in view the requirements of the forestry operations. Agriculture will acquire a secondary role in this economy, depending on the intencity of forestry-oriented activity, available manpower and appropriate choice for optimum use of land resources.

Active participation by the community in the planning and operation of the entire local economy will give them a sense of greater dependability and assured future. This will help in relieving the pressure on forest generated by keen desire for personal ownership of land, of whatever quality at whatever cost. This integrated plan could be worked out for each small area so that the decisions are taken in a face-to-face situation and the plan is within the comprehension of the participants. Institutional arrangement could be made at a higher level for providing wider frame within which all these smaller units can function harmoniously. Their leaders could participate in decision-making at that level.

An Integrated Plan

The Planning for tribal development and forestry development as mutually reinforcing elements, requires a careful analysis of the resource potential of each region as also of the socio-economic situation of the local community. The first essential step will be to evolve a consistent scheme for all areas according to the local factor-mix. The level of people's development is not the same in the entire tribal region. Similarly, the extent of forest resources are also not the same in all regions. If the programmes were to be prepared purely from forestry angle, the extremely backward areas will automatically get the highest priority because of their rich resources. But, here, the local community is not ready for a fast change, and social consequences of commercialisation of forest economy may be severe. It is, therefore, quite obvious that the pace of change in these areas should be slower than what could be dictated by purely forestry considerations. On the other extreme, where the pressure of population is heavy, the forest resources may have got completely depleted. On purely economic considerations, these areas could be left out. But it is these areas that ecological balance has got disturbed and, in many cases, the local population may be pressing hard against forest resources in distant regions. Therefore, on balance of considerations the forestry programmes in these areas may have to be more intensified than that may be dictated on purely commercial considerations. The intermediate areas, with moderate pressure of population and a reasonable forest resource potential, may have a suitable programme mix with elements of intensive forestry. In some cases, it may be possible to evolve forestry-based economies; in others, forests may be assigned a complementary role to the general tribal development programme.

The forestry programme in each area should comprise two parts. The first part should concern with the basic needs of the community in the region. The basic needs themselves will have to be carefully defined in the specific socio-economic context in each area. In the more backward regions, where the tribals' dependence on the forest is almost total, his entire subsistence has to be adequately taken care of in this part of the plan. As we move to the more advanced areas, this dependence gradually becomes lesser. The forest plan relatable to the basic needs, therefore, will also recede in the background.

The extent of dependence of a community for different components of their basic needs will also vary from one area to another. The dependence on the forest for food gets reduced in a comparatively earlier phase of development while the community continues to depend on them for shelter, like cousin material, till a very late stage of development The other aspects of economy like grazing of cattle, timber for making implements minor forest produce as a source of meeting cash requirements for a diversified economy, will also need to be carefully reviewed in each case.

Once the parameters of the first part of the forestry programme, viz., meeting the basic needs of the community have been defined, the second part can be planned with great emphasis on forestry proper. The impact of this programme on the local community and linkages with. Their economy, however, will have to be kept in view even in this part. For example, intensive forestry programmes may have to be avoided in the more backward areas so that the demographic structure is not suddenly changed. The preparedness of the people to accept a higher technology may provide an important boundary condition for determining the intensity and character of forestry operations. As we reach the lesser backward areas, forestry-based economies with appropriate mix of various elements could be planned. In advanced areas with high pressure of population and reasonable forest potential, intensive forestry programme could be taken up in the first stage itself. In the areas with depleted forest resources, the entire plan may be concerned with restoring the ecological balance as fast as possible.

The tribal development programme will also have to be suitably adapted so that they can be consistent with the local resource potential as also the skills and the aspirations of the people. It has to be appreciated that the economic forces can be moderated for a while, but the inherent contradiction will continue to increase and may reach, sooner or later, a limiting point. While the economic programmes will have to be adjusted with reference to the potential of the forests and possibility of their utilisation as the base of local economy, social services will have to be planned in advance. Sustained effort should be made in the more backward areas to ensure that the community acquires inner strength to face the new situation which may arise with the increasing tempo of economic activity in these areas in the near future Once the people become aware of their rights and they are enabled to partake in the benefits of new economic activity, an important constraint in planning for these areas will be removed and optimum utilisation of natural resources with necessary technical inputs and financial investment can be planned without hesitation. The local resources can be utilised with reference to the needs of the region, the State or the nation.

CONCLUSION

It is, thus, clear that development of the people and development of the forests, as two co-equal goals, are fully consistent. Certain basic needs of the local community must provide the solid foundation of rational utilisation of forest resources. The socio-economic conditions of tribal communities must be accepted as an important boundary condition for determining the level of technology and intensity of operations in an area. The basic needs themselves have to be assessed in a dynamic frame. The plan for tribal development must take the forest resources as the base on which tribal economy can progress with greatest confidence. The social services input must be provided on a priority basis in the more backward regions so that the initial handicaps of the tribals can be removed as early as possible and the resources can be optimally utilised for development of the region as a whole. As no two situations are entirely comparable, this will require careful planning at the micro-level. Planning without participation of the people and their active involvement cannot be expected to be realistic. The tribal should become a co-sharer in the new wealth created in these areas and should become an active participant in their management.

Forestry and Tribal Development

The oneset of State management of forests in mid-nineteenth century made deep inroads into the uses and benefits derived by tribals from forests. It marked the growing hiatus in perception towards forests of tribals on the one hand and forest authorities on the other. The thitherto unfettered rights and privileges were regulated and restricted by the 1984 Policy Resolution of the Government of India; the 1952 Resolution converted the "rights and privileges" into "rights and concession", as observed by the Dhebar Commission. We understand that a new policy resolution is on the anvil. It is our hope that the recommendations we make will be taken into consideration by the Ministry of Agriculture in framing the resolution.

FORESTRY AND TRIBAL DEVELOPMENT

At the time of launching of the 1952 Policy, it was averred that village communities in the neighbourhood of a forest were want to make excessive use of its products for satisfaction of domestic and agricultural needs, but such use should not be permitted at the cost of national interests. This is really the heart of the matter. While we agree that the management of forests and vegetal resources should be such as will provide for maximum goods and services for the well-being of all sections of the country's population, there has to be a judicious balance between the national needs such as defence, communications, industries, etc. and the local, particularly the tribal, needs. In fact, forest economy and tribal economy should be two co-equal goals. A strong forest economy should be geared to the requirements of employment and economic progress of the scheduled tribe communities living in the area. In any event, the two should not be antithetical to each other.

The national goal of covering one-third of the country's geographical area under forests can be achieved by careful evolving and observance of the land-use pattern. This requires identification of the area fit for agriculture; silviculture could be undertaken over the rest.

Before the era of State control of forests commencing from the middle of the last century, tree land was freely available for the use of the community, but with a much smaller population there was little danger of wastage exceeding increment. Today, with the pressure of population, reserved forests require to be demarcated for production forestry to meet the national needs of industries, communications, defence, etc. At the same time, the growing needs of the community in the way of fuel, fodder, agricultural implements, house construction, domestic furniture, fruit, flower, herbs and medicines, have to be satisfied through social forestry in village forests, protected forests and other waste-land around villages. The need for providing requirements of the local community is conceded by foresters, but forest plans have yet to be so oriented. Thirdly, the needs of environment and conservation can be met through tree cover planted on land falling outside the aforesaid two categories.

For the forest-based programmes to subserve tribal economy, comprehensive plans would need to be prepared for all integrated tribal development projects with sizeable forest area in which tribal development and forestry development share equal emphasis. In forest-rich regions, forestry-oriented tribal development programmes should be framed in which agriculture occupies a secondary position. In fact, for such ITDPs separate forest working plans or management plans would be necessary comprised of two parts, one in which the basic needs of the tribal economy are provided on a priority basis and the second related to considerations of forestry.

The Agencies

Apart from locating land separately for: (a) production forestry, (b) social and farm forestry, and (c) environmental forestry, the agency or agencies for carrying out the respective tasks need to be designated. The subject, forests, has been incorporated in List III, the Concurrent List in the Seventh Schedule of the Constitution. This perhaps implies that overall working and control of forests vests in the State Forest Departments while the policy and guidance has to come from the Ministry of Agriculture, Government of India.

We understand that among the objectives of the new policy would be to increase the area under forests and tree-land to bring it to the optimal one-third level and to accelerate the pace of reforestation and afforestation, eliminating deforestation and denudation. The effort involved in: (a) restocking the degraded and denuded 13 per cent out of the existing 23 per cent area notified as forests, and (b) raising the tree land cover from 23 per cent to 33 per cent will be colossal and the State Forest Departments by themselves may not be in a position to mount it, let alone achieve it. Further, the additional areas to make up to one-third might be comprised of degraded, marginal and sub-marginal lands lying far away from the existing operational and habitational areas. We suggest that the task be divided among: (i) the State Forest Departments who should look after the reserved forests, (ii) the village community or Panchayats or individuals charged with the responsibility of forestry in and around revenue villages, and (iii) a 'tree army' to be raised for undertaking silvicultural operations in the more distant, degraded, marginal and sub-marginal lands. We are fully aware that performance of the village community has not been uniform. In some State, Panchayats have not performed well. Notwithstanding the accounts given by the village and panchayat bodies, we would recommend the continuance of the experiment in the hope that, in the long-run, they will gather experience and render a more responsible amount of themselves. 'Tree-army' could function under a board of control and be constituted of forest labour cooperatives voluntary organisations as well as other official and non-official bodies.

In declaring the aim of maintaining one-third of the total land under forests, as a matter of broad perspective, in each State the area required for production forestry for the three or more national sectors (defence, communications, industries etc.) should be spelt out roughly. Simultaneously, the area for social forestry and the degraded and waste-land area which requires to be tree-covered also should be indicated approximately. The working plans of each State should detail these broad parameters for the guidance of not only the Forest Department but also for the people at large.

Partnership

We reiterate the recommendation of the Dhebar Commission that the State Forest Departments should consider themselves responsible for the development of the tribals as well as of the forests areas. There should not be any attempt to think in terms of an exclusive obligation to trees or vegetation; on the other hand, they should accept the responsibility of utilising forests as much as possible from the angle of economic development of the tribals residing in it. In return, the tribals should recognise the need to preserve forests. This call for a partnership approach. With its adoption, the tribal can be won over to the view that the Forest Department is his friend, interested in helping him. We suggest that this approach should inform the new policy under consideration in the Government of India.

We are aware that notwithstanding the communal outlook and the tendency to cooperative endeavour among many of the tribal communities, the modern trend of individualism and individual enterprises is making incursions in tribal areas. Much against what one may wish, the traditional fabric of community and village cohesion is under considerable strain, with the apprehension that, in the long-run, it may be rent under the weight of external antagonistic forces. Evidence of it is seen in the industrialised, industrialising and mining areas. In the rural areas also, unwittingly, the administration has helped the tendency, it has been found, for instance, that even in some areas where land traditionally belongs to the community, lacking apprehension of tribal customs and more the settlement authorities have recorded it in individual names. We are aware that the custom of communal ownership of land has been reported to have sometimes led to its abuse; in the north-east, for instance, some of the village functionaries or heads might have bent the system towards their personal aggrandisement, in Bihar, the khunkatti system has degenerated. Nevertheless, we feel that, cooperation having been accepted as one of the important instruments, those traditional communal institutions, which have it in-built in them, should not only not be lightly discarded but, on the other hand, full use of them should be made in furthering the goals. In fact, the attempt should be to resort to various alternative structural modules, choosing the one most appropriate in a given context. This may range from the Panchayat Samiti (at the Block level) at one end, through statutory Panchayats, the traditional regional and village organisations, to the individual at the other. Separate cooperatives is another form of organisation. The differing syndromes of the various tribal communities may call for an opposite strategy in each context.

The structural aspect is particularly relevant for social forestry. The general complaint made is that where Panchayats have been entrusted with land and responsibility for execution of the scheme, they have mostly failed. The critics would rather that an individual should be allowed the use of a land-holding (without conferment of title) as well as the right of usufruct, simultaneous with the responsibility for social forestry work on that land. Experience is not, however, uniform. Certain tribal communities have given a good account of themselves and there is no reason why this experiment should not be continued. We feel that it will yield dividends in certain typical tribal districts like Bastar and Koraput.

In fact, the best protective device for the existing forests and new additions is interest of the local community in the forest wealth. In Maharashtra and Gujarat, sustained movement of forest labour cooperative societies has been built up over the past four decades. The net income from working of coupes is shared between the State and the cooperatives. In effect, this means that profits flow to individual tribal members. We are happy at the decision of the XVIII meeting of the Central Board of Forestry eliminating contractors from forestry operations. The Forest Department, forest labour cooperatives and other cooperatives should step in their place, with the disappearance of the contractors, it is not too optimistic to hope for many of the malpractices to vanish. At the same time, we should be on guard against new malpractices springing up. Fair price will have to be ensured to tribals wanting to sell forest produce of their private lands. Although the forest labour cooperative system in Gujarat and Maharashtra may not be an unqualified success, we have no doubt that it is a distinct improvement over the exploitative contractors system. With the acceptance of the recommendation of the Central Board of Forestry, the States should substitute the co-operatives for the contractor.

Minor Forest Produce

Minor Forest Produce (MFP), meaning all forest products other than wood, plays an important role in tribal economy. In the first place, the various items of MFP form an ingredient in the family's domestic consumption. Further, studies conducted show that between 10 to 15 per cent of the income budget of an average tribal family in major tribal concentration states of Madhya Pradesh, Orissa, Bihar and Andhra Pradesh is obtained through sale of MFP, the rest being derived from agriculture. MFP items are important raw materials for cottage, small and village industries and contribute to national economy through export and import substitution. Notwithstanding these factors, the tribals have not been conceded full rights of collection of MFP by all States. States lagging behind may take steps necessary for conferring the right.

Marketing of MFP should channelised through co-operatives. There is a tendency to relate price to the labour input and, in some cases, wages lower than the statutory minimum are paid. The price to be paid to the tribal should be based on the market value of the item concerned. Linkages of primary cooperatives, (e.g., LAMPS) with secondary or apex bodies like Tribal Development Corporations and Forest Development Corporations will have to be: (a) strong to drive worth-while benefit, and (b) rational in respect of commodities the latter deal with. Further, the Forest Development Corporation should take in and not merely the commercial but also development aspects.

Apart from the tribal being merely regarded as a gatherer of forest produce, the inequity is compounded by the lack of any effort for value addition to produce. Various oilseeds like sal, Karanj, Kusum, Niger, Castor are sent out of tribal areas as such, without conversion into oil. Lac, gums and resins are hardly treated. Even de-seeding of certain produce, like tamarined, is more of an exception than the rule. Rolling of Kendu leaves into

Bidis is a simple affair, yet Kendu leaves are plucked and sent out as such. Reeling of tassar cocoons can be easily done and even weaving, as a lonelest art, can be picked up without much difficulty. There is a dire need of first processing of minor forest produce through cooperatives of primary collectors and ensuring value-addition. The requisite skills for such value-additions should be imparted.

Out of more than 21,000 botanical species reported from forest areas, so far less than 3000 species have been identified yielding minor forest produce of some commercial importance. With such dependence of a large segment of the tribal population on MFP, there is need for research and development of the various items by the various centres of Indian Council of Scientific and Industrial Research, Forest Research Institute, State Forest Research Institutes and other such bodies. These should relate to discovery and multiplication of improved varieties of species yielding higher production. Further, it would appear that a small percentage of the total potential of minor forest produce in the country is being tapped. Scientific collection and storage of these items cannot be ignored to avoid deterioration and value-reduction. As recommended by the National Commission on Agriculture, product-wise survey, proper method of collection and grading, improving resource-base, developing a system of marketing and distribution, ensuring proper processing and utilisation are necessary. The Commission recommended creation of product-wise corporations in rich forested states and a national organisation for tackling different matters connected with marketing, intelligence, export, etc. of MFP. We support this recommendation. We have suggested elsewhere constitution of TRIFED.

Mixed Plantation

The State working plans and ITDP working plans should keep carefully in view the proportions of commercial forestry (for industries, communications, defence, etc.), social forestry and environmental forestry. A situation of potential conflict is created by ignoring the needs of the local community. These needs can be met through mixed forestry, i.e., species which yield fuel-wood, various items of minor forest produce, fruit, fodder, timber (for house construction, agriculture implements and domestic furniture), herbs, etc. The resource-base of the local community should be strengthened through such mixed interspersal in all types of forests i.e., reserve forests, protected forests and village forests. The relative mix will depend on the present and projected local requirements.

Forest-based Industries

Reference has been made above of first processing of minor forest produce. This does not exhaust the potential in many situations. Infrastructure is available in many tribal areas and, in any event, its deficiency can be made up. In many States, conditions are favourable for establishment of forest-based industries in tribal areas. For instance, small pulp and paper plants, including hand-made paper, linked to availability of such species as bamboo, might be found feasible as cottage, village or small industry. It should be ensured, however, that these industries do not tend to develop into big establishments where the generally unskilled and unlettered tribals do not find a berth, while they are dispossessed of their land which is their only resource base. Steps for marketing of paper and pulp produced in small plant should be organised.

Forest Villages

The conference of State Forest Ministers held in 1978 recommended that forest villages should be converted into revenue villages and the tribals inhabiting them should be conferred tenancy rights over agricultural land. It would appear that this recommendation has, by and large, gone unnoticed by the State Governments. We urge that it should be implemented earnestly. Tribals living in the forest villages should be given heritable and inalienable rights over the land which they cultivate in the forest villages. All social and economic developmental programmes should be extended to these villages on the same lines as for residents of other tribal villages. Some of the tiny, cottage, village small and medium forest-based industries should preferably be located in the tribal area to take advantage of cheap supply of raw-material and infrastructure, provided marketing of the finished products is ensured through such agencies as the *All India Khadi and Village Industry Commission.*

Human Resource Development

The partnership concept between the forest authorities and the tribals implies that the tribals should be trained to participate in various activities like felling, logging, aforestation, cooperatives management, processing, etc. with the elimination of the contractors, motivation on the part of the forest department, the cooperatives and the individual tribal himself should be much stronger. In so far as social forestry and allied programmes are concerned, ultimately the cooperatives or the village community might allot small parcels of land to the individual tribal families. Hence, human resource development becomes the most important aspect for conversion of the natural resource endowment into a ready economic asset. The programmes of extension and training of tribals will, therefore, have to be vigorous. At the same time, training and orientation of the foresters will have to be paid special attention both in the Forest Research Institute, Dehra Dun and States' institutes.

Of late, the state of Gujarat has placed two useful schemes on tribal. In one, a tribal family is allotted a hectare of land (may be on a slope) for forestry purposes and the family undertakes silviculture as per departmental plans, receiving wages. At the expiry of gestation period the profits from the usufruct are to be shared on SO: SO basis between the family and the department. Secondly, in the district of Valsad, the Forest Development Corporation has undertaken on nearly a lakh of hectares a scheme of comprehensive forestry in which the various strands of forest and tribal economy are inter-woven with account on employment. Marketing and training arrangements also are being organised by the Forest Development Corporation. We would commend these two schemes to the other State Governments.

One good feature of the scheme of the Gujarat Forest Development Corporation has been that the Corporation has been able to attract institutional finance from the Agricultural Refinance Development Corporation. This bids fair for the promise of forestry programmes in States.

In the State of Andhra Pradesh, in a small way, tribals have been allowed to undertake 'Kumra' cultivation. They can grow crops like ginger, turmeric, horse-gram under tall teak and sal trees in reserved forests. For the purpose, they clear the ground.

Both the Forest Department and the tribals are beneficiaries of the schemes.

FOREST VILLAGES

Forestry

The National Forest Policy, 1952, while emphasising the need for evolving a system of balanced and complementary land use etablishment of tree lands and the need to maintain sustained supply of timber and other forest produce had not particularly visualised any clear-cut approach towards scheduled tribes who mostly inhabit forest land, however, recognised the problem of shifting cultivation and suggested regulating shifting cultivation by combining it with programme of forest regeneration. It was clear that the interest of tribals needs recognition in the forest development programme in the country to the mutual advantage of both. Awakening for improvement of economic standards grew amongst tribals with implementation of each succeeding five-year plan. The stress of eking out a livelihood following substantial denudation of forest growth made this awakening keener and the scheduled tribes became more chary of any infringement of their rights and privileges in forest and forest land. Growth of population and rise of political consciousness also gave a fillip to this idea. The general feeling of the country has now veered round view that forests and tribals have a symbiotic relationship and governmental policy on forestry regeneration and development should not detract from this relationship and should in every way further it actively.

With the adoption of the tribal sub-Plan strategy and subsequent emphasis on family-oriented programmes, several State Governments and Government of India started paying attention to devising suitable schemes in the forestry sector to support tribal families through these schemes with a view to bring them above the poverty line. Some schemes like Kishan nurseries of Gujarat, Arjun and Mulberry plantation for rearing tussary silk worms, raising forestry and cash crop plantations in individual beneficiary lend with subsidy under the IRDP have taken up with this end in view. Forestry regeneration programmes linking them to individual tribal families to ensure regular income to them have also been attempted. The earlier stress in forestry having been on maximisation of revenue through commercial plantations, only marginal attention has been paid to minor forest produce plantations on which tribals depend for a living. There has been some amount of unwillingness to take up minor forest produce plantations out of the Forestry Plan provisions, mainly on account of inadequacy of funds to be spared for this purpose; such plantations having been minimal and that mostly out of Special Central Assistance released by Home Ministry. In one word, while the interest of the scheduled tribes population has been recognised to be an important element in forestry policy formulation and implementation, sufficient attention has not yet been paid to strengthen the economic and resource base relevant to the tribals.

Following the recommendations of the National Commission on Agriculture, 1976, the Conference of Ministers in-charge of Forests and Tribals, 1978 and the National Committee on Development of Backward Areas, 1981, State Governments have paid considerable attention to departmental working of forests and control and nationalisation of trade of forest produce with a view to check exploitation of tribals and ensure a fair price for the primary tribal collectors of forest produce. Cooperativision of forest labour, particularly in Gujarat, Maharashtra, Rajasthan and Bihar, has been speeded up. Several measures for collection, processing and marketing of forest produce have been taken by a number of States through the auspices of Forest Development Corporations/Tribal Development Co-operative Corporations and by organising tribal cooperatives. Primary marketing societies under the Girijan Co-operative Corporation in Andhra Pradesh, the Girijan Service Co-operative Societies in Kerala, the Adivasi Co-operative Societies in Maharashtra and LAMPS in a number of States have taken to procurement and marketing of minor forest produce. In more and more States long-term leases of minor forest produce have been given to the co-operative or the corporate sectors, eliminating middlemen to a degree. In Karnataka, MFP leases have been given to LAMPS at concessional rate. Laws have been passed in Madhya Pradesh and Orissa nationalising trade in Kendu (Tendu) leaves and Sal seeds. However, the picture on nationalisation/departmentalisation of trade in forest produce and their complete channelisation through cooperative or corporate bodies is not yet complete and several States are yet to pass suitable laws invest their Governments with adequate powers *to* enable them to intervene in this sphere on behalf of the tribals in an effective manner.

The situation mentioned above applies more or less to organisation of apex co-operatives or co-operative corporations to guide control and coordinate marketing of forest produce at the State level. While most States having substantial tribal population and forest areas have Tribal Development Corporations or Forest Development Corporations, the items handled by them exclude several important minor forest produce like sal, kusum and other oil-seeds of tree-origin, katha, myrobalans, etc. The State of Madhya Pradesh which has nearly twenty-five per cent of the total tribal population in the country is yet to establish a minor forest produce corporation to deal with the tribal produce.

The brief resume of programme taken up in the forestry sector *vis-a-vis* the interests of the tribal population given above would indicate that the continuing emphasis on desirably orienting the programmes and policies in this sector to the mutual benefit of this sector on the one hand and the tribals on the other appears necessary. Nearly 22.8 per cent of the total land area of the country is under the occupation of the forest eco-system and forests constitute the major land use, next only to agriculture. The percentage will be higher if the area where soil and water conservation measures are taken up is added. If properly implemented the forestry programmes of the country can support a substantial portion of the tribal population in the poverty-reduction programme. This would also be true of the soil and water conservation sector to a considerable degree. In the above background we would suggest the following objectives to be adopted in these sectors during the Seventh Plan:

(1) There should be a close linkage between forest policy and programmes on the one hand and tribals and other traditional forest communities on the other. In other words, the national forest policy still under consideration, should take full cognisance of the needs of tribal communities while trying to harmonise the production, environmental and other objectives.

(2) As the vast mass of schedule tribes in the country depend upon forest, hilly and undulating areas of the country for their livelihood, all schemes in this sector

should give topmost priority to poverty-amelioration programmes consistent with ecological requirements. Economically viable schemes oriented to bring tribal families above the poverty-line should constitute the core schemes in this sector.

(3) It is possible to reframe and re-design many of the forestry development and conservation schemes whether relating to re-generation, upgradation of degraded forests, plantation of industrial raw-materials species, forest protection or providing a protective cover to catchments and slopes in such a manner that a good number of tribal families can be economically supported by such schemes on a continuing basis. It may be noted here that the emphasis should be on a regular flow of income to the concerned tribal families on a continuing basis and not on a sporadic or casual manner. A suitable mode of implementation with participation and involvement of tribals, with provision of usufructuary rights with stipulation to lift a certain number of tribal families above the poverty-line should form a specific chapter under all these schemes. The Ministry of Agriculture may, in consultation with the Ministry of Home Affairs, take up re-designing of the existing forestry and conservation scheme in this light and issue guidelines to the States.

(4) Social forestry should be encouraged and promoted in and around tribal villages, planting species relevant to tribal needs like food, fruit, fodder, fuel, fibre, timper, etc.

(5) Such forestry/agro-forestry/horticulture/minor forest produce species as are capable of yielding food-stuff and edible oil including raw-material for cottage, village and small industries in which tribals are already engaged should receive top-most priority in afforestation and plantation programmes.

(6) Minor forest produce regeneration, plantation and development besides collection, processing and marketing through cooperative and corporate sectors should receive high priority under the plan programmes.

(7) The local tribal population should be enabled to participate through their cooperatives in all commercially viable processing and production operations in timber, bamboo and other forest produce. The participation may include not only providing labour but also supply of forest raw materials and their plantation and up-keep in the captive area. Participation in equity and profit sharing may be attempted under public sector, joint sector as also in sector private enterprises.

(8) So far the tribal areas are concerned, project reports for family-oriented programmes in these sectors should be drawn up for ITDP/tribal pocket/primitive tribes project areas separately by a committee headed by the District/Divisional Forest Officer of the area in which the Project Administrator/Special Officer of the tribal projects, district level officers of soil conservation, tribal development, agriculture, irrigation and rural development should be represented as members. These projects should be discussed and cleared by the Project Implementation Committee for the Tribal Projects under the chairmanship of the District Collector. The Forest/ Soil Conservation Departments of the State Governments should issue firm instructions to their field agencies to this effect.

(9) The aim of the Seventh Plan should be to cover all activities, particularly in the forestry sector for implementation by: (i) departmental agencies; (ii) corporate sector; and (iii) co-operative sector. In particular a specific thrust has to be given to organisation of MFP cooperatives to cover all Gram Panchayats in tribal areas having good potential in forest growth, as complement to the LAMPS and similar other tribal cooperatives working in the area. While doing so, care may be taken to see that new societies are organised, they are tagged on to the nearby LAMPS to avoid duplication. The potential for minor forest produce to support poverty eradication programme in the country being very great. Minor Forest Corporations

may be formed. Social monitoring of the progress in this field may be done by Ministries of Agriculture and Home Affairs is called for.

(10) Intermediaries like forest contractors should be substituted by institutional bodies like labour cooperatives, tassar cooperatives, LAMPS, etc. However, except in a few States, the forest labour cooperatives have not even taken off the ground. No work has been entrusted to them by any other departments except minimally by the forest department. It is suggested that these cooperatives be organised and re-designated as Rural Labour Cooperatives for tribal areas with the stipulation that bodies forest department other departments/corporations of the State Governments like soil conservation, irrigation, power and horticulture departments, Cashew Development Corporation, Forest Development Corporation, MFP Corporation, Plantation Corporation, and Catchment Conservation Organisation should entrust work to these RLCS of the tribal areas to make them viable.

(11) Expeditious steps should be taken by all State Governments to assume adequate powers through suitable legislations to fix fair price of minor forest produce in the interest of tribal collectors.

(12) To provide support to the Tribal Development Corporations, Forest Development and MFP Corporations who are handling trade and the minor forest produce at the State level, the Tribal Marketing Federation (TRIFED) should be set-up at the national level before the Seventh Plan Period starts running.

(13) Cottage and small-scale industries like particle boards, small paper and pulp plants, match splint manufacture, leaf plates and cups, furniture-making, etc. should be promoted.

(14) Bullock carts may be provided to individual STs ensuring them work of transport of forest produce from coupes to forest repose for at least 150 days in a year.

(15) Elimination of the system of contractors in forestry operations including in hidden forms should receive

special attention. This should apply as much to the forest and other corporations working in this sector as to the forest departments.

(16) "Tribology" as a subject should form a part of the educational and training curriculum of officers belonging to the forest, revenue, soil conservation, welfare and rural development cadres in the States on the lines of the recommendations of the Committee on orientation of Forest Education in India (1983).

The report of the Committee on Forestry Programmes for Alleviation of Poverty (1984) has given several suggestions. These suggestions should be kept in view while formulating forestry programmes. The anti-exploitative measures in the forestry sector should also be expedited as recommended separately under the relevant chapter.

Forest Village

Originally created for meeting the man-power requirements for exploitation and regeneration of forest resources, the forest villages in the country present a confused a picture of tribal economy. Over two lakh tribal families residing in about five thousand forest villages (which may be more) possess no right on the land they cultivate. The tenurial arrangements for land in these villages run counter to the existing political and economic norms in the country and stand in the way of extension of full-fledged development benefits to these forest-dwellers.

The Ministry of Agriculture has, by their letter No. 11-39/83-FRY (Cons) dated 23rd March 1984 recently advised the States to confer long-term heritable but inalienable rights, say for 15-20 years, in respect of land belonging to tribals living in these villages. This is a good step and needs to be extended further in its dimension and scope. The burning problems so far as the forest villages are concerned can be said to be two:

(1) Being located inside forests and not having been declared as revenue villages, these habitants are outside the pale of direct development administration of blocks while it is necessary to extend all development schemes to the population, and

(2) The forest dwellers are deprived of assistance from institutional sources of finance as they have no recognised rights in their land/other property.

The Seventh Plan should pay specific attention to remove the above serious disabilities under which the inhabitants of the forest villages are labouring.

We would recommend the following positive steps to be taken during the Seventh Plan in respect of the forest villages:

(1) Forest villages in the country should, generally, be declared as revenue villages and made full recipient of all benefits flowing from the development administration. Such villages should be fully integrated into the near-by revenue and block administration. Where such integration is not possible, at present, on account of the interior location of the habitation lack of communication, etc. special schemes of development for such villages should be undertaken along with conferment of heritable and inalienable rights on the tribals in respect of their lands/other property.

(2) In the first category of forest villages which are declared as revenue villages and are integrated into the near-by block administration on account of their proximity to the block jurisdiction, all sectoral development schemes should be extended as early as possible by a conscious effort. In the second category of forest villages which are not declared as revenue villages (and this should happen only in rare cases where the villages are deep in interior of the forests), special extension staff for development of the villages or a group of such villages should be appointed under the auspices of the Forest Department of the State Government in consultation with the Community Development Department. Such extension staff should be attached to the near-by block for day-to-day supervision while the superior officers of the Forest Department and the Community Development Department oversee their work.

(3) In forest villages which are not integrated fully into the block administration on account of reasons mentioned

above, comprehensive schemes of development including education, health, drinking water supply, agriculture, animal husbandry, village industries, arts and crafts, etc. should be formulated. A Central sector scheme under the Ministry of Agriculture on the pattern of scheme for shifting cultivation since discontinued, should be instituted for the purpose.

Forests and Central Indian Tribes

Tribal Economy is characterised by the close relation between economy and the habitat. Not being powerful enough to modify the surroundings, the tribals learn to adapt themselves to it. Majumdar points out, "Primitive society has tried to work out some kind of adjustment between material needs and the potentialities of the environment. This is nowhere more clearly evident than in the adjustment of the tribal needs and efforts to the forests that beset them. The tribal dependence on forests for food, fuel, house-building materials, agricultural implements and minor produce for barter is considerable. Even settled agriculturists like the Bhils and Bhilalas look to forests for most of their needs. The food that they take is constantly supplemented by the green leaves growing in the forests and the small game abounding there. In times of scarcity and distress they depend on the wild roots, tubers, barks, leaves and fruits to provide them sustenance. Among the Saharias the dependence on forests is greater as compared with the Bhils, Bhilalas, Gonds and Korkus of the State. Their love for shifting cultivation continues even to this day. Acute shortage of land for cultivation and the poor nature of tribal land in general does not make for much dependence on agriculture. In this State of landlessness and poverty they look up to the forests for their livelihood. As forest labourers and gatherers of minor forest produce they have a large stake in the forests.

Looking to the tribal economy in the State it can be said that forest for the tribesman is the only insurance against famine.

FORESTS IN MADHYA BHARAT

Fortunately, Madhya Bharat has a large area under forests. According to the latest estimates 15,845,480 square miles is under forests. The forest area, amounts to roughly 29.94 per cent of the total land area of the state.

At the close of the year 1954-55 the area under different classes stood as below:

1.	Reserved	7,378.443 sq. miles
2.	Protected	7,594.78 sq. miles
3.	Unclassed	872.266 sq. miles
	Total	15,845.480 sq. miles

These forests are generally of the tropical deciduous type varying from teak to teak and mixed forest to almost pure stands of *Boswelia senata, Hardwickia binata,* and *Acacia catechu.*

The main types of forests are the following:

(a) Moist Deciduous Teak Forests

Occurring in the Kathiwara Range of the Dhar division in the Bhil belt where rainfall is 80″ to 100″. These forests are dense and attain large dimensions. The more important types of trees are: teak, sadad (Terminalia tomentosa), Semal (Bombax malabaricum), Mahua (Bassia latifolia), Dhaora (Anogeissus latifolia), Bija (Pterocarpus marsupium), Haldu (Adina cordifolia).

(b) Dry Deciduous Teak

These forests occur in Indore, Kargone, Kannod a major portion of Dhar and in parts of Guna Divisions. Here the rainfall varies from 25″ to 40″. The crop is somewhat open on hill-slopes and is dense in valleys.

These forests yield timber, fuel, fodder, grasses, gums, lac, temru leaves, mahua flowers and fruits, tanning material, etc.

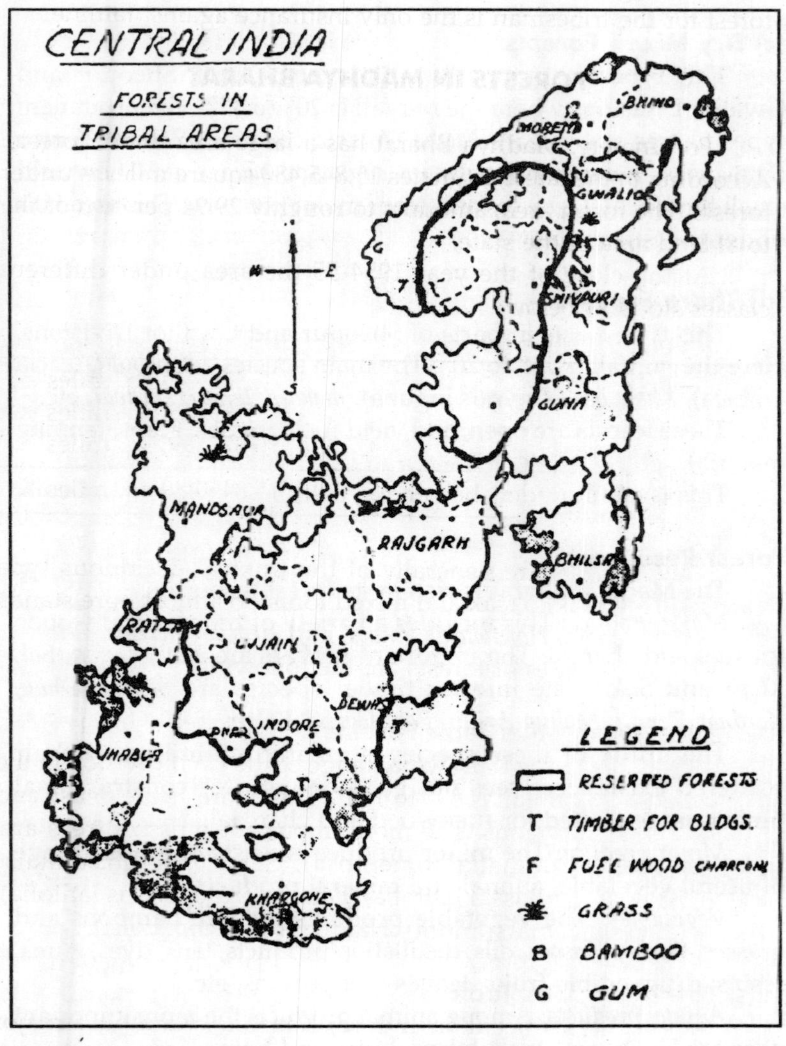
CENTRAL INDIA
FORESTS IN
TRIBAL AREAS
BHIND
GWALIOR
SHIVPURI
GUNA
MANDSAUR
RAJGARH
BHILSA
RATLAM
UJJAIN
DEWAS
INDORE
DHAR
JHABUA
KHARGONE
N
E
S
LEGEND
RESERVED FORESTS
T TIMBER FOR BLDGS.
F FUEL WOOD CHARCOAL
GRASS
B BAMBOO
G GUM

Except Indore the rest of the area under this type is inhabited by the tribal people—Khargone and Dhar by Bhils and Bhilalas; Kannod by Gonds and Korkus and Guna by Saharias.

(c) Dry Mixed Forests

This type exists mostly in Shivpuri, Guna, Sheopur and Gwalior Divisions where the rainfall is 20″ to 35″. The prominent types of tree species are *kattha* (Acacia catechu), Sadad, Temru (Diospyros melanoxylon), *dhaora, aonla* and *bahera,* etc. They yield small timber, fuel, grasses and other minor produce. This area falls under the Saharia belt.

(d) Thoru Forests

This type exists in parts of Sheopur and Gwalior Divisions. Here the rainfall is 15″ to 20″. The main species are *babul* (Acacia arabica), *Khair ber* (Zizypus juguba), *makora, tendu, kardpai,* etc.

These forests are open, and yield fuel, grasses, gums, tanning materials, etc.

This is again under the Saharia belt.

Forest Resources

The Madhya Bharat is rich in its forest resources.

Major produce: This includes a variety of timbers and woods for fuel and charcol. The important timbers are *Teak, Anjan, Sal, Khair* and *Salai.* The inferior timber species are *Sental, Dhao, Kardhai, Tendu, Mahua Arjun, Baheda* and *Kalam.*

The utility of these species is greatly minimised by their scattered existence. Trees not good enough for constructional timber are exploited for fuel-wood and charcoal.

Minor produce: The minor produce consists of a wide range of useful vegetable, animal and mineral products.

Vegetables: The vegetable products include bamboos and grasses, fibres, Masses, oils, distillation products, tans, dyes, gums, resins, drug, edible fruits, leaves and poisons, etc.

Animal products: Among animal products the more important ones are lac, honey, wax, horns, hides and bones.

Minerals: Important rocks and minerals are sandstone, basalt, gneiss, granite, slate, limestone, shales, quartite and ores of iron and manganese.

Forests and the Scheduled Tribes—A Flash Back

The Scheduled area of Madhya Bharat consists of the whole or part of the territories of eleven conventing States. These states are: *Ratlam* (*Bajna teshil*), *Sailana* (Raoti tehsil), *Alirajpur* (Bhabra, Chandpur, Chbakatala Nanpur and Rath tehsils), *Barwani* (Pansemal, Rajpur and Sitawad parganas), *Jhabua* (Jhabua, Rambhapur, Ranapur and Thandla tehsil, and Umrao and minor jagirs), *Indore* (Nisarpur, Petlawad. Seagon and Sendhwa parganas), *Gwalior* (Sardarpu district), *Dhar* (Mandu, Kukshi and Nimanpur district), *Jobat* (whole), *Kathiwara* (whole), *Mathwar* (whole).

These States had different policies with regard to the tribals. In the tribal areas of the former Gwalior and Indore States a nominal commutation fee of Rupee one or two per plough-unit of land (15 acres) was charged from the tribal people. In lieu of this commutation fee the following concessions were allowed: Building timber at concessional rates for *bonafide* domestic use, free timber for agricultural implements, grass for thatching the roof, head loads of certain leaves for house-building, dead-wood for fuel, cart loads of minerals like stones, kankar and muram and free grazing of a pair of bullocks in the forests, etc. Special areas in the forests were designated as commuted areas in which these privileges were allowed. In other States like Dhar, Alirajpur, Jhabua, Barwani, Sailana, etc., similar concessions were allowed to the tribal people.

There is a feeling among the tribal people that the concessions and privileges that they enjoyed under the princely order were much more liberal and useful than what they now enjoy. One reason behind this felling is objectively true. Except the States of Indore, Gwalior, Barwani and Dhar most of the States had no definite scientific forest policy of continuity of management. As such, the tribals were permitted to carry on reckless felling of trees for timber and fuelwood, as well as for shifting cultivation. Secondly, the headquarters of the administrative units (states) were generally at a very short distance from the different parts of the State. The people of these small States had, for generations, looked to the Central Authority for a settlement of their problems. They had got accustomed to it. The reorganisation changed the picture completely and the tribal, who, in the past, had easy access to the Ruler of the State, now found the junior executive officer a very poor substitute.

FOREST CONCESSIONS TO THE TRIBALS IN MADHYA BHARAT

'Van Nistar'

'Van Nistar' refers to the concessions in the former princely States, under which certain groups of villages in or near the forest areas, were allowed to enjoy the forest produce required for their bonafide use in lieu of nominal fees paid by them to the Government annually. We have seen that the tribal people were affected greatly by the *van nistar* system prevalent in the various areas. After the ceration of Madhya Bharat the different systems of *van nistar* continued to be in force in the various parts of the State. Broadly these systems could be summarised as under:

1. *Haqdari*, and
2. Commutation System.

Haqdari is derived from the word *Haq* meaning the right. It refers to the special rights enjoyed by certain villagers over the forest produce. Such villages were known as *Haqdari* villages. This system was prevalent in the former Gwalior State and goes as far back as 1910 when the reserved forests created. At that time, the then Government, created some *Hakdar* villages and vested them with rights to use certain forest produce for their own bonafide use for a nominal annual fee. The rights so granted came to be known as *Haqdari*. Under the *Haqdari* the *haqdars* could get useful wood from the *muafi* (free) coupes. *Haqdars* were entitled to headloads of fuelwood and grass free of charge from the Reserve Forests. *Non-haqdars,* theoretically had no such right. But in practice, anybody could get these articles in headloads free of cost. The animals belonging to the *haqdars* were provided grazing in Reserve Forests at half the rates normally charged from the *non-haqdars. Haqdars* were allowed to graze one buffalo, two bullocks, heifers and colts and the riding pony free of cost per every ten rupees of land revenue. From Protected Forests the *haqdars* could meet all their agricultural requirements from specified trees.

Commutation system was prevalent in the former Indore State and was adopted as far back as 1906. It is also known as *Halbandi* or *Halot*. Under this system the payee was entitled to remove from the specified forests certain kinds of forest produce on payment of a stipulated nominal fee once a year. This was designated as commutation fee. The fee was nominal and much below the value of the produce removed by the commuters. The commuters in practice, used to get all the wood and other forest produce they required for agricultural purposes from the Reserve Forests. This was against the provision that these requirements were to be met from *Abadi* forests. This led to a destruction of forest of wealth.

Nistar Committee

In 1953 the State Government appointed two committees for the northern and southern conservancies of the forest for making the *Nistar* rights and privileges uniform throughout the State. The aim was to stop the system of commutation and adopt a uniform schedule for both the conservancies. This Committee felt that as the forests were a national wealth they ought to be used for the common benefit of all. It agreed that the forest populations would continue to make greater use of the forests. But it was against the recognition of many special rights in the forests. The Committee recommended that in the course of next five years the special rights should be gradually abolished. At the same time the Committee recommended that the provision should be made to supply the required forest produce to the cultivators at the normal rate. Before the *Haqdari* and commutation systems are abolished steps should be taken to supply the normal forest requirements of the villagers at a reasonable distance. This, in the view of the Committee, would put an end to the illicit felling of trees.

Abolition of Special Rights

In 1954 the Government abolished the *Haqdari* and the Commutation systems. The Government also published a Schedule of rates for various forest produce as well as the rates of grazing to make the *nistar* rights common throughout the State. The existing *Haqdari* and Commutation rights shall lapse in 1959.

The special concessional rates of grazing prevalent in the Scheduled Area would also be abolished in 1959. The special facilities given for grazing in Jhabua would coutinue till the next settlement. But the tribal cooperative societies would continue to get bamboos and other raw materials for cottage industries at half the rates.

With a view to give economic relief to the tribals the Government decided in 1954 to allow them, together with general forest population, to extract a number of minor forest produce free of royalty. The list of articles not allowed to be used gratis is as follows:

Bhil Belt

1. Khargone Division—Gums, honey, wax, lac, temru leaves, rosba grass.
2. Dhar—Gums, honey, wax, temru leaves, mahua flowers and fruits, rosha grass.

Gond-Korku Belt

Nemawar—Temru leaves, rosha grass.

Saharia Belt

1. Shivpuri—Lac, katha, honey wax, temru leaves, gums, rosha grass.
2. Guna—Lac, katha, honey, wax, temru leaves, gums rosha grass.
3. Sheopur—Katha, honey, wax, temru leaves, gums, rosha oil.

New rate schedule of forest produce is as given below:

	Produce	*Quantity*	*Rates*		
			Rs.	*As.*	*P.*
1.	Fuel wood	Per cart load of dry wood	1	0	0
		(For big cities)	2	0	0
		Per head load of dry wood	0	2	0
		(For small towns)	0	1	0
2.	Thorns	Per cart load	0	4	0
3.	Suvari, nirgu and Khajur leaves	Per cart load	2	0	0
		Per head load	0	2	0
	For cottage industries	Per cart load	0	12	0
4.	Tendu leaves	Per md.	1	0	0
5.	Gums (Babul)	"	7	8	0
	Katha	"	5	0	0
	Kare	"	10	0	0
	Salaveed	"	5	0	0

	Produce	Quantity	Rates		
			Rs.	As	P.
6.	Wax	"	10	0	0
7.	Hing	"	5	0	0
8.	Lac	"	10	0	0
9.	Katha	"	25	0	0
10.	Rosha oil	"	100	0	0
11.	Aritha	"	2	0	0
12.	Barks (Anjan)	"	1	0	0
13.	Semal lint	"	5	0	0

Thus, we see that two things have happened to the forest rights of the tribal people. One, most of the rights and privileges they had been enjoying in the forests were suddenly restricted on creation of the Madhya Bharat. Under the new system of forest administration it was hard for the tribals to get the forest produce for their household needs and for barter, as such permissions were not granted by the officers on the spot. Getting permission from higher officers located at distant places meant great deal of time and money. The supervision, now, also became more strict. Every encroachment was now a punishable act under the new Forest Law. Secondly, the *van nistar* committee prohibited the free use of most of the articles. Perhaps except dead wood and grass no other forest produce could be bad gratis.

This, naturally, means a great economic handicap to the tribals. The things they used to get free have now been priced. And even at the high rates fixed it is not possible for them to get the forest produce in the quantity needed at the time desired.

Tongya Cultivation

Another forest policy namely Tongya cultivation also touches the forest dwelling tribals quite considerably, particularly the landless persons.

Tongya (or Taungya) cultivation is the practice of allowing a cultivator to cultivate a piece of land for a certain number of years in return for planting of young forest trees. Tongya system was first evolved in Burma. In the Burmese Tongya literally means hill cultivation. It has been defined as a scientific method of raising plantation with field crops under skilled control generally on level or moderately sloping grounds. In Madhya Bharat it has been defined as "the raising of crop of trees of forest species in conjunction with agriculture in a given plot of land."

In Madhya Bharat roughly 27,670 acres of land is available in the forest areas which is clear of forest trees. The forest villages also have nearly 2,19,771 acres of fallow land which can be safely utilized for either new forest plantations or agricultural purposes.

This land is being distributed for a period of six years for Taungya cultivation. The land is being allotted on a temporary lease on the basis of one ploughland (about 15 acras) per family. The preference is being given to the landless tribals. Harijans and other backward class peoples. Each lessee is being provided with a pair of bullocks and necessary agricultural implements. The rent for 15 acres of land for six year has been fixed as Rs. 15 only.

Except the nominal rent the conditions of lease are quite rigorous. In the first year of lease the lessee is required to fell all the deformed and useless tree in his holding. He is allowed to a clear, 3 acres of land for his own use and may sow it with kharif or rabi. Next year the land cleared and cultivated by him shall be used for afforestation. The rest of the plot be can clear again and cultivate. The labour for digging one foot wide and one foot deep seedling lines is to be provided by the cultivator free of cost. The maintenance and weeding of the seedling lines is also a responsibility of the lessee. Next year again 3 acres of cultivated land is used for silvicultural purposes. This progressing, his cultivated area keeps on diminishing and the labour requirements keep on increasing. After the expiry of the lease the agriculturist is again landless. The hard labour he puts into the clearing and cultivation of the piece is of no use to him. Nor is this system found to be consistent with greater yields. Moreover, the rules of Taungya cultivation place restrictions on the growing of certain crops like makka and sugar-cane which may compete with forest seedlings. Particularly the restriction on makka is resented by the Bhil and the Bhilala cultivators for whom makka in the staple food.

As a result of these features the system has not found favour with the tribal people. It is doubtful if this system can help to solve the problem of the landless tribals. At best Taungya cultivation can give some relief to the landless for a very short period. From the point of view of the broad pattern of tribal economy the Taungya cultivation does not touch even the fringe of the problem.

Forest Crimes

The forest in the State are administered under various Acts. Any act done in contravention of the above Acts becomes a forest crime. The sudden change in the rules and regulations of the forest administration without any consideration of the needs of the tribals has created an acute problem. What the tribal had come to regard as perfectly legitimate and rightful by long usage and custom, over-night became an illegal act punishable by law. The normal pursuance for food gathering and collection of minor produce has become a crime which the ignorant and poor tribal cannot comprehend. There is no effort to explain this change in values to him. Nor does he know of any alternative that may substitute the freedom of the wilds he had been enjoying since centuries.

Tightening of the forest administration is slowly leading to an increase in the violations of the new rules. Looking to the State as a whole the forest crime position was as follows:

TABLE 9.1

Forest Crime in the State of Madhya Bharat for 2 Years

Years	*Injury by fire*	*Felling*	*Grazing*	*Under Games Act*	*Other offences*	*Total*
1949-50	48	3,487	1,141	19	191	4,886
1954-55	4	6,116	1,073	4	2,585	9,782

The table shows that the crimes are on the increase. As far as the nature of the forest crimes is concerned, the most common type is the unauthorised felling of trees and unauthorised grazing of cattle in the reserved areas. The fellings of trees useful as timber and wood both. They are mostly taken for agricultural and home use, and very rarely for commercial purposes. The system of permits and restrictions on the use of certain blocks for fellings may be very necessary and even useful from the point of view of silviculture. But it does not accord with the economic requirements and practises of the tribal people. The wood and other forest produce they are allowed to get does not suffice for their purposes. They are willing to pay more than the stipulated fee for getting their normal requirements. Whenever they fail to get permits they throw the law to the winds and take to the axe.

Grazing crimes are explained by shortage of sufficient pasture land near about villages. Gaming offences are few because the tribal likes the fowl and goat for his food. He is not interested in the game generally prohibited.

The problem of the rise in the crime rate is very closely connected with the economic condition of the people living in or near the forest areas. In good years these crimes go down. In years of scarcity the crimes go up. This is indicated by the above table. The year 1949-50 mentioned in the table was a normal year. The year 1953-54 was the year following two years of scarcity and famine. And we see the number of crimes shooting up in the bad year as compared to a normal or good year. But, as generally a good year in these areas is a rare phenomenon and bad year the rule, the crime rate is usually high.

Causes of High Crime Rate

The economic pattern of the tribal areas has remained the same. Therefore, the high rate of crimes should be the effect of other cause. The biggest cause as we have mentioned earlier, is the changed forest administration which has restricted the freedom of the tribal *vis-a-vis* the use of forests. The Rulers of the former States were the absolute masters of the forests and the forests were treated as their personal property, where no adverse rights existed. In some States the people in general and the tribal people in particular were granted very liberal forest concessions. The new administration of Madhya Bharat views the forest as a source of revenue to the State, and has regularised and restricted the rights of the tribals. Red tape, bureaucracy and sometimes the desire of illegal gratification led the forest staff to delay the granting of permits for the supply of timber and wood, etc. The non-availability of these essentials on time even after the tribal was willing to pay for them, created great difficulties for him. Three reasons are generally advanced for the upward trends in the illicit fellings.

1. "Criminally minded" people resort to illicit fellings because they are forced to do so due to the persisting scarcity conditions in order to maintain their livelihood.

2. They find it the easiest method of earning a living.
3. Undesirable elements encourage them to do so.

These forest areas are mostly inhabited by the Bhils and Bhilalas. It is admitted even by the forest authorities that due to low fertility of land and poverty, under unavoidable circumstances the tribals resort to illicit fellings."

It is not accurate to explain the illicit felling as due to criminal mindedness! Habitually the tribals are not so. In years of distress their very existence depends on the forests. In the form of wild berries, roots, leaves and barks the hungry tribals get sustenance from the forests. As a source of income and employment also the collection and sale of forest produce helps them to earn an income, so indispensable for their very existence. The tribal regards forests as his very own. Not only his food but also his gods and spirits are derived from it. The way he regards the forests is very well illustrated by a very interesting practice among the Saharias. At the time of the marriage of his daughter a Saharia will bequeath a certain forest to her. This forest he shall never use for his requirements. He would regard it strictly a property of his daughter and son-in-law, and as such it would be a taboo to him.

The forests are an important factor in balancing the economy of the tribal whether he be a cultivator or a labourer. It is his only security against a bad year or unemployment. To be declared a criminal for doing what he has been doing for generations without let and hindrance fails the comprehension of the unsophisticated tribal.

The other aspect of the problem is more tragic and alarming. Instances are plenty when a contractor eggs the ignorant and unsuspecting tribal to do the felling knowing full well that what he is commissioning him for is an illegal act. The process is simple. The contractor gets hold of a tribal. Asks him to supply him the wood of a particular tree from a block that does not belong to him. The tribal commences the felling and if apprehended he comes under the heavy axe of the law. The contractor who instigated him and who stood to gain the most, does not figure anywhere in the charge-sheet.

Thus, the forest crime is a misnomer. It is an indication of the wrong forest policy which has ignored the welfare of the tribal altogether. Tribal welfare and the sound forest management on the principle of sustained yields are not inconsistent.

Forest Policy

Despite the presence of good deal of forest wealth in the Stage the tribal people continue to be in very bad plight. Forest wealth worth 61 lakhs of rupees should be a good source of subsidiary income. Agriculture and forest taken together should have given to the tribal people gainful employment throughout the year with sufficiently high incomes. But this is not so. The forest wealth either fills the coffers of the State or increases the bank balance of the contractor. As wage earner the tribal gets very little out of the natural wealth that is a part of his habitat and environment.

This problem is intimately related to the method of utilization of the forest produce.

Utilization

The forest produce is utilized by the following agencies:

(a) Departmental agency.
(b) Purchasers.

The departmental agency exploits some forest coupes only. The major part of exploitation is done by the purchasers. The Forest Department sets apart coupes for utilization which are put to auction. The highest bidder gets the lease of the coupe for the season. The major forest produce is utilized in this manner through the agency of the purchasers. These purchases are generally moneyed people who employ the tribal people to work for them as labourers. The utilization of forests through actions, thus, brings the contractors on the scene. On the one hand that means restrictions of the rights and privileges of the tribals in the forests. On the other hand it leads to exploitation of the tribal labour. This is an experience common to all tribal areas, Aiyappan, reporting on the socio-economic conditions of the aboriginal tribes in Madras Province, says, "The Forest Department can do a lot for the tribes. It is the duty of the Department to help the tribesmen in their own interests to be more efficient and to be better off economically. If more forest work is done departmentally the Government themselves would become the largest employer of tribal labour and the contractor will not be in a position to exploit them". On the basis of his wide experience Aiyappan makes a strong recommendation for the Depart ental management, particularly of minor produce. Grigson, the Aboriginal Tribes Enquiry Officer in the C.P., writing on the conditions prevailing in the C.P. recommends that "Departmental working should replace contracts wherever possible, and a clause should be inserted in Forest Contracts prescribing minimum wages for forest labourers." In Madhya Bharat there is neither a large volume of departmental working of the forests nor is there any safeguard of a fair wage to the tribal labour. The contractor is the master of the forest block for the season and he pays the wages he likes. Bahadur, Dey and Ramaswamy suggest, "if the backward classes are to be benefitted, the existing system should be changed." There is unanimity on the adverse effect the system of auction is having on the economy of the tribesmen. The system of contracts has turned the tribal labour as virtual slaves. But there appears to be a good deal of difference of opinion regarding the substitution of the forest contractors with the Departmental mode of working. The Departmental workings, unfortunately have been marked by the ill-treatment of the tribals by the petty officials of the Forest Department. The funds allotted are not properly used. Embezzlements and misuse of the funds are also not uncommon. Constituted as the department is at present, it gives no hope of serving the interests of the tribal any better. Moreover, if the Department could successfully undertake this work, it would fail to generate among the tribals that spirit of independence and mutual help and thrift which is so essential for their regeneration and revitalization. The Department may, if ideally worked, provide various types of amenities like medical care, education, recreation, etc. in a shorter time. But the tribal will continue to look to others for his needs. Not merely the economic welfare but also the social and political welfare as well calls for the ceration of cooperative institution to undertake this responsibility.

State has made experiments in the cooperative utilisation of forest produce in the Sheopur Forest Division. These experiments have not been very successful. There have been two major handicaps leading to the failure of the most of these attempts:

1. Technical nature of the business, and
2. Unreliable personnel.

The highly technical nature of marketing of forest produce led to the failure of some co-operative ventures of the Saharia societies in the Sheopur district. The society made the mistake of stocking a large amount of the produce, particularly Gums. But the market price suddenly went down. The society ran into a big loss in the very initial years of its work when it had no reserves to absorb the shock.

The other defect has been the wrong type of persons who come into such societies. These unscrupulous elements bank on the ignorance of the tribal and exploit him.

These defects are inherent in co-operation in general and the tribal co-operative in particular. The answer will lie, perhaps, in quasi-co-operatives operating in areas smaller than that allotted usually to the contractors, with a strict Government supervision and control and liberal financing by the Government.

Bombay State has recently seen some excellent experiments in Forest Labourers' Co-operative Societies. Referring to the successful experiments made by Bombay in this field the First Five Year Plan suggests, "It should be the object of State policy throughout India to organise the tribes into co-operatives for the collection of forest produce, and for this a phased programme should be drawn up." Defining the role of forest departments the Plan lay down that the responsibility of organising the tribal forest co-operative should lie on the shoulders of the Forest Department.

In its lucid exposition of the forest policy *vis-a-vis* the tribal people the Second Plan envisages the exploitation of the forest wealth with due consideration to the economic welfare of the tribal people. The Plan lays down, "It is desirable that tribal communities should be made the primary agents for the care and development of the forests and the exploitation of forest resources."

ADIVASIS OF CENTRAL INDIA

The Adivasis and forests are mutually connected. All the Adivasi tribes inhabiting the forest areas of Madhya Bharat, except the Sabarias dwelling in the Northern districts, are notified scheduled tribes, (*vide* the Scheduled Tribes Order of 1950, issued by the President of the Indian Republic, under the Constitution of India). According to this order, 16 Tahsils, (i.e., the Revenue district of Jhabua, the Tehsils of Sandhwa, Barwani, Rajpur, Khargone, Bhikangaon and Maheshwar of the revenue district of Nimar, Sailana Tahsil of the revenue district of Ratlam, and Sardarpur, Kukshi, Dhar and Manawar Tahsils of the revenue district of Dhar) have been declared as "Scheduled Area". This area falls in the Dhar, Nimar and Indore Forest Divisions. The total population of the scheduled tribes in Madhya Bharat is 11 lacs. This is mostly found in the jungles and hilly tracts in the Narbada valley embracing greater portion of the said Schedule Area.

The Madhya Bharat Forest Department administers about 12,000 sq. miles of Government owned, reserved, protected and unclassed forests. Besides this, approximately 4000 sq. miles of forests exist in the ex-jagirs and zamindaries, which is under transfer to the Forest Department. These forests contain 803 scattered villages, with a total population of about 40,000 persons under the control of the Forest Department. In addition to this, approximately 50,000 Adivasi persons dwell in the forests, either for working in the forest coupes under exploitation or for exploiting minor and major forest produce through the purchasers' agency.

The total area under cultivation in the 803 forest villages as well as that of the scattered holdings in the Government forests, is approximately 90,000 acres. The land assessment charged from these villagers is only nominal, varying from Rs. 5 to Rs. 10 per plough holding. The forest villages are administered under the rules made under Chapter VI of the Madhya Bharat Forest Act, Section 40(1). These rules are simple executive instructions, and are mainly designed for the welfare of the villagers.

The revenue villages (other than the forest villages) in the vicinity of the forests are commuted nominal fee, for their forest "nistar". Almost all the villages in the said Adivasi areas are commuted with the Forest Department for their "nistar".

The main occupation of the Adivasis is agriculture. They supplement their earnings by forest labour. The collection of minor forest produce, such as gums, temru leaves, lac, honey, mahua flowers and mahua fruits, etc., and its selling in the local markets is another supplementary occupation to them. Hunting and fishing is their hobby. Their indiscriminate shooting and killing of wild animals and birds has rendered the Scheduled Area barren of the natural fauna.

The economic conditions of the Adivasis in Madhya Bharat is, on the whole, poor. It is mainly due to their lazy habits and, partly due to the poor quality of local soil and practising primitive methods of agriculture. The agricultural returns earned by these people is also very low. With all the facilities given, the income they earn is hardly sufficient to provide them with two square meals.

The Forest Department makes all possible efforts for the welfare of the Adivasis. The Department provides them with labour and gives them fair wages in the remote forests. It does also look to their social, economic and educational needs and arranges to open schools, through the Education Department, and panchayats, and distributes taccavies, medicines, etc. Special provision is made in the contract rules for fair and timely payment of wages to the forest labour. If timely and adequate wages are not paid, in any case, to the adivasis, the Divisional Forest Officer has got the power to sell or auction the contractor's material and pay wages to the claimants.

The Adivasis are given the forest produce required for their *bonafide* consumption, gratis or at a very nominal payment. No fee, whatsoever, is charged to the Forest villagers, while the amount charged to the rest of the Adivasis is very nominal, varying from Re. 1 to Rs. 2, per family per year. The details of the forest produce so allowed to these people is given in the booklet "मध्यभारत में वन सम्बन्धी सुविधाएं".

In general, the concessions given by way of forest produce for the *bonafide* consumption of the Adivasis are, as under:

1. Timber, to the extent available, for construction of their dwelling huts.
2. Small timber required for their agricultural implements.
3. Grass, leaves and thorns required for feeding their cattle and for thatching and fencing respectively.
4. Dead and dry fuelwood.
5. Stones, Kankar, murum, sand and earth.
6. Free grazing of plough cattle.
7. Free collection of edible fruits, such as mahua fruits, mahua flowers, temru fruits, chironji, etc.

Soon after the formation of Madhya Bharat generally, and

during the past three years specially, this Department has been responsible for various activities for the welfare of the Adivasis.

Departmental working of the forest coupes was started in the Adivasi areas to give economic relief of the local people by providing them with labour. 9 coupes, of an area of 1268 acres, were worked at a cost of Rs. 31,675 during the year 1952-53. The timber and fuelwood obtained from the coupes worked departmentally was given to Adivasis, at concessional rates, which was much lower than the prevailing rates in the local markets. The Adivasis sold fuel and timber in the adjoining local markets, and made profits.

To alleviate fodder scarcity in the Adivasi areas, the Department did grass operations in Dhar, Khatiwara, Alirajpur, Jhabua, Ratlam, Manpur, Sendhwa and Kathiwara Ranges and collected 94,76,043 lbs. of grass. Out of this, 15,00,000 lbs. of grass was distributed free among the Adivasis. An amount of Rs. 1,35,337 was spent by the Department on this work. Grass, by headloads, was allowed to be brought from the Government forests without paying any royalty, while the rate for bringing the grass by cartload was reduced to annas 4 per cart-load. Grass depots at various places in the scarcity areas were opened and the grass sold at concessional rates of Rs. 2 per maund, 28,34,311 lbs. of grass in Jhabua District, 16,180 lbs. of grass in Ratlam District and 9,91,767 lbs. of grass in Nimar District were sold to public at concessional rates.

The grass coupes and birs in the Adivasi areas were not put to auction, but were opened to the local public to cut and collect grass for their own requirements.

The Adivasi area has experienced acute scarcity of water during the last two years. In order to provide water facilities to the Forest villages, the Department dug and constructed new well and ziras and repaired the old ones. Wells and ziras were dug, constructed or repaired in 98 Fores villages, at a cost of 2,61,200, during the past two years.

The Department has recently revised the rates of grazing fees in Madhya Bharat. The grazing rates fixed for the scheduled areas is only nominal. The grazing rates fixed for the scheduled areas as compared with other areas in Madhya Bharat.

The Forest Department has started training of the Adivasis in cottage industries run on forest products, such as manufacture

Annual Rates of Grazing

Name of the animal	Southern Circle						Northern Circle											
	Indore, Kannod and Khargone Divisions excluding Barwani Range			Ratlam and Dhar Divisions including Barwani Range of Khargone Division			Gwalior, Shivpuri, Sheopur and Bhilsa Divisions			Guna			Rajgarh Division			Garoth Division		
							Haqdar			Gair Haqdar								
	Rs.	a.	p.	Rs.	a.	p.	Rs.	a.	p.	Rs.	a.	p.	Rs.	a.	p.	Rs.	a.	p.
Elephant	10	0	0	5	0	0	0	8	0*	1	0	0*	10	0	0	10	0	0
Camel	2	8	0	0	10	0	2	0	0	4	0	0	1	0	0	2	8	0
Buffalo	0	12	0	0	3	0	1	8	0	3	0	0	0	6	0	0	12	0
Buffalo calves	0	12	0	0	3	0	0	12	0	1	8	0	0	6	0	0	12	0
Bullocks	0	6	0	0	2	0	0	8	0	1	0	0	0	4	0	0	6	0
Nata-bullocks	0	6	0	0	2	0	0	6	0	0	12	0	0	4	0	0	6	0
Sheep	0		0	0	2	0	0	2	0	0	4	0	0	2	0	0	6	0
Goat	0	6	0	0	2	0	0	4	0	0	8	0	0	2	0	0	6	0
Horse	0	8	0	0	2	6	0	8	0	1	0	0	0	4	0	0	8	0
Ass	0	8	0	0	2	6	0	2	0	0	4	0	0	4	0	0	8	0
Cow		Free			Free			Free			Free			Free			Free	

* The per day rate is only for the elephant of the Haqdar and Gair-Haqdar villages.

Note: No grazing fee shall be charged from the cultivators in the former Jhabua State area for their cattle as the land assessment in that State included the grazing fees.

biris from temru leaves, making of baskets and tattas from bamboos and sirali, wood works, turney, etc. The Forest Guards are given a special training in this sphere, at the Burwaha Forest Guards Training Centre, so that when posted in the Adivasi areas they may be able to train the Adivasis in this work. During the year 1952-53, the training-*cum*-production centres of cottage industries functioned at the following places:

Name of the Range	*Name of the Centre*
Jhabua	Ranapur
Alirajpur	Alirajpur
"	Borkua
Kathiwara	Kathiwara
"	Bhabra
"	Amkhut
Sardarpur	Tanda
"	Longsiri
"	Gandhwani
"	Kukshi

An amount of Rs. 13,000 was spent during 1952-53 on these centres. During the year 1953-54, these activities are extended to the following 14 centres. The total amount expected to be spent is Rs. 20,000. The programme of the work is as under:

Dhar Forest Division (District Dhar)

	Name of the Centre	*Amount Sanctioned*		
		Rs.	a.	p.
1.	Gandhwani	1,500	0	0
2.	Tanda	1,500	0	0
3.	Kukshi	1,500	0	0
4.	Longsarai	1,500	0	0
5.	Mandu, Nalchha	1,500	0	0
		7,500	0	0

Dhar Forest Division (Distt. Jhabua)

1.	Amkhut	1,500	0	0
3.	Ranapur	1,000	0	0
3.	Alirajpur	1,500	0	0
4.	Borkua	1,000	0	0
5.	Kathiwara	1,500	0	0
6.	Bhabra	1,500	0	0
		8,000	0	0

Forest Division, Khargone (District Nimar)

Pansemal	1,500	0	0
Palsood	1,500	0	0
	3,000	0	0

Forest Division, Indore (District Nimar)

Bablai	1,500	0	0
	1,500	0	0
Grand Total	20,000	0	0

In addition to the special works mentioned above, the Department gave the following facilities and concessions to the Adivasis, during the years 1952-53 and 1953-54:

1. Manufacture and sale of charcoal from dead and dry wood.
2. The Adivasis were allowed to collect and sell to the local contractors the minor forest produce, such as mahua flowers, mahua fruits, honey, gum, wax, chironji, temru leaves, etc.
3. Anjan leaves were allowed to be brought from the Government forest by head loads 10 feed the cattle.
4. Dead and dry fuelwood was allowed to be brought from the forests, without any royalty, and was allowed to be sold in the local markets.
5. The rates of fuelwood were reduced from Rs. 1/8 per cart-load to anas 6 per cart-load. They were allowed to sell this fuelwood in the local markets.
6. The Adivasis were allowed to remove the timber and fuelwood cut by the Forest Department in the departmently worked coupes at large concessional rates and were also allowed to sell this material in the local markets.

The benefit derived by the Adivasis due to these concessions was worth Rs. 1,12,000.

The Five Year Plan of the Department makes ample

provisions for the development of the Adivasi areas. Out of the total amount Rs. 50,00,000 sanctioned under the Plan for this Department, approximately an amount of Rs. 20,00,000 would be spent in the Adivasi areas.

The works expected to be completed by the end of 1953-54, under the Plan, are as under:

	Name of Project	*Target expected to for completed*	*Amount expected to be spent*		
			Rs.	a.	p.
1.	Survey and Demarcation of Forests	Survey and demarcation of 415 miles 7 furlongs, 9 chains long lines	15.663	3	6
2.	Firelines.	Clean cutting of 45 miles 4 furlongs long fire-lines	4.471	1	0
3.	Buildings	Construction of 1 Range quarter, 4 Dy. Range quarters	62,000	0	0
4.	Communications	Constructions of— 1. Dhaoli Kabri Road. 2. Alirajpur Mathwar. 3. Alirajpur Amkhut. 4. Amkhut Kathiwara. 5. Amkhut Bhabra fair weather roads	2,38,000	0	0
5.	Forest Improvement and Development works.	Thinking and cultural operation in 2803 acres	18,905	0	0
6.	Forest Industries	Running of training-*cum*-production centres of cottage industries. 10 centres during 1952-53, and 14 centres during 1953-54	24,171	0	3
7.	Division of Forests into Blocks and compartments.	Clear-cutting of 251 miles 2 furlongs long block lines	7,759	12	0

The future policy of the Department for the exploitation of major and minor forest produce is to encourage the Adivasi Co-operative Societies against the contractors. Forest contracts are given to Adivasi societies, at up-set prices, without auctioning them. By this way, the profits earned by the contractors go to the co-operative societies of Adivasis. Such societies have actually started functioning in Sheopur and Guna Forest Divisions.

TRIBAL LIFE AND FORESTS IN BIHAR

The total area of forests in Bihar is of the order of 12,345 sq. miles, comprising 19.3 (or to be more precise, 19.27) per cent of the total area of the State. Before the organisation of the States in 1956 the total area of forests in Bihar was 13,652 sq. miles in 1951-52 and 13,887 sq. miles in 1954-55. When the absolute figures of the areas of the forests in different States of India are taken into account, Bihar's rank turns out to be ninth. Table 9.2 is illustrative of this. The private forests constitute 85 per cent of the total area of forests in the State.

As would appear from Table 9.2, although Bihar's position from the standpoint of forests is stronger compared to some other States such as West Bengal and Uttar Pradesh in the country, yet the area of forests as percentage of total area is below the all-India average. Bihar occupies the fifth position among the States mentioned in the table in the matter of the area of forests as percentage of the total area.

Per capita forest area amounted to about 0.5 acre in India and 0.2 acre in Bihar, which was one of the lowest in India, as can be seen from Table 9.3.

About 80 per cent of the total forest area is concentrated in Chhotanagpur plateau region. The densely populated districts of North Bihar have not much of forest excepting an area of 356 sq. miles on the border of Nepal in Champaran district.

Out of about 13,000 sq. miles of the existing forests, 11,000 sq. miles, i.e., about 85 percent, constitute the erstwhile private forests which came under the Government management about fifteen years ago. These forests were in a very degraded and denuded condition when their control was taken over. They failed to fulfil the task as conservers of soil and moisture. Erosion was found to be common in these private forests, the main reason for this being unplanned and unrestricted cutting, incessantly heavy grazing and recurring annual hot season fires. Along with these private forests extensive areas of blank eroded lands and scrub jungles came under the Forest Department.

TABLE 9.2

States	I Area (In Sq. Miles)		1960-61 (In '000 Rs.)	II Revenue and Expenditure	
	1951-52[a]	1954-55[a]		Revenue 1951-52	Expenditure 1951-52
Andhra Pradesh	N.A.	13,673 (8)	24,032 (4)	N.A.	N.A.
Assam	30,391 (12)	19,444 (4)	17,605 (5)	6,575 (7)	4,775 (7)
Bihar	13,652 (6)	13,887 (7)	12,345 (9)	6,177 (9)	5,146 (6)
Gujarat	N.A.	N.A.	6,875 (12)	N.A.	N.A.
Jammu & Kashmir	12,822 (8)	11,058 (11)	8,028 (11)	6,287 (12)	2.658 (12)
Kerala	N.A.	N.A.	6,122 (13)	N.A.	N.A.
Madhya Pradesh	66.851 (1)	62,604 (1)	56,023 (1)	43,719 (1)	11,770 (2)
Madras	20,832 (3)	9,993 (10)	8,298 (10)	20,785 (4)	8,012 (4)
Maharashtra	20,314 (5)[b]	20,863 (3)[b]	26.191 (2)	35,819 (2)	12,230 (1)
Mysore	4,705 (11)	5,202(12)	13,994 (8)	9,331 (6)	3,749 (9)
Orissa	20,617 (4)	24,245 (2)	25,789 (3)	9,982 (5)	3,240 (10)
Punjab	5,104 (10)	5,621 (11)	2,094 (15)	5,795 (10)	4,457 (8)
Rajasthan	N.A.	16,045 (5)	16,752 (6)	3,878 (12)	3,043 (11)
Uttar Pradesh	13,410 (7)	14.930 (6)	16,025 (7)	35.033 (3)	10,232 (3)
West Bengal	5,256 (9)	5,167 (13)	4,548 (14)	5,707 (11)	5,433 (5)
All-India	2,64,041	2,80,896	3,60,453	2,53,639	1,01,807

(Contd.)

TABLE 9.2 (*Contd.*)

States	III *Revenue and Expenditure (In '000 Rs.)*			
	Revenue 1954-55	*Expenditure 1954-55*	*Revenue 1960-61*	*Expenditure 1960-61*
Andhra Pradesh	8,913 (7)	3,130 (11)	34,172 (7)	11,494 (9)
Assam	6,707 (11)	5,291 (7)	15,887 (13)	11,855 (8)
Bihar	7,633 (9)	6,514 (5)	19,756 (11)	15,341 (6)
Gujarat	N.A.	N.A.	26,773 (8)	9,357 (12)
Jammu & Kashmir	8,021 (8)	3,039 (12)	36,161 (6)	7,611 (14)
Kerala	N.A.	N.A.	43,194 (5)	11,134 (10)
Madhya Pradesh	40,960 (3)	14,428 (3)	1,01,163 (1)	31,415 (1)
Madras	13,188 (5)	5,371 (6)	19,935 (10)	10,657 (11)
Maharashtra	48,203 (1)	15,144 (2)	48,535 (4)	21,841 (4)
Mysore	12,961 (6)	4,152 (10)	76,195 (2)	29,562 (3)
Orissa	14,288 (4)	4,337 (9)	25,604 (9)	10,278 (12)
Punjab	4,757 (12)	4,533 (8)	14,768 (14)	11,681 (7)
Rajasthan	4,116 (13)	2,721 (3)	7,790 (15)	8,117 (13)
Uttar Pradesh	41,404 (2)	16,692 (1)	69,114 (3)	30,909 (2)
West Bengal	7,345 (10)	6,865 (4)	16,759 (12)	19,727 (5)
All-India	2,71,209	1,25,898	4.91,431	2,61,487

Notes: Figures in brackets indicate the ranking of the States.
(a) Indicates the figures before the reorganisation of the States.
(b) Indicates the figures for Gujarat.

TABLE 9.3

Percentage Area of Forests in Selected States (1956)

States	*Area of Forests as Percentage of Total Area*
Andhra Pradesh	22.8 (4)
Bihar	19.3 (5)
Kerala	26.4 (3)
Madras	17.0 (6)
Madhya Pradesh	31.5 (2)
Orissa	42.0 (1)
Punjab	3.0 (10)
Rajasthan	3.3 (9)
Uttar Pradesh	13.5 (8)
West Bengal	13.9 (7)
All-India	22.3

Note: Figures in brackets indicate ranks.

Government Policy: Its Achievements and Failures

All the private forests were taken over by the Bihar Government for management much before the Land Reforms Act came in. The Land Reforms Act has been of great help to the Forest Department inasmuch as the Government, instead of being merely managers of the forest property, are gradually becoming their owners as well. With the change in ownership, the management is bound to improve as also the conservation of the forest property will be rendered easier.

The First Five-Year Plan concentrated attention on the survey and demarcation, recruitment and training of staff and preparation of working schemes in relation to the private forests. A sum of Rs. 124.50 lakhs was spent and nearly 100 lakh miles of forest boundaries were demarcated. An experiment to associate village panchayats in the management of forests was first made in 1958 in the districts of Ranchi and Palamau. Forests in 190 villages began to be, thus, managed and 7 forest co-operative societies were formed. These societies purchased surplus coupes from the Forest Department and disposed of the produce. During the First Plan new forests over an area of 1,500 acres were planted. 1,100 miles of roads were constructed in important areas. During the First Plan the private forest management was consolidated. Plans were compiled for their working. Partial housing accommodation for the staff was provided. Steps were taken for their gradual training.

The Second Plan provided mainly for afforestation of the waste lands on a large scale and fencing of derelict forest lands regeneration areas. 1,395 miles of roads were constructed. It provided not only for afforestation, and building up of roads for the development of lac culture but also for the opening of saw mills, seasoning kilns and timber treating plants. A sum of Rs. 292,00 lakhs was spent.

TABLE 9.4

States	*Per Capita Forest Area (In Acre)*
Andhra Pradesh	0.54 (6)
Assam	2.6 (1)
Bihar	0.20 (12)
Gujarat	2.26 (9)
Maharashtra	0.52 (7)
Jammu and Kashmir	1.69 (3)
Kerala	0.18 (13)
Madhya Pradesh	1.74 (2)
Madras	0.18 (13)
Mysore	0.46 (8)
Orissa	1.11 (4)
Punjab	0.22 (11)
Rajasthan	0.81 (5)
Uttar Pradesh	0.23 (10)
West Bengal	0.12 (14)

Note: Figures in brackets indicate ranks.

The imbalance in the regional distribution of forests was sought to be mitigated to a certain extent by undertaking afforestation in 7,000 acres in North Bihar and by bamboo plantation during the Third Plan.

The Third Plan proposed to carry out afforestation work on 41,000 acres of land, to raise the economic plantation of teak, match-wood and bamboo on 26,000 acres, to manage 2,500 sq. miles of forests intensively through working plans, to extend new forest roads over 1,600 miles and to take up soil conservation measures. It provided for an outlay of nearly Rs. 473 lakhs. It was proposed to do afforestation over about 2 lakh acres as against 1 lakh acres during the Second Plan. The three plans together achieved the consolidation of erstwhile private forests.

During the Third Plan it was expected that about 2 lakh acres would come under afforestation. In addition, 15,000 acres of bamboo and 10,000 acres of teak would have been planted. The production of timber was expected to increase from 11 lakh cubic feet at the beginning of the second Plan to 14 lakh cubic feet at the end of the Third Plan. Similarly, the production of bamboo would have increased from 1.30 lakh tons at the beginning of the Second Plan to 2 lakh tons at the end of the Third Plan. During the same period annual revenues would have registered an increase from Rs. 2 crores to about Rs. 2.75 crores.

Table 9.3 shows that both the total revenue from and the expenditure on all the forests, private and State, in Bihar have tended to rise during the Plan period. However, as Table 9.5 will show, gross revenue in Bihar per sq. kilometer is among the lowest. This speaks of the utterly low productivity of the forests in the State. The revenue from the private forests in Bihar showed a marked increase mainly due to scientific management construction of new roads in inaccessible area; improvement of forests, tighter control on leakage and strengthening of the personnel from Rs. 4,77,135 in 1947-48 to about Rs. 70,00,000 in 1960-61 and not due to rise in the price of timber (which was of the order of 30 per cent only). During the same period the expenditure on the administration of these forests increased from Rs. 12,43,094 to Rs. 45,04.211.

Problems

Our forests contain a large number of miscellaneous products like myrobalans, honey, silk, cotton, medicinal hurbs, etc., which all have immense commercial possibilities.

Bihar is renowned for its *sal* trees, most common in the forests of Singhbbum district. This timber is hard and durable and is used for the railway sleepers, beams, rafters, etc.

The private forests were and are more heavily burdened with rights in Bihar than anywhere else in India, almost all of which the Government has been honouring. Thus, all rightholders are allowed to take their requirements free from the annual coupes. Their grazing right have not at all been interferred with. The main factors responsible for this are poor condition of the crop over large tracts, requiring afforestation lack of proper communications in the interior, and lack of utilization of lesser known, secondary timber.

TABLE 9.5

Productivity of Forests in the States and the Union Territories of India (1959-60)

States	*Gross Revenue (In Rs.) (Per sq. Km.)*
Andhra Pradesh	431 (15)
Assam	338 (16)
Bihar	460 (14)
Gujarat	1,383 (5)
Himachal Pradesh	1,743 (3)
Jammu and Kashmir	978 (8)
Kerala	2,620 (1)
Madhya Pradesh	509 (12)
Madras	791 (11)
Maharashtra	1,795 (2)
Mysore	859 (10)
Orissa	477 (13)
Punjab	916 (9)
Rajasthan	186 (17)
Uttar Pradesh	1,069 (7)
West Bengal	1,296 (6)
Andaman and Nicobar	1,612 (4)
Delhi	100 (19)
Manipur	47 (20)
Tripura	132 (18)

Note: Figures in brackets indicate ranks.

The survey and demarcation of the private forests was carried out rather in a hurry. Consequently, some cultivated lands of the farmers got included by mistake. By sustained efforts the Forest Department was able to exclude later on all such lands from the demarcation. However, the cry for more land release persists. This is mainly due to the increasing hunger for land. The Bihar Government has laid down a policy that only that land lying on the fringe of the forests, which is fit for permanent agriculture on an economic basis, will be considered for release. About 40,000 acres of land were thus, excluded from demarcation during the Second Plan.

We are still unaware of the total forest resources in the State. All that we know is the area under forests. Timber, firewood, bamboo and a host of other valuable minor forest products exist in our forests. We do not as yet know definitely the extent of the area over which various kinds of produce are found and in what quantity.

The strength of well-trained personnel is inadequate. Sustained efforts, no doubt, have been made to increase the strength of the subordinate staff at the level of the Forest Guards, Foresters and Forest Rangers. But Bihar has not as yet reached the norms prevailing in a number of other States in India. The Government, therefore, wants to standardise the normal charge of these people to 5 sq. miles, 25 sq. miles and 100 sq. miles of the forest area respectively.

Research organisation in Bihar has long been rather rudimentary in nature. The Forest Department has not even the basic arrangement for soil analysis.

Although the demarcation of the private forests was generally completed during the First Plan, the boundary posts were all *Kacha*. Encroachment for cultivation within the demarcated forests has not, therefore, been infrequent. The *Kacha* boundary posts can be demolished as well as re-erected easily.

Due to inadequate attention, uncontrolled grazing, recurring fires and repeated cutting in the past, extensive areas in the erstwhile private forests have been reduced to a stage where only bushy growth is found on the ground. Experience shows that such areas respond remarkably to closure to grazing and protection against fire after some initial cultural operations.

The present set-up of the Forest Department is wholly inadequate to cope with the normal organisational work, let alone the heavy developmental programme envisage.

Large quantities of firewood at present remain unutilized notably in the forests of Singhbhum district, adding considerably to the fire hazards. These need to be made available to the populated agricultural tracts of North Bihar and at such other places of the State where the local supply of fuel and small timber is not adequate.

In recent years agriculture and industry are both threatening to reduce the forest area of the State. The rural population wants more and more of the forest lands to be released for cultivation. More and more such lands are being claimed for mining and other industrial purposes. In 1960-61 about 7,000 acres of these lands were released for these purposes. While this cannot be helped in an expanding economy, it must, nonetheless be seen that forests do not suffer heavily on this account. In the United Kingdom there is a law according to which wherever forest lands are given over to a concern for mining, it becomes its responsibility to restore the area back to forests after mining is done. Some such laws will have to be passed and enforced in India too.

As pointed out above, fires damage our forests heavily. They have become almost a regular feature, particularly in the erstwhile private forests. Their adverse effects are well-known. The ground vegetation including young seedlings and saplings is killed outright and even the grown-up trees get a serious set-back and lose the major part of their annual growth. The watersheds lose their soil and water conservation value. In the absence of ground cover rich fertile top soil is washed away in subsequent rain and regeneration is hard to establish. The ultimate effects of this are becoming apparent in parts of Palamau and Hazaribagh districts where young and middle-aged sal trees are dying in large numbers. The tribal hunts and habit of lighting fire underneath *mahua* trees for the facility of collecting mahua flowers, careless throwing of *bidi* stubs, etc., are the chief causes of these fires. The future of the forests will continue to be gloomy so long as serious steps are not taken to combat their menace.

The present availability of bamboo in our forests is insufficient for the increasing demands of the Rohtas Industries. The output of sabai grass is less now than before. Much of sugar-cane bagasse produced in the North Bihar sugar mills is consumed as fuel. Only 3 per cent of it was used for pulp-making in 1956-57.

Forests in Bihar have no suitable trees for match wood. They are not in a position to provide the timber requirements for the State's own projects.

The demand for timber and other forest products is developing fast and is likely to increase rapidly in view of the growing industrial complex at several places like Barauni. Bokaro, Ranchi, Adityapur, and so on. To meet this demand it is imperative to increase the production of the existing forests to the maximum extent possible.

Chhotanagpur can boast of producing the largest quantity of lac in India. India is the greatest exporter of lac in the world market. Bihar produces 4.5 lakh maunds of stick lac, i.e., about 40 per cent of the total in the India Union. Only small quantities of lac are produced in the Pakur sub-division of Santhal Parganas and Aurangabad sub-division of Gaya district. Due to heavy concentration of lac cultivation in this region, the lac industry has grown mostly in Chhotanagpur. Out of 360 manufacturing centres for lac in India, about 120 are in Bihar and, with an exception of a few, all are located in Chhotanagpur, mostly in and around Ranchi.

Lac is an essential raw-material for industries which require properties of adhesiveness, insulation and water-proofing. It is an important constituent in the plastics, printing ink, electrical adhesive, grinding wheels, leather and wood-finishing industries. The gramophone records industry is the single largest consumer of shellac. Polish prepared with shellac-in-spirit gives high glaze to wood and metal surpassing in excellence that given by synthetic polishes. From this it is obvious that only highly industrialised countries can have scope for consuming lac and, in fact, the U.S.A., U.K., Russia, Germany, Japan and others are the largest importers of the Indian lac. India's home consumption of indigenous lac is only 8 per cent of the total produce, the rest, that is, 92 per cent is exported to the above-mentioned countries. The average value of annual exports works-out to Rs. 10.24 crores. The estimated share of Bihar in this is about Rs. 5 crores. Lac is, thus, a great foreign exchange earner. Table 9.6 gives an idea of the inter-State distribution and production of the lac industry in India.

The actual production of stick lac in India in 1962-63 was 41,672 tons as against 38,558 tons in 1961-62. India is the chief source of the supply of stick lac and till 1950 it accounted for 85 per cent of the total world production and now Thailand has become India's chief competitor and India's share has come down to 30 per cent of the world production. About 90 per cent of the total quantity of the processed goods is exported from India, U.S.A. being the chief customer, followed by U.K., Germany, U.S.S.R., etc.

To ensure steady export of lac, the industry needs vigilant

attention of our Government in the matter of stabilisation of the price of lac which fluctuates very widely. The lac market is dictated by the ruling price in Calcutta which in turn is conditioned by the speculative activities in Wall street and London. This operates to the detriment of the manufacturers and the poor Adivasi lac growers of Chhotanagpur.

TABLE 9.6

Average Production of Stick Lac in Different States

States	*Average of 1946 to 1953 (in maunds)*	*Average of 1946 to 1956 (in maunds)*	*1952-62 (in tons)*
Assam	21,379 (5)	17,000 (5)	381 (8)
Bihar	6,73,019 (1)	4,53,500 (1)	18,057 (1)
Gujarat	N.A.	N.A.	299 (9)
Madhya Pradesh	2,90,914 (2)	2,38,500 (2)	13.005 (2)
Maharashtra	15,211[a] (7)	64,000[a](3)	1,915 (4)
Orissa	20,349 (6)	17,000 (5)	679 (6)
Uttar Pradesh	11,633 (8)	12,500 (6)	826 (5)
West Bengal	48,535 (3)	2,38,500 (2)	5,947 (3)
Others	27,480 (4)	20,500 (4)	521 (7)
Total	11,41,819[b]	11,16,000	41,630

Note: Figures in brackets indicate ranks.
(a) Including the figure for Gujarat.
(b) Including 33,272 maunds for Vindhya Pradesh.

Because of this factor our lac industry is generally unstable and disorganised. The units, being small, have no staying power with the result that in times of boom a large number of manufacturing establishments crop up only to close down no sooner than the price factor becomes unfavourable. Over and above this, the synthetic substitutes are competing with natural lac, specially in the U.S.A., where India has lost much ground. This irregular foreign demand, therefore, leads at times to glut and crisis in our lac industry.

The cultivators grow lac as a source of subsidiary income for it is a good cash crop. About 7,000 workers are engaged in the manufacturing centres. So if the industry is not put on a sound footing, both the producers and the workers will be hard hit.

The first step towards it would be for the Government to fix a floor price for lac or to introduce such other measures that stabilise its price.

The main difficulty in increasing the production of lac is the inadequate supply of brood-lac and unscientific methods adopted by growers in the cultivation of lac.

As stated above, lac culture is concentrated in the Chhotanagpur plateau region. Lac occupies a significant position in India's export trade. About 90 per cent of it is exported in the form of seedlac and shellac. The value of the average annual export of lac exceeds Rs. 10 crores.

The main difficulties of the shellac industry, to sum up, are: wide fluctuations in the production of stick lac and the consequent fluctuations in prices, dependence on foreign markets, competition from synthetic products and dependence of the producers on the brokers and shippers at Calcutta for marketing their products. There is need for the standardisation of production.

The private forests need enormous capital for investment in the afforestation of the barren and denuded lands and the construction of roads and buildings over a long period of time.

According to the National Forest Policy laid down by the Government of India in 1952, Bihar should have a well distributed forest area up to 35 per cent of its total area. This means that the existing forest area in Bihar has to be nearly doubled but this increase is not feasible. The immediate task will, therefore, be to develop our existing forests to their optimum productivity.

Under the First Plan the activities of the Forest Department were mainly confined to the management of the private forests. Initially, when the private forests were taken over, the areas were tagged on to the existing. Forest Divisions, with the result that most of these Divisions became extremely unwieldy. The Second and the Third Plans have done a lot to rectify the situation but even then much remains yet to be done.

The coverage of the private forests is so wide that even now it is not possible to produce detailed working plans of the same standard as apply to the State-owned forests. The work of afforestation is so vast that the Afforestation Division cannot alone tackle it effectively. For afforestation to make real progress, it is necessary to have a number of such divisions. It will be the responsibility of the Fourth Plan to make up the leeway.

Forest Labour Co-operative Societies in Maharashtra and Gujarat—Their Significance in Tribal Development

G.M. Gare* and D.T. Birari**

The life of Adivasis in India is vitally interrelated, intermingled and intertwined with forest and agriculture economy. The Adivasis, as aboriginals of India, have dwelt and are still dwelling mainly within the forests and on the outskirts of the forests, and that is why they have provided a good deal of labour force for the exploitation of the forest resources. This chapter discusses the deep-rooted link of the Adivasis with the Forest Labourers Co-operative Societies in particular as the strategic weapon used to exploit the forests.

Since the topic has many dimensions, for the sake of brevity, it is restricted to some important dimensions of the topic only.

The following areas of the movement have been considered in this chapter.

*Director, Tribal Research and Training Institute, Pune.
**Research Officer, Tribal Research and Training Institute, Pune.

(1) The Forest Labourers Co-operative Societies (FLCS) movement in its historical perspective.
(2) Organisational structure of FLCS in Maharashtra and Gujarat.
(3) Working of FLCS in general.
(4) Economic and social aspects of their working.
(5) Some issues involved.
(6) Reflections of the viability of the societies to achieve short-term economic goal as well as the long-term goal of all-around development of tribal people.

1. THE FOREST LABOURERS CO-OPERATIVE SOCIETIES (FLCS) MOVEMENT IN ITS HISTORICAL PERSPECTIVE

Almost all the districts of Maharashtra and Gujarat have some forests but it is predominent in only some districts. For example, in Maharashtra forest concentration is significant in districts like Thane, Dhule, Nasik, Kulaba, Ahmednagar, Chandrapur, Yavatmal, Amravati and Nanded. Similarly, in Gujarat, Dangs District is prominent for forest concentration and tribal population. Thane, Dhule and Nasik pioneered the movement and they have the large concentration of both forest area as well as Adivasi population. One may say that greater the proportion of the forest, the greater is the proportion of the tribal population.

In the pre-independent era, the forests were being exploited with the help of contractors and the contractors in turn used to exploit the Adivasis. The contractors used to employ them as labourers on meagre wages. The labourer was given some advance at exorbitant rates of interest and in turn the labour pledged his hands and feet to the contractors. Since this Adivasi labour had no sources of income other than cultivation of their low-yielding land and labour on other farms, he had no other alternative but to work for the contractors. There were no developmental and other welfare programmes as of today for these Adivasis and hence these labourers for generations used to serve the contractors who dictated their own terms.

The forest labour co-operative movement was first launched on 5th April, 1947, by B.G. Kher—the then Chief Minister of Bombay Province. Behind this great event lies the well-known report of Symington who was appointed by the Bombay Government to inquire into the problem of Adivasis. He suggested some schemes for the amelioration of the plight of Adivasis and Government decided to implement these schemes. One of the measures was to pay minimum daily wages to the Adivasi labourer which was announced by Shri B.G. Kher on 5th April 1947 at Mahalaxmi in Thane District at a conference of the Adivasis. Thus, the movement took its birth here and then the objectives of the movement were: (a) to eliminate the agency of forest contractors progressively, (b) to give a fair wage and share of profit to the Adivasi in his work, (c) to impart training to Adivasi in the management of these societies, and (d) to achieve an all-round development of the Adivasi people.

To achieve these objectives, the following concessions were given:

(i) Coupes were allotted to societies at fixed price for saving Adivasis from open competition,
(ii) Societies were allowed to select convenient coupes, and
(iii) Exemption was given from payment of deposits and part of the upset prices of the coupe.

The societies were given the following financial assistance:

(i) Rs. 3000 towards share capital for the first year,
(ii) Rs. 1200 per year for 2 years towards managerial subsidy, and
(iii) Rs. 1500 per year for 3 years as subsidy for welfare schemes.

This financial assistance gave a great fillip to the movement. There was a great spur in organising new societies. Soon there was a steady progress in the movement. In the first decade of planning a significant awakening in the Adivasi areas of the then Bombay Province was noticed, as was seen in progressively greater participation of Adivasis in the societies, along with the sympathisers. Especially, more and more appointive posts were taken by Adivasis.

The following tables relating to organisation of societies and membership indicate the growth of the movement. The first table for the period 1948-58 gives consolidated position for both Maharashtra and Gujarat.

The Table 10.1 reveals a steady progress of the movement. The societies increased 28 times within twelve (12) years. Later on the Bombay state was reorganised. Two separate States, Maharashtra and Gujarat came into existance. The picture in Maharashtra after bifurcation is as in the table.

TABLE 10.1

Registered Societies and their Membership in Maharashtra and Gujarat

Year	*No. of Regd. Societies*	*No. of members*	*Average membership per society*
1947-48	11	508	46
1948-49	29	2,421	83
1949-50	61	6,920	113
1950-51	100	16,996	170
1951-52	108	20,440	189
1952-53	118	22,521	191
1953-54	124	28,367	228
1954-55	145	34,742	239
1955-56	179	41,879	235
1956-57	216	42,538	197
1957-58	275	45,781	166
1958-59	308	51,405	166

Registered Societies and their Membership in Maharashtra State

Year	*No. of Registered Societies*	*No. of Members*	*Average membership per society*
1959-60	212	23,457	111
1961-62	319	30,879	96
1963-64	379	37,048	98
1966-67	465	46,649	100
1967-68	472	46,872	99
1968-69	464	47,012	101
1971-72	443	53,047	120
1973-74	442	55,298	125
1974-75	418	55,651	135
1975-76	417	47.651	114
1976-77	409	59.294	145

The Share capital growth and number of coupes worked, value of business carried out, profits/loss made, wages paid and amount spent on social welfare will give an idea of the development of these societies. These details are in the table on next page.

The figures given in table on next page impressive picture of the development of the movement upto 1977 in Maharashtra. There were 409 societies with a total membership of 59,294 out of which Adivasi members constituted 81 per cent. They employed 1,896 employees out of which 72 per cent were Adivasis. So far as Gujarat is concerned at present there are 142 societies with 60,000 members. The membership is mainly spread in districts like Baroda, Bharuch, Valsad and Dangs. This figure compares favourably with Maharashtra. As against 59,294 membership of 409 societies of Maharashtra, Gujarat has membership of 60,000 for 142 societies showing that the size of membership is greater in Gujarat and that the movement could bring in its fold more members in Gujarat.

So far as wages paid are concerned, Gujarat Societies paid to the tune of Rs. 1,93,56,000 during the year 1975-76, while Maharashtra Societies, nearly three-fold in number paid Rs. 48,18,496 in 1973-74. It shows that on an average, business carried out is more in Gujarat as compared to that in Maharashtra. The developmental aspects in Maharashtra can be summed up as under.

As against 11 societies in 1947-48, working over 13 coupes and doing business of Rs. 2 lakhs there was vast increase in the number of societies, up to 409 in 1977. Taking the year 1970-71, (which marks the two decades of development) there were 453 societies working over 821 coupes and doing business of Rs. 400 lakhs. An amount of Rs. 65.30 lakhs was paid as wages for coupe exploitation and the aggregate share capital reached Rs. 17-52 lakhs with reserve funds of Rs. 22.74 lakhs and other funds to the tune of Rs. 31.18 lakhs.

Out of 1.861 coupes exploited (in 1971-72), 876 were exploited by the societies and 664 were allotted to forest contractors, and 321 were worked departmentally. Thus, upto 1971-72, elimination percentage of contractors was about 65 per cent; 47 per cent of the coupes were worked by societies and 18 per cent by the Department. The percentage is significant but not impressive.

Year	Share Capital	No. of Coupes worked	Value of Business	Profit	Loss	Wages Paid	Amount Spent on Social Welfare
1	2	3	4	5	6	7	8
1947-48	8,936	12	1,87,500	1,16,491	—	—	
1955-56	4,12,847	309	1,27,09,006	38,81,566	2,13,427	20,86,202	1,05,779
1958-59	10,41,384	456	1,87,00,185	51,92,985	81,170	48,32,918	2,11,467
1959-60	6,37,078	370	99,61,795	31.66,135	2,74,872	43,32,066	1,01310
1963-64	10,92,391	534	1,46,12,116	25,02,608	1,59,025	32,79,737	1,74,459
1965-66	15,65,721	687	1,80,88.103	17,16,523	2,26,353	49,14,097	2,35,875
1970-71	17,52,648	712	3,40,95,933	37,58,770	—	65,22,961	2,52,988
1973-74	15,18,187	777	4,99,75,164	46/77,568	—	48,18,496	4,93,743
1974-75	16,44,688	674	94,90,970	32,64,289	7,84,503	—	—
1975-76	15,96,492	640	98,02,587	39,69,539	17,67,361	—	—
1976-77	15,24,524	635	1,06,18,567	5,42,44,297	13,67,018	—	—

For the year 1970-71 we find that 87 per cent of the members were Adivasis and 70 per cent of the Adivasis were on the managing committees of the societies. For the year 1976, 82 per cent of the chairmen were Adivasis in the societies, 60 per cent were chairmen of District Federations which had 66.42 per cent as Adivasi members on their Managing Boards. As pointed out earlier. 72 per cent employees in the societies are Adivasis, 32 per cent Secretaries, 75 per cent as Accountants, 51 per cent as Depot Clerks 90 per cent as coupe-agents, 97 per cent as Mukadams, 90 per cent as watchmen, 76 per cent as peons, 51 per cent as Clerks and 50 per cent as Drivers and Cleaners. These percentages of Adivasi participation in Maharashtra is on the whole impressive viewed from the angle of leadership training. But this is a quantitative aspect of the achievement. We have to look to its qualitative aspect also.

The first objective of elimination of forest contractors has, although not fully achieved within 24 years upto 1971-72, it has been achieved in a great measure. Nearly 50 per cent of the coupes are worked by societies. This shows that there is still much scope for further improvement and the movement needs to be strengthened further. There has been a three-fold increase in the share capital. A society on an average, carried out business worth about Rs. 40 to 50 thousands per year. The societies in the aggregate are running in profit. The wage distribution per society was much higher in the first few years of the movement. It dropped down during 1961 to 1965 and against maintained a level around ten thousand rupees after 1965-66. The average annual bonus paid to members varied from Rs. 60 to Rs. 175 per society. Bonus distribution is only 1 to 2 per cent of the wage distribution. There is some increase in the amount spent over social welfare say around Rs. 450 to 550. It was spent on amenities provided at the coupes. However, the turnover shows a declining tendency. The proportion of non-member workers in the total work force as gone down. But very few societies have shown a tendency to obtain additional sources of employment other than forest coupes for their members. Only 42 per cent and 65 per cent societies could obtain A and B audit class, respectively.

But the end of June 1970, the total membership of societies in the country was 1.50 lakhs. More than l/3rd of it belonged to Maharashtra and little less than l/3rd to Gujarat. This means that nearly 2/3rd of the membership of these societies in India comes from these two States. Nearly half of the share capital has been accounted for by Maharashtra. However, so far as reserve funds are concerned, Gujarat is ahead of Maharashtra. This also true in case of working capital.

As far as the financial position is concerned a strong base has been created only in Maharashtra and Gujarat for sustaining and expansion of the movement.

2. ORGANISATIONAL STRUCTURE IN MAHARASHTRA AND GUJARAT

The structural design of the Forest Labour Co-operatives in the two States has been evolved through 30 years of experience and sincere efforts of the government and devotion of the leading social workers.

Maharashtra have a three-tier system of organisation and administration, in the form of State Federation, District Federations and the societies. In detail, the organisational design is made up of the following:

1. State Council for Forest Labourers Co-operative Societies.
2. State Federation of F.L.C. Societies.
3. District Federations of F.L.C. Societies.
4. Circle Wage Board.
5. Central Training School.
6. Primary Forest L.O. Societies.

The organisational chart is as follows:

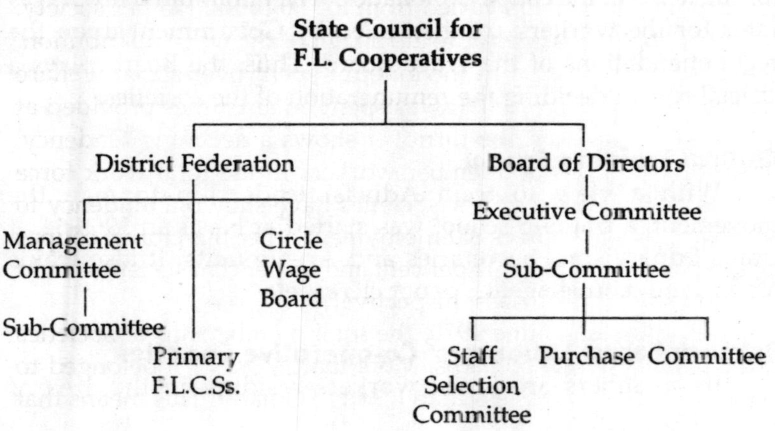

State Council

The Planning Committee which functioned at State level upto 1962 gave way to the State Council. It gives directions and guidance to the whole movement. It formulates a programme of phased expansion.

State Federation

This has been organised in 1966. It attends to the needs of societies in marketing, processing, forest-based industries. It makes available raw materials, tools, equipments, marketing assistance, commercial intelligence and organises conferences, periodicals, libraries. It has opened sales depot at Pune and it effected sales of Rs. 71,583 during 1976-77.

District Federation

With the increase in the number of societies, a need was felt for district federation of the societies. They replaced the former sponsoring agencies and the District Coordination Committees. They sponsor, supervise and guide the primary societies, recommend allotment of coupes and entertain complaints of societies regarding allotment. There are 12 district Federations and one District Federation at Kolhapur is under liquidation.

Circle Wage Boards

The Board consists of the Conservator of Forests for the Circle, one representative of the societies from each division in the Circle, Divisional Forest Officer and Labour Officer. It fixes rates for the items in the coupe exploitation. The minimum daily wages rates for the workers are then fixed by Government upon the recommendations of the Wage Board. Thus, the Board plays a crucial role in deciding the remuneration of the societies.

Central Training School

With a view to train Adivasi leadership to man the movement, a training school was started at Nasik in 1963-64. It trains Supervisors, Secretaries and Accountants. It also trains Mukadams, coupe agents, depot clerks, etc.

Primary Forest Labourers' Co-operative Societies

Its members are forest workers residing in the area of

operation of the society and social workers. The society has a manageing committee with 4 to 6 elected representatives, one or two representatives of social service organisations and one nominee of the financing agency.

Annual Conference

These are held annually in the Adivasi areas and arouse awakening among the Adivasis. The Adivasis from the neighbourhood and society members from all over the State participate in large numbers. Grievances are heard and suggestions are made. Government takes note of these suggestions.

So far as Gujarat is concerned, the State provides for the organisational set-up similar to that of Maharashtra The only exception is that they do not provide for the State Federation of the Forest Labour Cooperatives. Instead at the State level, there is a State Advisory Council for the Forest Labourers' Co-operative Societies and Labour Contract Co-operative Societies. The following chart depicts the set-up in Gujarat:

State Advisory Council
for F.L. Coop, and Labour Contract Cooperative Societies

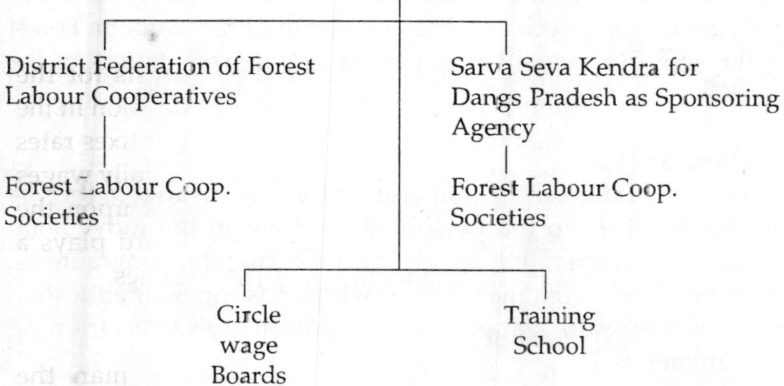

State Advisory Committee

The State Government has appointed a State Advisory Committee under the Chairmanship of the State Minister for Cooperation for giving guidance to the Forest Labour Co-operative

Societies in respect of their problems, administration and other matters.

District Federation/Sponsoring Agencies

In the light of the recommendation of the Evaluation Committee, the State Government has agreed to organise the district Unions of the Forest Labour Societies. Accordingly, in most of the districts, such Federations have been set-up, as in Maharashtra, with similar functions. They have taken up the sponsoring activities of the societies. Where such Federations are not working properly, some social agencies have been recognised as sponsoring agencies. So far as Dangs Pradesh is concerned, Sarva Seva Kendra Billimore has been the main sponsoring agency with its 15 societies. It is learnt that very recently Gujarat has ordered for the abolition of the District Federations and Sponsoring agencies. There will then be branches of the State Advisory Council in each District. The branch offices are to be manned by 2/3rd Government officers and l/3rd officials Collector, D.F.O. and District Deputy Registrar will look after the administration of these branches.

Circle Wage Boards

As in Maharashtra, Gujarat also provides for a machinery to fix wages for these societies. They consist of Conservator on Forest for the area, Divisional Forest Officer and representatives of the societies.

Training School

As in Maharashtra, Gujarat State has arranged for the training facilities to the personnel working in the movement. Balsad Zilla Cooperative Sangh conducts training programmes. It receives funds from the societies which pass on their education fund to the said Sangh for utilisation towards training programmes.

3. WORKING OF THE FOREST LABOURERS' CO-OPERATIVE SOCIETIES

These societies are registered by the Deputy Registrar of Co-operative societies under the Co-operative Societies Act, 1961. There should be at least 10 promoters above the age of 18 years and 20 to 30 members. It must raise at least Rs. 500 as initial share capital and adopt model bye-laws with suitable modifications. The society should be sponsored by the District Federation.

The society gets financial assistance towards share capital, management subsidy and subsidy for welfare activities as described earlier. Besides, the District Federation also grants financial assistance.

The allotment of coupes is done by the Conservator of Forests if the Society has cleared off dues to the Forest Department and that it has adequate borrowing capacity and it has the recommendations of the District Federation. There is affixed time-table for allotment and exploitation of coupes.

In this connection a Research Report of Tata Institute of Social Sciences, Bombay, can be referred to know the working of the Forest Labourers' Cooperative Societies. This survey was conducted in Thane, Nasik and Kolaba districts. The findings show that the working of these societies is not very satisfactory to achieve the objectives of the movement. There are organisational, structural, administrative and financial problems faced by the societies. For example, societies need to be reorganised by eliminating sympathisers and non-working members, non-member workers need to be made members, inefficient staff at the society and at coupes who are largely responsible for poor management and malpractices need to be replaced by trained and qualified staff and the society should help tribals financially for various purposes:

(i) As regards the working of the coupes it was found that the items included in the operational cost are inadequate and there are differences which occur between the society and the Forest Department leading to disputes. For example, differences over amounts allowed for construction of approach roads, transport charges, welfare expenses at coupes and salary of coupe-agents, Mukadam and peons, etc.

(ii) The financial position of the societies is unsatisfactory because of the delay in the coupe operation due to lack of proper guidance and supervision by the staff, delays in disposal of material and delay in submission of audited statements.

(iii) Regarding the management of accounts it was observed that accounts are not maintained up to date and there is shortage of adequately trained staff for maintaining the accounts.

(iv) All the members do not work on coups because in general, some members do not need work. Further, coupes are distantly located and, therefore, some members who are ill and are of old age cannot undertake the work.

(v) Management Committees are largely dominated by non-working members and societies have very old bye-laws. There is also lack of proper supervisory staff at the coup. Forest Department takes long time in sanctioning expenditure on variable items and transport. It is also very rigid regarding the time schedule. Moreover, coup staff is frequently changed.

(vi) Regarding the mal-practice it was found that the working of the society is fraught with bogus attendance theft of material, illicit cutting of trees, extravagancy in coupe operations, false vouchers and thumb impressions, making less payments to the labourers, etc.

(vii) Regarding the participation of tribals in the movement it was observed that the active participation of the tribal is mainly absent.

Besides the above research report, the Tribal Research and Training Institute, Maharashtra, Pune had also conducted a survey of the working of these societies in Dhule District in 1976. Some of the findings are enumerated below:

(i) Out of 23 societies surveyed, the management of 13 societies is still with the non-Adivasis.

(ii) The participation of Adivasis in posts like Secretaries, Accountants and Clerks was negligible.

(iii) Similarly, none of the persons trained as supervisors, Secretaries and Accountants at the Central Training Institute, Nasik have been appointed to posts for which they were trained and the existing office bearers from the Adivasis were not sent for training because they either did not fulfil the conditions for admission or there was disinclination on the part of the Adivasis.

(iv) The societies surveyed had failed to provide adequate employment to their members. 50 per cent of the societies could provide employment for 600 to 700 Adivasis and that too for a part of the year. The movement failed in minimising the unemployment problem amongst the tribals.

(v) The societies provided an income of Rs. 60 to 70 on an average during the whole year. This meagre income cannot solve the problems of unemployment and raising the socio-economic conditions of the Adivasis.

(vi) It was also revealed that some societies assign the coupe operation on sub-contract basis, thus, defeating the very purpose of the movement.

(vii) Coupes allotted were also often small in size which resulted in making societies non-viable economic units.

(viii) The societies in general had not shown interest in works other than coup operations, for example, collection and disposal of minor forests produce, road construction, forest industries, processing units, etc.

(ix) So far as the welfare activities of the societies were concerned, very little had been done. The maximum expenditure per member per year was Rs. 6 in Dhule district. On an average they spent one to two rupees per head. They had no concrete programme under welfare activities.

(x) Investment of big amounts by some societies was found on items which could not provide any substantial benefit to the members.

(xi) The old forest contractors were still there on the scene as transport agents. More than 20 to 25 per cent of the expenditure by the societies had gone to non-tribal transport agents. The very object of helping the tribals by eliminating contractors could not be achieved fully. On the other hand in Dhule district it was found that out of 340 labourers contacted 98 workers were having bullocks and carts, but they were not given the transport work by the societies. In short, the employment providing outlook is lacking in these societies.

(xii) None of the societies surveyed had distributed profits or dividends to their members during the last 5 years. The societies surveyed were not functioning in the real sense as commercial as well as welfare organisations. They spent more funds towards pay and allowances and transport charges rather than on payment of wages to the forest labourers and Adivasi members. It could also be concluded that the movement helped more in elevating the social status of the social workers, mostly non-tribals, rather than eliminating contractor and raising the socio-economic standards of the tribals.

4. ECONOMIC AND SOCIAL ASPECTS OF THEIR WORKING

While dealing with the working of the societies, we have knowingly as well as unknowingly, touched the economic aspects of these societies. However, at this juncture, we are trying to examine in detail the economics of their working form the angle of costs and returns and to determine ultimately their economic viability.

While regulating and developing this movement Government of Maharashtra and Gujarat, have modified from time to time their directives based on experience and suggestion regarding the costs and returns. From a quantitative aspect the movement may be adjudged to have progressed well in Maharashtra in view of the following considerations:

(i) F.L.Cs. have succeeded in bringing a very large number of forest labourers within its fold,
(ii) They are sharing profits and bonus,
(iii) A large number of contractors have been eliminated, and
(iv) Owned resources of F.L.Cs are growing.

However, it is desirable to derive the correct picture by having an insight through evaluation of costs and returns.

As stated earlier, there is a time schedule for coupe-operation and exploitation. From 1947 to 1958-59, these societies and the Forest Department were sharing the profits and losses on the working of the coupes on 50 : 50 basis. Under this pattern, the upset price was fixed on the basis of the estimates of yield minus total operational costs. At the end of the year estimated value of the estimated yield minus 10 per cent operational cost, was compared with the actual realisation and the resultant loss or profit was shared by Government and the society on 50 : 50 basis.

This formula was subsequently found unsatisfactory as it led to many disputes in the matter of fixation of upset price and other difficulties such as excess expenditure on extra yield, etc.

Revised Formula of 1959

A revised formula was, therefore, brought into effect from 1959-60. The procedure of fixing upset price and advance estimation was discontinued. At the close of the yearly felling operations, the societies shared the profits with the Government on fixed proportion of the net profit. The exploitation and sale of the coupe material took place under the supervision of the staff of the Forest Department. The net realisation was arrived at by deducting actual expenditure over 33 admissible items specified, from the gross sale proceeds. Rates of these items were fixed. The following table shows the scheme of sharing net realisation.

Age of the Society	*Society's Share*	*Government's Share*
Upto 1 year old	25	75
More than 3 but upto 6 years old	20	80
More than 6 but upto 9 years old	15	85
More than 9 years old	10	90

Modified Revised Formula

The societies were not satisfied with the expenses on 33 items. They had to incur expenditure even on other additional items. More and more items were being suggested by societies for inclusion in admissible cost. So in November 1967, all the societies were given 20 per cent share irrespective of the period of their establishment. Later on, Government began thinking in terms of replacing this system by another system known as logging system, under which the societies are responsible for all operations in the coupe and delivery at the Depot. The material is sold by the Forest Department. Societies get the operational expenditure on the prescribed items, plus 10 per cent of the operational costs to cover their overhead expenses. The Department also gives advances to the societies to meet the working expenditure.

At present, every year the coupes are allotted to the societies from their operational area by the Conservator of Forests of the Circle concerned. If the societies are in A and B Audit classification, coupes are given to them on the revised formula, i.e., 20 per cent profit is given to the society and if they fall in C and D Audit classification, the coupes are given to them on logging formula. In this formula 20 per cent profit is given on expenditure incurred.

In the case of Gujarat, the societies are allotted coupes by the Forest Department. Keeping in view the recommendations of the sponsoring agencies and the cooperative Department recently, Government has appointed District Committees under the Chairmanship of the District Collector to deal with disputes amongst the societies in respect of the allotment of coupes. After arriving at the net profit on the realisation of the sale, the profit is shared between the society and Government on 20 : 80 basis.

Economic Viability of the Societies in Maharashtra to Achieve the Objectives of the Movement

Broadly speaking, expenditure is incurred on coupe work, transport, depot work, office management, welfare programmes, etc. It is observed that the costs on coupe work and transport account for nearly 60 to 80 per cent of the total costs in majority cases of societies. About 10 to 20 per cent costs are on office management and a similar percentage on depot work. Coupe work is the prominent source of wage-distribution and employment. Wages for coupe work account for 40 to 50 per cent of the costs and supervisory charges come to 5 per cent.

Today, A and B class societies only get the benefit of revised formula of sharing profits and they will prosper wherever the coupes allotted are adequate and fetch a good deal of sale proceeds. Their wage-component would remain as explained here. But in case of other societies which are allotted coupes on logging system, their wage component would be reduced because the logging basis dispenses with the need of the society to transport the material and establishment of a depot for its sale. They would, therefore, handle only 30 to 40 percent of the present total costs which are costs over coupe-work and 10 to 15 per cent of the costs which are costs over office-management and welfare. This would give a wage component of 40 to 50 per cent under the revised formula. This wage loss would be due to loss of wages over truck loading, road loading, road construction and depot work. Depot work gives employment opportunities to the extent of 4 to 8 per cent of the costs. The loss of employment over transport would be a great loss to the society because it is seen that 30 to 40 per cent of the cost is on transport. Since the logging system would take away some labour-intensive activities from the societies, the income-generating and employment boosting sources of the members would diminish and it would also mean non-employment of members who are cartmen. The contractors may usurp these activities from the Forest Department. Thus, it is feared that the already reduced economic viability of the societies would be further reduced with the wider application of the logging system to many societies.

Another effect would be on the management costs, which already amount to 10 to 15 per cent of the costs. Now the depot clerk would be unnecessary. With the societies losing nearly half of the present costs as the costs over transport and depot work, the proportion of office management costs would go up further.

Profit and Loss

The actual expenditure on 33 items of work is in many cases more than the expenditure held admissible by the Forest Department. This inadmissible extra expenditure besides the other expenses in some cases reduce the income of the societies. Some societies maintain jeeps at costs which they cannot afford to meet. Peons are employed and the expenditure on them is inadmissible. Societies pay audit fees equal to 1 per cent of the total value of the coupe and this high expenditure is met from the reduced income of the societies. The district Federations collect 2 per cent of the operational costs as their fees.

The forests in Maharashtra with some exception of Melghat, Chandrapur and some areas in Satpura, are not that rich to give handsome sale preceeds to the societies in general. Many coupes are not rich in teak wood. They have more of fire-woods. This picture is not found in Dangs area of Gujarat. The societies are getting good profits in Dangs area for which the mean reason is good coupes giving handsome yields to the societies.

Thus, in general the economic viability of the societies is very much less in majority of cases in Maharashtra. Further, the fulfilling of the main objective of economic uplift of the tribal community whose main source of livelihood is the forest is not adequately met.

The economic viability gets further reduced because the societies in general have failed to tap other sources of income and employment except the coupes. The other sources are collection of minor forest produce, construction works (roads, buildings, percolation tanks, etc.) in the area. Sincere efforts to secure these works are not made by majority of the societies. On the other hand, expenditure on pay and allowances, meetings, rent of office, etc. is increasing. This is also one of the main reasons as to why societies are unable to pay bonus or profits to their members in majority of the cases.

The survey of Dhule district revealed that despite the movement, quite a substantial forest revenue is collected either through the agency of forest contractors or by the Department itself. This explains the need to boost the economic viability of these societies. Out of 56 societies in Dhule District, 17 are defunct. Of the remaining some are subsisting on marginal profits. Thus, many are not economically in a sound state. For the purpose of determining the viability of the society, it is necessary that a society should annually get coupes having a minimum estimated gross realisation of Rs. 1 lakh from the sale of the material.

Social and Cultural Aspect

Coming to the social and cultural aspects of the working of these societies, we have to think of the welfare activities undertaken by the societies. The only available data is regarding the amount spent on this item. This amount has the following three sources, viz., one per cent of wage as per formula, grants-in-aid and owned funds.

It is seen in Maharashtra that grants-in-aid account for a major share of the funds utilised for welfare activities and that the societies contribution out of its own profits is very meagre. Every new society used to get Rs. 1500 as grant for the first three years. The findings of the survey reveal that many of the societies could not furnish the details of the socio-cultural activities undertaken by them. The office bearers are not clear about the welfare activities. The labourers contacted at coupes seated that they themselves managed to get the drinking water. Very few society really constructed good sheds for residence. The Forest and Co-operation Department too are not seen taking adequate interest in this matter. A negligible amount of Rs. 2 to Rs. 5 per member is spent for welfare activities, like providing drinking water during coupe operations and in very few cases on distribution of slates and books. Some of the societies out of the accrued amount of profit have taken such works which directly or indirectly do not provide any benefit to the members in that area.

On the contrary, we find a picture quite contrast in Dangs Pradesh of Gujarat. Here the main sponsoring agency is the Sarva Seva Kendra. It runs 31 Balwadis, 30 Adult Education Classes and have distributed 450 Ambar Charkhas to Adivasis in the area which gives each family a wage of Rs. 7 to Rs. 8 per day. This agency is able to spend also on welfare programmes like sanctioning medical aid and educational assistance to its members. The agency can sanction lumpsum amounts upto Rs. 100 to the members whose children are college-going. Similarly, cash upto Rs. 53 is given as medical aid in deserving cases. It is seen that agency could spend on social welfare activities like:

(a) Distribution of food grains free of cost,
(b) Medical aid,
(c) Educational aid,
(d) Contribution of Relief Fund of the Chief Minister,
(e) Governor's Relief Fund,
(f) Dangs Shibirs,
(g) Contribution to Prime Minister's Relief Fund, and
(h) Other assistance.

The total expenditure on welfare activities for 1976 was Rs. 1,85,419. This explains the interest taken by the said Agency in welfare activities for the benefit of the members and the society in general.

One conclusion that may be drawn is that on the whole, the societies were well on economic front, but they have a poor progress on social and cultural fronts.

SOME ISSUES INVOLVED

The major administrative issues involved in the management of the societies are:

(1) Inadequate expenditure allowed on admissible items,
(2) Inadequate coverage of the items of expenditure and its consequences on the financial position of the societies,
(3) Delay in the settlement of final accounts,
(4) Inadequate coverage of allocation for welfare programmes,
(5) System of auditing, and
(6) Vague realisation or ways for achievement of goals.

One of the major complaints of the societies against the Forest Department is that they have to spend huge amount from their share of net realisation to meet extra expenses on admissible and uncovered items. Hence, they incur losses. It is also true that many societies tend to be extravagant or poor in their management which accounts for excess expenditure.

As regards final settlement of accounts, although, societies lag behind in submitting proper accounts in time, the Forest Department should come out with more imagination, innovation and understanding in handing this issue. Similarly, the nature of auditing should be more problem-solving and consultative rather than inspectional.

In order to minimise the malpractices in the management of societies, it is necessary that:

(a) Literacy campaign should be organised by the Societies and Federations among the tribals,
(b) Members of societies should be educated about their rights and responsibilities,
(c) Frequent and effective supervision of coupes and sale depots need to be arranged, and
(d) Better quality of staff at all levels should be appointed.

As regards achieving of goal, it is felt by most people who are associated with the movement that the societies have largely, if not utterly, failed in creating additional employment. They are able to provide employment in Maharashtra for not more than 100 days in a year per worker.

REFLECTIONS REGARDING THE IMPACT OF THE MOVEMENT WITH REFERENCE TO VIABILITY OF THE SOCIETIES

It would not be wrong if we contend that the short-term goals of the movement are ensuring growth of the movement by setting up adequate number of societies, and ensuring fair wages by removing exploitative practices, and the long-term goals are of building up leadership in Adivasis to run the movement and bringing about all round development of the tribal people.

From the point of view of achieving the goal of adequate number of societies it can be said that both the States, *prima facie* have achieved an adequate spread of the primary forest labour cooperatives. However, it would require in depth study to know whether there are really adequate number of societies to cover that size of Adivasi population which requires the benevolences at the auspices of these societies. Also, although the number of societies seems to have considerably gone up in both the States and looks quite impressive, the real question is that of the efficient functioning of the societies and their total viability to achieve the objectives. The progressive decline in the number of societies setting A and B audit classes does not assure us of the viability of the societies to that effect more and more societies are getting involved in misappropriation and the number of defunct societies and societies on the verge of meagre profits is slowly increasing at the aggregate level. The size of the society is a point on which hinges the economics of the society. What should be the optimum size of the society to lend it viability to achieve its short-term as well as long-term goals. This is also a matter of empirical study. The size of the societies is growing smaller in Maharashtra and this is not a happy sign towards achieving viability. Besides, the problem posed by size, we have to note other matters like growing extent of non-participation of members in the actual work undertaken by the societies, their growing reliance on non-members, somewhat declining tendencies in turnover with the exception of Dangs Pradesh and some few other areas in Maharashtra, declining trend in giving more employment and income and growing involvement in cases of misappropriations, etc. Do these problems give us a feeling that the societies are optimally viable to achieve the desired objectives? No. It is necessary and urgent to pay attention to the problems being faced by the societies in particular and the movement in general. For this, the cooperative and the Forest Departments should both show more imagination, innovation and understanding in guiding the movement.

One thing is sure that the growth of the movement mainly brings on the growing availability of the forest coupes and planned phased development of forest-based industries simultaneously. Upon these two factors, depend the optimum growth of the society to lend it viability to do good to its members as well as to the forest-based community. But the movement in general seems to be faltering exactly on these very counts. One should not be surprised to witness the stunted growth of the movement very soon.

So far as Gujarat is concerned, except Southern Gujarat, there are no dense forests in the State. That is why we witness a good deal of viability amongst majority of societies in Dangs Pradesh compared to societies in other areas in that State. The majority of the society in Gujarat are organised in Dangs Pradesh, Baroda, Bharuch, Surat and Balsad areas. It is also heartening to note that in most of the societies of the above districts, the actual management is in the hands of tribals. But, even then we cannot claim that they have covered all the Adivasis and all their villages fully and ameliorated the living conditions of Adivasis to an appreciable extent.

In Maharashtra a little more than 1/4th of the families in the villages from which the societies draw their membership are associated with the societies. There are still a number of villages from which they could not draw more than 5 members. Not a very large number of families of members and non-member workers have been directly benefited by the societies. There is still the serious phenomenon of indebtedness among a large number of member and non-member families of Adivasis. During the course of a survey of Dhule District conducted in 1973-74, as many as 94 families in a sample of 193 families were found indebted to the money lenders, despite efforts of debt resumption. The picture may be different in other districts but it shows that societies have not succeeded in giving more income and employment to the Adivasis and save them from the clutches of *Sahukars.* Of course, we cannot blame societies alone. The viability of the societies gets further reduced because besides their problems of getting good coupes, they have on the whole failed to tap other additional sources of employment as explained earlier. There are exceptions to this picture here and there.

Regarding the objective of ensuring fair wages, the forest labourers societies have helped to eliminate the contractor's agency to some extent. Still substantial share of earnings and profits in the forest working goes to contractors engaged in transport and processing units practically owned by the private sector. The Federations could not adequately and satisfactorily develop the forest-based industries. Forest-based industries and their simultaneous phased development along with coupe-operations assume great importance for developing the tribal community and the forest areas. Adivasis in many areas depend to a great extent on the forestry operations. By and large, they do not have skilled workers and hence they have less scope for employment in outside industrial belts. That is why forest areas increasingly require more forest-based and processing industries which will induce intensive and extensive utilisation of human and natural resources of the forest area and which ultimately will provide large scale employment to the tribal community. To their misfortune, although this requirement is realised by the concerned authorities, it has not been acted upon fully and here the whole federal structure of the Forest Labour Co-operatives showed its inefficacy. Especially, the forests of Melghat in Amravati and that of Chandrapur district in Maharashtra are rich in forest resources which provides a great challenge to the administration for establishment of large scale and small scale forest-based industries. The Federal structure could have done much to start adequate training-*cum*-production centres. The officials of Maharashtra Rajya Jungle Kamgar Sahakari Sangh Limited conducted a market survey with the assistance of Small Scale Industries Services Institute of the Central Government and it was found that there is a great promise for the establishment of small scale multipurpose workshops for manufacture of doors, windows, packing cases, photo frames, agricultural implements, furniture, etc. The Sangh prepared projects for starting production-*cum*-training centres in Thane, Nasik, and Dhule Districts and these have been approved. Similar centres are to be set-up in Nagpur and Kinwat also. For their success, Government needs to provide adequate funds and assure supply of raw material at reasonable rates.

With the establishment of Forest Development Corporation, many of the forest areas covered by the area of operation of the Forest Labour Co-operatives especially in Thane and Nasik circles have been transferred to the Corporation and the very existence of the societies is at stake. These societies need to be suitably accommodated in the working of the Corporation and ensured that they are not turned into labour contract societies only.

Now, coming to the long-term objective of building up Adivasi leadership in the movement in particular, the statistics are impressive. For example, 81 per cent members of these societies are Adivasis, 82 per cent Chairmen of these societies are Adivasis, 60 per cent Chairmen of the District Federations are Adivasis and 66.42 per cent Adivasis are on the committees of District Federations.

Regarding the employment of tribals in this set-up, the position is as follows:

(i) 72 per cent are Adivasi employees,
(ii) 32 per cent are Adivasi Secretaries,
(iii) 75 per cent are Adivasi Accountants,
(iv) 51 per cent are Adivasi Depot Clerks,
(v) 90 per cent are Adivasi Coupe Agents,
(vi) 97 per cent are Adivasi Mukadams,
(vii) 90 per cent are Adivasi Coupe Watchmen,
(viii) 76 per cent are Adivasi Peons,
(ix) 51 per cent are Adivasi Clerks,
(x) 50 per cent are Adivasi Drivers and Cleaners,
(xi) 24.2 per cent are Adivasi employees in District Federations,
(xii) 50 per cent are Adivasi Accountants in District Federations,
(xiii) 25.6 per cent are Adivasi Supervisors in the District Federations, and
(xiv) 27 per cent are Adivasi Clerks in District Federations.

From the above statistics, it is seen that the major impact of the movement is in creating leadership from among the Adivasi themselves. The District Federations in later phases could replace much the role of sympathisers and private sponsoring agencies.

The organisation of the societies on a large scale was responsible for the creation of new leadership of Adivasis which today serves the needs not only of the Forest Labourers Co-operative Societies but also of the other social and economic spheres of the Adivasi life to some extent in general. However, this is a quantitative achievement. The qualitative achievement is not satisfactory on the criterion of effective participation in the movement. The extent of employment of Adivasis in the societies and the Federations is much satisfactory. But by now, the employment of the Adivasis in them should have been complete and full.

Coming to the long-term objective of bringing about all-round development of the tribal community, the movement has shown its weakness fully. The Forest Labour Co-operative Societies have as one of their objectives, the general welfare of the Forest Labourers especially the members. In the jurisdiction of the managing committee and of its duties, the bye-laws state that in consultation with the District Federation, the committee may chalk out an annual programme of the welfare activities and obtain the approval of the Federation. This programme is comprehensive enough to include housing, water-supply, medical aid, creating hygienic conditions, inducing social worker to come and stay with the labourers and to educate them, undertaking educational and recreational programmes, supply of vegetables, oil, jaggery, etc., conducting Ashram Schools, hostels, etc., or giving aid to agencies which are engaged in maintaining Institutions, creating facilities for agricultural development, advancing loans towards the purchases of bullock carts, implements, etc. All these activities which are intended to bring about slowly but surely the all round development of the members and non-member workers directly and of other people in the area under the jurisdiction of the society indirectly.

How far these activities are undertaken by the societies? Is it that the societies could do almost nothing in this respect, why? Has it to do with the lack of total viability of the societies in general? And if these activities are undertaken, are they adequate and whether they are equally distributed among the members and among the villages? If not, why? If these activities are undertaken what is the change they could bring about in the socio-economic and cultural position of the villages? What all round developmental activities are taken at the village level and what welfare activities are taken at the family level? It would be interesting to know if these activities led the members to other co-operative efforts in other sphere of life, that is whether the co-operation in Forest Labour led the members to further cooperative efforts in agricultural operations, hunting, fishing, housing, marketing, education, etc.

The answer to these pertinent questions can be given after conducting a purposive survey to that effect. Presently, our impressions are that, though not all, a few of the societies in Maharashtra have provided some amenities and auxiliary benefits to the members in the area around them. The societies in Thana District had helped the schools and the famine relief workers and had taken part in extension activities to educate their members. In Dhule, one society had started a saw mill and another was running a shop for the benefit of the area. The major activities were those of giving medical aid and shelter in coupes. Recreational activities were also being provided by a few societies. Slates, pencils and books were distributed to children in some cases. A few of the members had received poles for house construction at concessional rates. Some societies have taken up works which directly or indirectly do not provide any benefit to the members in the area. So far as Gujarat is concerned in Dangs Pradesh, we witness some appreciable welfare activities undertaken by one sponsoring agency. But on the whole the societies have not even touched the fringe of the problem of bringing about all round development of the people. During the last 30 years, the movement could not create confidence and economic stability amongst the tribals. We cannot say confidently today that the movement has created appreciable affinity in the minds of the members as a whole about the societies, by providing at least rather adequate supply of schooling assistance, medical aid, housing, water supply, agricultural assistance, hygienic conditions, etc. They could not undertake, with some exceptions, activities like helping members for purchasing bullocks, carts, seeds, agricultural implements, fertilizers, etc.

Similarly, from the point of view of income and employment raising of the people associated in the working of the societies leading to betterment of their lives and of their families, if at all there is any increase in their employment in the area during the working in the coupes, it can be said that it may be attributable to policies of the Forest Department and not to the organisation of the societies. We have noted earlier that in general the societies have failed to generate additional income and employment in the area. The majority achievement of the societies is the rationalisation of the wage rate which was otherwise low and fluctuating much according to the interests of the contractors. Although there might be some grievance in this respect here and there, the workers are satisfied with the higher wage rate and continuity of employment in the coupe work. They are freed from the exploitative clutches of the contractors. However, this alone could not improve their housing conditions, number of live stock with them and also could not tackle indebtedness amongst them. Even today members are more from the upper stratum of the tribal community than from the lower stratum, and the latter are mere working members. To change this picture, much remains to be done at the upper levels of the organisational structure of the Forest Labourers Co-operative Societies. For all-round development of the people, the State and the District Federations have to be geared to the developmental project in the tribal areas. The upper federal structure could still be expected to plan and implement forest-based industries to develop the area. If large-scale industries are undertaken through the State and District federations it is possible that ancillary component manufacturing industries could be assigned even to the individual forest labour co-operatives. For want of adequate job done at this level, even today it is seen that only a little over 1/4th of the families in the villages are drawn to membership. So far the coverage is poor because of lack of total viability of the societies in general.

Thus the objective of bringing about an all round development of Adivasi community and that of the area is not achieved. However, considerable progress has been achieved in creating leadership, bringing Adivasi people to some urban contact and ensuring rationalised wages. Of course, one can not underestimate the role of these societies in tribal development. The best societies assures us that such societies can become the instrument of betterment of the lives of the Adivasis. Our need today is that of developing the primary units into viable societies, although it is conceded that more societies is also a need of the area and the tribal people.

Forest Economy

About 74.74 million ha. or 22.7 per cent of the land area of India is classified as forest, but only 40 per cent of this area is actually under tree cover. The large scale deforestation and over-felling of trees have set in motion a chain of events that have threatened the ecological security of the nation and have created a situation where:

(i) Out of 328 million ha. as much as 175 million ha. is believed to have been affected by soil erosion, salinity and water-logging and another 40 million ha. is flood prone every year.[1] Yet another estimate indicate that 85 million ha. land has gone out of production for such reasons.

(ii) Crop lands have become devoid of protective cover from desiccating and soil eroking winds. Nearly 4.0 million ha. is badly gullied and ravined and expanding at the rate of almost 8000 ha. every year. More than 6000 million tonnes of top soil (about 9 tonnes per person) carrying 5.32 million tonnes of nutrients slip away each year.

(iii) Siltation of 487 reservoirs of major and medium irrigation and hydel projects has become a great concern for the nation. Surveys indicate that storage capacity of Nizamsagar lake in Andhra Pradesh has been reduced by 63 per cent in 44 years; of Mayurakshi and Mainthon reservoir by 10 per cent in 20 years; of Panchi reservoir by 12 per cent in 19 years; and of Bhakra reservoir by 6 per cent in 16 years.

(iv) The Himalayan eco-system has considerably deteriorated due to which floods ravage the Indo-Gangetic plains almost every year taking their toll in terms of human life and property. Land slides are causing immense damage by uprooting many habitations annually.

(v) Floods and droughts have almost become an annual feature. Nearly 8 million ha. of land, 26.5 million people and 42.37 million ha. of cropped area were affected by droughts during 1982-83 in 15 states, union territories.

(vi) The volume of annual rainfall is estimated at 370 million ha. metres (mhm) of which less than 80 mhm is available as ground water which is a direct source for drinking and irrigation. Deforestation has caused lowering of ground water table due to less percolation of rain-water in the ground.

(vii) In cold and hot deserts ecological degradation is of far greater consequence to the community and rehabilitation of the ecology has to be taken up with far greater urgency and priority. Immobilisation of desert brooks no delay.

(viii) In coastal areas descaturing winds and spread of saline water have done immense damage to the human and cattle populations besides affecting production.

Forests and wasteland cover about one-third of the geographical area of the country and nearly 540 million rural people depend on forests for their daily needs such as fuelwood, fodder, fibre, timber and bamboo needed for agricultural implements, cattle sheds, hutments and fencing material, edible roots, rhizomes, leaves, flowers, fruits and nuts, etc. The onus is on forestry sector, therefore, to extend following benefits to the population:

(i) Mankind has used fuelwood to cook food and for warmth from times immemorial. Wood is the dominent domestic fuel for rural poor and for many of the urban poor as well. Fuelwood is preferred because it can be used without complex equipment, both for use and distribution and can be acquired at little cost. For the poor there is often no alternative to fuelwood or other locally available organic materials. It is of interest that about 10 Mega-jules (MJ) per person per day energy intake is required as food whereas about 12–15 MJ daily per person is required for minimum levels of cooking. The Fuelwood Study Committee[2] observed that as against the present requirement of about 133 million tonnes of fuelwood per annum, the recorded annual production from forest land is only 15 million tonnes. The Committee recommended stepping up the annual fuelwood plantation programmes upto 1.5 million ha. per year during the 10 years period besides distribution of 800 million seedlings per year to meet the projected demand of fuelwood.

(ii) Nearly 10 per cent of the world's livestock population live in the country and due in concentration of bovine population in the forest areas overgrazing and erosion are rampant. The drain on forests by domesticated animals is estimated to be twice that of fuelwood in terms of biomass. Over-grazing has largely deteriorated the soil productivity and net production of forests besides inhibiting natural regeneration of tree species. Livestock development has lately become a major rural development programme, but the objective of this programme, will most certainly remain unrealised in the absence of a strong fodder base which determines the productivity of the animals. In addition to the development of forest and waste lands it is necessary to motivate the beneficiaries to increase the grass and top feed production.

(iii) Roundwood timber requirement is estimated as 65 million m^3 by 2000 AD for agricultural implements, cattle sheds, hutments, fencing material, houses and for forest-based industries, etc. as against present production of about 12 million m^3 during 1980-81. It is estimated that shortages in housing in rural areas have crossed 17 million dwelling units. Similarly, shortages of raw materials are felt by forest-based units producing plywood, hardboard, paper, newsprint, rayon, etc. To meet the demands, it is necessary to practice intensive forestry, social forestry and farm forestry for increasing production of timber and other forest produce.

(iv) According to the National Commission on Agriculture, Minor Forest Produce (MFP) have the potential to bring about an economic revolution for tribal and other rural people. During drought and adverse climatic condition, the forest-dwellers mainly depend on MFP collection. Regeneration, collection, processing and marketing of MFP can generate 20 million standard Person Year employment. Development of MFP can make the country self-sufficient in respect of edible and non-edible oils, tannins, gums, essential oils, and in production of medicines, etc.

(v) There were about 250 communities of scheduled tribes in the country with a population of about 40 million in 1971. This population is estimated to be about 50 million in 1981. Forests represent for them a way of life; a home, a culture; for worship; food and other wherewithal; employment and income. Nearly 6 per cent of the tribal population of the country is involved in shifting cultivation, 2 per cent reside in forest villages and about 5 per cent are encroachers of forest lands. It is necessary to link forestry development programmes with economic development of tribals.[3]

(vi) Unemployment and underemployment pose a chronic problem in rural areas. This gets accentuated during the lean period of agricultural operations. The National Rural Employment Programme has been designed to generate 300 million to 400 million mandays employment every year. The Rural Landless Employment Guarantee Scheme envisages to provide 100 days' employment to one member of every landless household every year. Forestry has to play a major role in generation of employment under the above scheme.

(vii) The forest dwellers largely derive their sustenance directly from bush-meat, honey, a wide variety of tubers, rhizomes, leaves, secculent shoots, flowers, fruits, nuts, etc. It is necessary to integrate production of these items with timber and other forest-produce.

(viii) Nitrogen is a limiting factor for increasing agricultural production. These have a manurial value which can be realised in the form of leaf manure or through atmospheric-nitrogen fixation by leguminous plants. Use of bio-fertilizers needs to be promoted.

Forest is gaining worldwide importance in national development. The current world strategy for development of forestry in rural areas of the developing countries identified the following priorities:

(i) eradication of poverty on the basis of greater access of rural people to benefits generated by forestry activities;

(ii) equitable participation of the rural people in forestry and forest-based activities; and

(iii) integration of percepts of wise environmental management and performance of the forest resource-base required to secure optimal flow of benefits for the present and future.

India's strategy for forestry development now identifies two priorities. Firstly, through social forestry programmes to supply fuelwood, fodder, small timber and MFP to the rural population, and secondly, to develop production forestry to supply the growing needs of forest industries, defence and communications. Social forestry programme has to be essentially people-oriented. Forestry profession has already started growing trees in collaboration with local communities for multiple purposes in non-forest areas. Amongst other things the strategy includes:

(i) multiple choice of suitable species for different habitats and purposes;

(ii) spatially diffused small-scale production units; and

(iii) devolution of authority of forest department by allowing autonomous management by user groups.

The conquest of poverty and unemployment has been a major concern of the successive five year plans. In spite of sustained efforts over the last 30 years, the incidence of poverty in the country is high. In 1977-78, about 48 per cent of the people were living below the poverty line and in rural areas the percentage was still higher at about 51 per cent. Such population includes mainly landless labourers, small and marginal farmers, rural artisans, scheduled castes and scheduled tribes. These people have either no asset or asset with low productivity, few relevant skills and no regular full time jobs or very lowly paid jobs. Following three broad types of beneficiary programmes in forestry sector can improve their economy and bring them above the poverty line within a stipulated period—

(i) Land-based activities viz., development of forest villages, settlement of shifting cultivation, etc.
(ii) Forest development-based activities inside as well as outside the forest areas.
(iii) Minor Forest Produce-based activities.

HISTORICAL PERSPECTIVE

Forest Economy in Pre-British Days

It is difficult to reconstruct the picture of the economy of the 'forest dwellers' before the British intervention. Such reconstruction has to be done largely from the waitings of the colonial administrators themselves. It would seem, however, that by and large the rural communities enjoyed untramelled use of the forests and wasteland in their vicinity. This would be true to villages practising settled (plains) agriculture as well as those that depended more directly on their forest habital. In Garhwal for example, "the waste and forest lands never . . . attracted the attention of former (i.e. pre-British) Governments". While the native kings did subject the produce of the forests (such as medicinal plants) to a small cess as and when they were exported, the products of the forests consumed by the people themselves were not taken into account. Similarly, it was reported from Madras that villages had traditionally owned all forests within their boundaries. Such a situation would have arisen in a state of equilibrium, arrived at through a process of conflict and struggle between the Forest State and the village communities under its aegis. This equilibrium entailed payment of a certain tribute by the peasantry to the feudal authority, which in turn recognised the existence and continuation of certain communally-held rights in relation to forest and waste land. The freedom enjoyed here was extensive—according to an official handbook of the Forest Department (hereafter FD), under the "oriental governments" that preceded the Raj, "anyone was accustomed, without led or hindrance, to get what he wanted from the forest to graze his cattle where he liked, and to clear jungle growth for cultivation wherever he listed."[4]

The forest dwellers, of course, depended on their natural habitat in a multitude of ways. An adequate forest cover was ecologically necessary to sustain cultivation on hilly terrain, whether it was *jhum* (shifting cultivation) or cultivation of the terraced variety. In addition, the forests themselves provided a reserve of food that could be consumed throughout the year. The Indian Famine Commission of 1881, has detailed 31 species of trees whose produce was consumed as food by the tribes of the Satpura Hills, in different seasons—including fruits, flowers, buds, young shoots, seeds, etc. both in raw and cooked form (In fact, peasants and tribals in forest areas normally know of over a hundred natural products, besides the staples that can be gathered without cultivation). Where animal husbandry was a valuable appendage to cultivation (as in the Himalayan foot hills), the forests were a prime source of fodder.

It is important to stress that this dependence was institutionalised through a variety of cultural and religious mechanisms which enable the forest dwellers to sustain their existence. It is striking to see how, in many of the myths and legends, the deep sense of identity with the forest is emphasised even today. The area cultivated by different families under *jhum* adhered to boundaries established and respected by tradition. Dietrich Brandis, the first Inspector General of Forests (hereafter IGF), found that the sacred groves, the traditional form of sacred presentation were very numerous and existed in nearly all the provinces of British India. As late as in 1953, an eminent botanist reported that, "the largest *deodar* (Himalayan Cedar) are those which are planted near temples and which are venerated and protected from injury."[5]

Early Period of British Rule

Among British colonies,"India stood pre-eminent by reason of its vastness, the density of the population and the seemingly immeasurable extent of its natural resources". The first show of interest in forestry—the reservation of teak in Malabar in 1806—was predictably dictated by imperialist considerations. With oaks forest vanishing in England, a permanent supply of suitable timber was required for the Royal Navy and "for the safety of the empire depended on its wooden walls."[6] This was the period of fierce competition between the colonial powers, and Indian teak, the most durable of shipbuilding timbers, saved England during the war with Napoleon and the later maritime expansion Ships were built in dockyards in Goa and on the Malabar coast, as well as from teak imported into England.

The Railways

The early years of railways expansion saw unprecedented assault on the more accessible forests. Great chunks of forest were destroyed to meet the demand for railway sleepers. No supervision was exercised over the felling operations, and a large number of trees being felled whose logs could not be utilised. The sub-Himalayan forests of Garhwal and Kumaon, for example, were all "felled in even to desolation," while "thousands of trees were felled which were never removed, nor was their removal possible."[7] Private contractors, both Indian and European, were chiefly responsible for this devastation the forests of native rajahs not escaping their hand. Before the coal mines of Raniganj became fully operative, the railways companies also indulged in widespread use of local timbers as fuel for the locomotives. In the North-Western Provinces, the railway companies drew their fuel directly—and cheaply—from local timber until 1880s, causing considerable deforestation in the Doab.

This depredation finally awoke the colonial authorities to the fact that India's forests were not inexhaustible. Railways expansion continued unabated and the methods by which private enterprise were working the forests forced the States to step in to safeguard "their long-term imperial interests."[8] Dubbing the forest administration upto the mutiny a "melancholy failure", the Governor General had in 1862 called for the establishment of a department that could ensure the sustained availability of the enormous requirements of the different railways for sleepers. As one officer later remionisced: "The Forest Department was started because government became aware that the magnificent forests of India and Burma were being worked by private enterprises in a reckless and wasteful manner, and were likely to become exhausted if supervision were not exercised."[9] The crisis was all the more acute since only three Indian timbers—teak, *sal*—and *deodar*— were strong enough in their natural state to be utilised as railway sleepers. *Sal* and teak, being available near railway lines in peninsular India, were very heavily worked out in early years necessitating expeditions into the North-Western Himalayas to search for deodar forest. The *Deodar* of the Satlej valley was rapidly exhausted in the years following the inception of the FD, leaving only some *deodar* forests in the Jamuna valley as a possible reserve. From these latter forests alone, over 6,50,000 deodar sleepers were supplied in the period 1869-85.[10]

It was in this situation that the imperial FD was formed, in 1864 with the assistance of German foresters. However, the task of checking the deforestation of the earlier decades and "consolidation of the forest estate" could not be accomplished without the assertion of State monopoly right over forest. It was in this dual sense that the railways proved to be the watershed with respect to forest administration in India—the need was felt to start an appropriate department and for its effective functioning the enactment of legislation to curtail the previously exercised unlimited rights of users was required. The latter feature marked the beginning of a progressive curtailment of these rights, and was an especially difficult task since it ran contrary not only to the traditional practices of villages and especially tribal communities, but also to earlier colonial agrarian policy in India. While, by and large, the British followed a *laissez-faire* policy that allowed the villagers to freely roam about in the forests and utilise its produce, there is also definite evidence from certain areas that "all land of every description was made over in absolute right to the community, subjects only to the yearly payment of rent fixed."[11]

The first attempt at asserting State monopoly right was through the Indian Forest Act of 1865, which was replaced by a much more comprehensive piece of legislation 13 years later. The provisions of the 1878 Act ensured that the State could demarcate 'valuable' tracts of forest, needed especially for railway purposes, and retain enough flexibility over the remaining extent of forest land to revise its policy from time to time. Monopoly right was established by a legal sleight of hand, which sought to establish that the customary use of forest by the villagers was based not on 'right' but on 'privilege' and that this 'privilege' was exercised only at the mercy of the local rulers. Since the British were the rulers, the rights of absolute ownership were held to be vested in them. As one officer bluntly stated in 1873, "the right of conquest is the strongest of all rights—it is a right against which there is no appeal."[12] The Act was the means by which the success of this sleight of hand was assured.

ALIENATION OF FOREST DWELLERS

This progressive diminution of 'rights' and the consequent loss of control over their natural resources evoked a sharp reaction from the forest communities. From the early days of forest administration, there have been revolts in different tribal areas centred around the question of forests. These revolts, which attempted to restore a 'golden past' where the tribal roamed freely in his forest habitat were swiftly crushed by the colonial State. Nevertheless, they recurred throughout the period in almost all tribal areas where "forests have always been the citadel of social movements against successive Government".

Even where the discontent did not manifest itself in popular revolt, the loss of control over forests was acutely felt by the rural communities, thus, deprived. The reservation of forests in Garhwal in 1913 was followed by extensive social movements in 1916 and 1921, the latter coinciding with the first non-cooperation movement and engulfing large areas of Garhwal and Kumaon. While these upsurges forced the government to de-reserve large forest areas, the discontent over the onerous forests restrictions was manifested in the continuing unwillingness of the villagers to cooperate with the FD in its tasks. This historical process had several salient features that need to be commented upon. Fundamentally, the demarcation and fencing of large tracts of reserved forest meant an effective loss of control by the forest dwellers over their habitat—a control so necessary of the sustinance of their existence. Inevitably, increased pressure was felt on the forests that did remain open to them, thereby hastening their destruction.

Secondly, though the State had, in certain areas, made over some forests under the settlement for the villagers to utilise (the so-called "third class" or "village" forests), the loss of community ownership had effectively broken the link between man and forests. Thus, the superintendent of Dehradun, commenting on the attitude of the villagers of Jaunsar-Bawar towards the forest settlement, said that "not altogether without reason, the villagers believe that any self-denial or trouble they may exercise in preserving and improving their third class forests will end in appropriation of the forests by the forest department as soon as they become commercially valuable."[13] The anthropologist, V. Elvin too has talked about the "melancholy" effect forest reservation had on the tribals of Middle India, for whom nothing aroused more resentment against the government than the taking away of the forest they regarded as "their own property."[14]

Thirdly, the large areas of forests under the Indian rajahs were also drawn in, though indirectly into the orbit of colonial capitalist expansion (This was notably the case in the North-West Himalayas, where the finest stands of *deodar* were found in the forests of Tehri Garhwal and the Punjab Hill Chiefs.) The exploitation of these forests, either by agency of the colonial State or in the later stages directly by the raja, introduce qualitative change in the relationships between ruler and the subject. Over time, the native rulers became "generally very much alive to the value of their forest properties," they severely curtailed the traditionally held rights of the subject communities. Thus, the raja of Tehri Garhwal leased valuable tracts of *deodar* forest to the British which diverted of any existing rights of user on part of the surrounding villages were worked from 1885 to 1925. The enormous value of the forests being evidenced by the average annual profit of over Rs. 1.6 lakh between 1910 and 1925. He did not renew the lease and henceforth worked the forests (with professional help from the colonial FD) exclusively for his own profit. As a result, there were sporadic *dhandaks* or forest movements in Tehri Garhwal since the early years of the century.

This history of conflict and struggle can be seen essentially as emanating from alternative conceptions of property rights and obligations. There did not exist a developed notion of private property in these tribal and peasant communities where the relationship to the overload was expressed in terms of mutual obligations which had to be fulfilled. Colonial rule, on the other hand, was based on a notion of private property that ran contrary to the experience of these communities. Moreover, the State dealt with its subjects individually in an impersonal fashion by the medium of an abstract rule of law that was theoretically neutral. As a consequence, the individual was now brought directly under the subjugation of the colonial State without the benefit of the mutual aid system of the community acting as a cushion. The tribals were confronted with the vagaries of the colonial market economy that continually eroded their life-styles—simultaneously, the assertion of State primacy over natural resources deprived them of an important subsidiary means of subsistence. J.V. Voelcker, an agricultural export, called in by the colonial authorities, summed it up thus: "The tendency of our system of Government has, to a considerable extent, been to break up village communities, and now for the most part they are heterogeneous bodies rather than communities."[15]

Bureaucratic Response

The circumstances in which State monopoly right was asserted and the unrest in its wake brought to the fore the division within the colonial bureaucracy—a division between the revenue and law and order administration, on the one hand, and the forest department; on the other. This schism was based on antagonism, of interest and differences of stand point.

The district officer, entrusted with the maintenance of law and order, was concerned at the discontent engendered by the new forest, the revenue-generating possibilities of forest land were not immediately apparent. The roots of this antagonism were succinctly stated by C.F. Amery in the first volume of the "Indian Forester:

> Upto a very few years ago the district officer had sole control of all lands in his district, and the unoccupied lands were his chief means of conferring patronage; he could give or lease them or confer or confirm privileges in them. If troubled with lawless tribes *budmashes* he could offer them land as an inducement to settle to honest pursuits. And if a keen shikari, the forests were his sole and undisputed game preserves.

> Apart too from all departmental and personal interests, his standpoint is different, his recollection carries him back to days when the forest as such yielded to little revenue, that it was often as well to let the people help themselves to its products and graze their cattle in it, as to be at the worry and cost of collecting the revenue; when every acre broken up for cultivation yielded more revenue than a hundred acres of forest land besides enlarging the capabilities of the district and promoting the well-being of the people; to a time when in fact the amount of forest broken up for cultivation became the recognised measure of a district officer's capability tact.

Interestingly, the objections to the work of FD, though essentially relating to the increased threat to law and order, were often couched in more readily comprehensible terms Voelcker, for example criticising the FD for not directly serving the interest of agriculture, advocated the creation of "Fuel and Fodder Reserves". He justified the policy on the grounds that, in the long-run, any "possible diminution" of forest revenue "may be attended by increased revenue to the State from cultivated land".

The FD on their part strongly resented the impediments put in their path by the district administration. The early years of the "Indian Forester" contain several attacks on district officials who, though knowing "nothing of forest matters", had an influence on forest administration out of all proportion to their knowledge and "steadily opposed the rational treatment of the forests". Another frequent complaint was that the district officers were reluctant to hand over forests and waste lands that came under the operations of the Forest Act—and when they did, the endeavour was to enlarge the record-or-rights to the fullest extent. Forests were, thus, unnecessarily burdened with rights to the detriment of the government's legitimate revenue".

The State's response to this division was to entrust each arm of the bureaucracy with separate, apparently conflicting tasks. At the behest of Beden-Powel, one of the architects of the 1878 Act, forest settlements were effected in all cases by a land revenue or "civil" official, who was to ascertain the FD's requirements from the forest to be reserved, and then see "how far these requirements can be met". The civil officials, in addition, were to be in-charge of the punitive sanctions of the forest act, so as to "prevent any further interference with the people than is necessary for efficient protection". This 'carrot and stick' approach was called for by the 1894 resolution on forest policy, one necessitated by the "strict forest administration which has prevailed of late years (and) has given rise to serious discontent among the agricultural classes". This more 'lenient' policy, ostensibly dictated by considerations of serving the peasantry more directly, asked for more liberal provisions of fuel, fodder, grazing, etc. However, this provision for local requirements was to be made only "to the utmost point that is consistent with imperial interests".

This forest policy, which guided colonial administration upto 1947, envisaged the benevolent paternalism of the district official acting as an arbiter between the FD and the people. Closer cooperation and constant consultation between the FD and revenue officials was urged the maxim prescribed for the forest officer was one of *festina lente* (hasten gently) even if this involved a deviation from perfect measure of regeneration or the extraction of trees for local use over and above that laid down by the record-of-rights. At the same time it was stressed that the detailed application of these principles must depend on local conditions—whenever concessions were granted to the local population (such as the throwing open of reserved forests for grazing), it was best to make them for a limited period say 10 or 20 years so that they could be reviewed as circumstances changed.[16]

Forest Policy upto 1947

The administration of the forest 'estate' of British India was contingent on the strategic 'imperial interests is served—first, during the period of railways expansion, and later during the two world wars. At the same time, however, the FD had to generate an adequate revenue to justify its existence in keeping with a fundamental tenet of imperial policy viz.; that the administrative machinery had to be self-supporting. As such, a constant endeavour was to find markets for the multiple species of India's tropical forests—a difficult task, since in these rich mixed forests only a few species often comprising less than 10 per cent of the total crop were saleable. Another difficulty was that of communication—many forests, though containing commercially valuable species, were 'useless' due to their inaccessibility. The stagnant nature of industrial development in the colonial period thus, inhibited full commercial utilisation of forest produce.

Nevertheless, the FD consistantly showed a handsome surplus on account (Table 11.1). This was made possible by the requirements of urban centres for fuelwood, furniture, building materials, etc., while supply was facilitated by the improved communications, the railway network brought about. Thus, the forest of Garhwal provided bamboo and *sal* for the urban markets of Punjab and the United Provinces and for the military cantonments and hill stations that were a creation of colonial rule. The railways continued to be an important buyer and as late as in 1929, a government committee urged that the FD and the railways work closely together especially with regard to the treatment of railways sleepers pointing out that "in many cases the interests of the two departments are identical."[17]

TABLE 11.1

Revenue and Surplus of Forest Department, 1869-1925

Yearly average for the Period	*Revenue (Rs. million)*	*Surplus (Rs. million)*	*Percentage of Column 3 to Column 2*
1	2	3	4
1869-70 to 1873-74	5.6	1.7	30
1874-75 to 1878-79	6.7	2.1	31
1879-80 to 1883-84	8.8	3.2	36
1884-85 to 1888-89	11.7	4.2	36
1889-90 to 1893-94	15.9	7.3	46
1894-95 to 1898-99	17.7	7.9	45
1899-1900 to 1903-34	19.7	8.4	43
1904-05 to 1908-09	25.7	11.6	45
1909-10 to 1913-14	29.6	13.2	45
1914-15 to 1918-19	37.1	16.0	43
1919-20 to 1923-24	55.2	18.5	34
1924 to 1925	56.7	21.3	38

After years of research, the antiseptic treatment of inferior timbers (such as the *chir* and blue pines) for use as railway sleepers was made possible on a commercial scale in 1912. In the following year, the extensive pine forests of Garhwal were reserved—thus, largely obviating any need to import wood or to search for metal and concrete substitutes. The task export trade continued to be paying with over one million pounds of teak wood being imported annually into Britain from India and other countries. The development of Minor Forest Produce (MFP) was also taken up in the twentieth century. These MFP were found to have a variety of industrial uses abroad. As India was the only source in the Empire for several of the more valuable ones—e.g., resin and turpentine, tanning materials such as kuth and myrabolans and essential oils—the foreign trade in these products showed a rapid rise.

A feature common to different types of forest exploitation regardless of the end use was the exclusion of these communities into whose habitat such policies intruded. For the colonial administrators, forests which did not contain marketable produce were considered to have no value. According to G.P. Paul, when timber that floated down the Himalayan rivers had reached the catching stations in the plains, it hence forward entered into the useful necessities for the comfort of the human race thereby implying either the forests had no value for the hill agriculturists or were not meant for their use. Such an elitist orientation consistently denied the right of the forest dwellers over the natural resources in their vicinity—at the same time the mercantile interests of British colonial rule ensured that ecological considerations were generally of secondary importance. Historically, this attitude has been the precursor of the class orientation of Indian forestry right upto the present time.

The Two World Wars

The world wars saw India's forests being requisitioned for the imperial cause. In fact, it was only during the "Great War" that the enormous potential value of India's forests for the Empire was fully realised. Every possible effort was made to substitute indigenous timbers for imported ones. Timber and bamboos were supplied for construction of bridges, piers, wharves, buildings, huts and lines, and ships. In little over a year (April 1917 to October 1918) 228,076 tonnes of timber (excluding railway sleepers) were supplied by the specially created "'Timber Branch" of the Munitions Board, while 50,000 tonnes of fodder grasses were exported (in the same period) to help military operations in Egypt and Iraq. Approximately 1.7 million cubic feet of timber mostly teak) were exported annually between 1914 and 1919 and the indigenous resin industry proved to be a great boon at a time when American and French supplies were unavailable. Due to the war, various species previously unsaleable were no longer so.[18]

The impact of the second world war was more severely felt on the Indian forests. Early in 1940, a Timber Directorate was set-up in Delhi to channel supplies of forest produce from the provinces. India was the sole supplier of timber to the Middle Eastern theatre of war and later on the Allied Forces in Iraq and the Persian Gulf. The war become an over-ridding objective as timbers had to be found to replace the few that had hitherto ruled the market and were now unobtainable—the Forest Research Institute dedicated itself solely to this task. The cessation of the import of structural steel brought an urgent demand for wood substitutes too.

Table 11.2 gives an indication of the war demand and efforts to meet it. The figures relate to recorded fellings in State forests only, the available evidence points to considerable over-fellings in forests of both private owners and native States, as well as to unrecorded fellings in government forests—all to meet the war demand. While "fellings and sawings were pushed into the remotest forest jungles of the western Ghats", the only limit to the exploitation of previously unworked forests was the availability of labour. The recorded figures show an increase over pre-war out-turn of about 65 per cent. However, it was admitted that due to the varying circumstances in which felling took place, an accurate estimate of the damage done to forest capital was not possible for the government forests. On an average these excess fellings were estimated to be nearly six annual yields. The working plan prescriptions in reserved forests were "considerably upset by excess fellings during World War II. As can be seen from Table 11.2, the accelerated fellings in the last years of the war coincided with a sharp drop in the area covered by working plans implying much felling was carried out without the supervision required to ensure proper regeneration.

At the time of the building of the railway network, Indian forests proved to be an important strategic raw material in the imperial scheme of things. Having learnt their lesson at the time of the reservation of the forests, the colonial rules thenceforth retained control over forest resources especially those conveniently situated and containing timbers such as teak, *sal*, pine, and *deodar*. This naturally entailed a restriction on the use of forests by the surrounding population—a restriction regarded as 'invitable' if the paramount imperial interest was to be served.

The 1952 statement affirms that the 1894 policy "constitute the basis for the forest policy of India upto this day", while its "fundamental concepts," still hold good. Apart from the populist rhetoric in which it is couched, this policy share with its predecessor certain other important features:

TABLE 11.2

India's Forest and Second World War

Year	*Out-turn of Timber and Fuel (m. cu. ft.)*	*Out-turn of FD (Rs.)*	*Revenue of MFP (Rs.)*	*Surplus of FD (Rs.)*	*Area under sanctioned working plans (sq. miles)*
1937-38	270	11.9	—	—	62,532
1938-39	299	12.3	29.4*	7.2*	64,789
1939-40	294	12.1	32.0	7.5	64,976
1940-41	386	12.5	37.1	13.3	66,401
1941-42	310	12.7	46.2	19.4	66,583
1942-43	336	12.9	65.0	26.7	51,364
1943-44	374	15.5	101.5	44.4	59,474
1944-45	439	16.5	124.4	48.9	50,440

*Average for the period 1934-35 to 1938-39.

There is an explicit assertion of State monopoly right at the expense of the forest communities. This exclusion is legitimised in the name of the "national interest" so as to ensure that the "country as a whole" is not deprived of a "national asset" by the mere "accident of a village being situated close to a forest."

As in the 1894 statement, there is an enumeration of objectives without any examination of how far these aims could be conflicting both at the local and national levels. Thus, the main prongs of the policy were identified as six-fold, viz., the need for: (a) balanced and complementary land use, (b) checking denudation, (c) afforestation, (d) increased supplies of fuel, grazing, and small timber to the agriculturists, (e) sustained supply of timber and other forest produce requirement for defence, communications, and industry, and finally, (f) the need for the relation of maximum annual revenue in perpetuity consistant with objectives: (a) to (e). Yet there is no awareness of whether objective, (f) could at all be compatible with: (a) to (e) especially in a so-called "Welfare State". Moreover, the listing of objectives, without any clear priority being assigned among them, is understandable only in the context of the retention of the flexibility germane to the successful (from its own standpoint) implementation of colonial policy.

With increased forest exploitation, the forest communities have experienced a progressive loss of control over their habits. This deprivation has been manifest in a series of movements. While there were intermittent uprisings in the fifties and sixties, at the present time we find "unrest" in most forest areas. These movements, ranging from Uttarakhand in the North to Jharkhand in the East and Thane/Dhulia in the West, have been individually studied and reported on. The increasingly militant struggles have centred around the question of regaining community control over land and forest.

Given the history of continuing alienation and protest, the experience of Van (forest) Panchayats in Garhwal is instructive. A recent survey concluded that many of the panchayat forests managed by the villagers in Garhwal are in better condition than the reserved forests of the area.

The fuelwood crisis, though given prominence only of late has been affecting Indian agriculture—by the diversion of dung from manure to fuel—for at least a century. Voelcker had urged the creation of "fuel and fodder reserves" out of Government Waste lands while Howard in 1944 had mentioned that the wanted of villagers for fuel and small timber was the most important problem facing the FD, at the same time being "the most difficult of solutions". Despite this recognition, the Government diverted its own forest land (utilised for commercial forestry) to directly serve the agricultural population.

The last official reactiot to the firewood shortage has been to launch a Social Forestry (SF) programme. It "involves the people at all levels with raising forests as their own assets for their own use" while its main objective is to provide forest goods and services in rural areas where these are needed most."[19]

Government committees have recommended dynamic schemes for overcoming the shortage of firewood. Various organisational changes have also been suggested to ensure that SF schemes are properly implemented.

The need for "farm forestry" i.e., for each farm to be self-sufficient with respect to its requirements of fuel, fodder, and small timber had been talked of for some time. Similarly, with regard to the claim that the wonder tree 'Ku-babul' renamed Subabul by the Prime Minister at a national seminar in early 1981 will solve the problems of rural poverty and unemployment. It can be noted that the tree was introduced into India as early as in 1962. Its propagation by the State, however, comes only at a time when its usefulness as a source of paper pulp has also been established. At the same time, the paper industry has been severely hit by raw material shortages caused by its own over-exploitation of bamboo stocks. The Industry has been petitioning the government not only to lower pollution standards already very lax compared to those elsewhere and lift the ban on the export of certain varieties of paper, but also to raise "industry of certain varieties of paper, and also to raise industry-oriented" plantations, both in government forests and on private lands though SF schemes.

Since 1951, over 3.4 million ha. of forest land have been sequestered for different purposes, such as for agricultural use, road building, and river valley projects. The net result has been a considerable disturbance in the ecological balance leading to the increased incidence of floods, silting up of dams, drying up of perennial sources of water, etc.

In a sharply stratified Indian society, there are inherent compulsions towards the deterioration of the environment. While the rich destroy the environment indirectly through resource-wasteful lifestyles, and directly through exploitation of nature for profit, the poor are often forced to fall back upon nature for their very survival thereby using up resources in an unsustainable manner.

Though the needs of the rural communities have been explicitly recognised and articulated in the populist rhetoric of many policy documents, the actual implementation of policy has invariable concentrated on realising the productive function of the forests. If we want to stem the tide of rising poverty and all that goes with it, there is no escape from implementing programmes of planting trees and raising village forests on a massive scale particularly in thickly populated areas where there are very little forests and a large number of villagers are living below the grinding poverty line by making available the necessary funds and by creating an effective organisation to implement it by involving people.

DEPENDENCE OF TRIBALS ON FORESTS

Tribal people have abundant self-respect and are conscious to preserve their social and cultural identity. On account of various pressures exerted on them they retreated into forests and hill tracts over the centuries. They are simple, nascinating, sincere, innocent, colourful, hospitable and as lively as they are lovely. Majority of them are poor and lead a hard life but not a discontented one. They are physically tough and adapted to the rugged terrain which they inhabit. Civilisation has not spoilt them, sophistication has not polluted them, violence has not encroached upon their peaceful pursuits to which they are dedicated. Their wants are primarily basic needs of life like food, shelter and clothing.

Forests are their cherished home through generations. It is an abode of their mother-deity. The tribal communities could subsist for thousands of years with reasonable standards of health and abode mainly because forests provided them food, water, shelter, clothes, medicines and employment.

In times of distress like famine, forests are their last succour. Even in areas where forests do not exist, the tribals still visit the distant forests periodically and try to get their traditional requirements from there, however, insignificant they may appear to be.

The Scheduled Tribes traditionally collect many items of daily use from the forests which are necessary for their day-to-day sustenance. Food items from forest are gathered by the young, old and the women-folk. A survey done in forest regions of Gujarat revealed that nearly 22 per cent to 27 per cent of the elderly persons and 70-72 per cent of the children go to forest for collection of tubers, leaf vegetables, bamboo, shoots and a host of other products. Another survey (1980-81) in Bastar district indicated that average household (having two adult members, one child and one old person) on an average earns Rs. 1500 a year (against total annual income of Rs. 1750) from sale of MEP without any initial input or risk. The size of the contribution to the family income is significant and cannot be overlooked in the context of rural situation in the country and more so of the subsistence economy of tribal areas.

Fuelwood in the context of tribal people is not merely used for cooking but also for warmth and lighting purposes. By and large, these people do not have any warm clothes to protect them from the winter and the only method by which they keep themselves warm is by being near the fire. The fire also gives them light in the absence of any other means of lighting in the area. Fire also helps them in keeping the wild animals at bay. In fact, the material existence of the people depends on forest to such an extent that this cannot be visualised in the absence of the forests.

Tribals and forests are ecologically and economically inseparable. They have co-existed since times immemorial and will continue to coexist in a mutually reinforcing relationship.

Tribals have always been sentimentally attached to the forests and considered them to be nature's gift. Their folklore is full of references to the forest. There are several rites and rituals in which some forest produce is used one way or the other. Many of the leaves, climbers, etc. needed in magico-religious rites are procured from these forests. Few trees in the indigenous forests are considered to be the abode of deities and are worshipped as such.

In tribal area, agriculture and its allied activities are dependent on forests to a large extent. Agricultural implements and tools are made from wooden poles and bamboos. The maintenance of cattle for agriculture purposes depends to a great extent on the existence of grazing facility. Animal husbandry and dairy development programmes are related to the availability of grass fodder, leaves, etc.

House construction in tribal areas is undertaken with the materials collected from forests. Timber, bamboo and grass are used in house-construction. Even for the purpose of binding or fixing the poles in such construction, creepers or barks are used instead of iron nails. The importance of forest produce in house construction activity is evident from the fact that a number of villagers shifted from the forests due to submergence or mining activities could not construct suitable houses being away from the forest.

However, with the passage of time their own untramelled peaceful habitat has been disturbed. The balance between these forests dwellers and nature has titled due to extraneous pressure of burgeoning population and entry of outsiders in their peaceful home, construction of Dams, power stations, steel and aluminium plants, mines, Railways and Telecommunication installations and related townships have thought in armies of skilled workers. In all this activity, the tribal has been a very small participant or beneficiary. On the contrary he has become an outsider in his own home exploited by others and alienated. The so-called modern culture has ruthlessly destroyed the forest. The exploitative system has made an all oat attack on their basic right, to live and work in the forest.

The problem of forest conservation and protection cannot be separated from the lives of forest dwellers and local population. A new understanding and programme that develops new and healthier relationships between forest department and the masses must be evolved to avoid tribal movement. The local tribal community which has symbiotic relations with the forest should be accepted as partner in the local forestry development efforts in each area. Unless this promise is accepted and built into the system, it may not be possible to avoid conflicting situation at the local level. The best protective device for the existing forests and new additions is to create an interest of the local community in the forest wealth.

Tribal economy and forest development are actually interdependent. The use of forest resources in industrial development need not be regarded as an unmitigated evil. What most be sought is a right balance, to avoid destruction of forest and tribal life in the name of industrial programmes? Trees have an important place in the economic and cultural lives of tribals and this tie can be strengthened by adopting following programmes:

(i) The economic uplift of tribals be integrated with maintenance and development of their forest habitat.
(ii) Forest development programmes should aim at internalising its components into the rural production system as a whole.
(iii) The working plans should contain suitable prescriptions

providing for tribal development and their active participation in the development of their habitat.

(iv) The development of tribal cooperative societies should be encouraged and as far as possible the exploitation of forest and trading of its produce, especially minor forest produce, should be entrusted to such societies. The agency of contractor should be eliminated.

(v) The tribals should be given training in various forest-based operations such as logging, collection of minor forest produce, intensive cultivation of medicinal herbs and other skills and they should be provided gainful employment in forestry operations all the year round.

(vi) Forest-based cottage industries should be established within tribal areas. First stage processing of minor forest produce should be by local people in order to economically benefit the primary collector.

(vii) All social and economic development programmes should be extended to the forest villagers.

(viii) Integrated programmes with family-based approach aiming proper land use practices should be adopted for settlement of shifting cultivators.

(ix) Assistance be given to the rural families for developing income generating programmes based on ago-forestry to develop local interest towards forestry.

(x) Financial allocation for social forestry and development of minor forest produce should commensurate with the role they can play.

(xi) There should be close and sustained association of forest managers with the tribal development. The approach of foresters towards tribals should be in the spirit of friend, philosopher and guide aiming at educating and training them so that tribals could earn their livelihood in the process of developing the forest.

Forest-Based Tribal Development Programme

Pre-Independence Tribal Scene

Before Independence, the British followed a policy of isolation of tribals from the mainstream of national life. Gandhiji reacted sharply to the segregation of forest community particularly the tribals. In strategically situated Assam in 1946 he reminded the people that, "it was their shame that the Adivasis should be isolated from the rest of the nation of which they were an inalienable part".

India is one of the very few countries of the world which enshrined in its constitution development of tribals, forests and environment. Article 46 enjoin on the State to promote with special care the education and economic interest of the scheduled tribes and protecting them from social injustice and all forms of exploitation. As per Article 48-A the State should endeavour to protect and improve the environment and safeguard the forests and wild-life. Since the tribals live in the forest areas hence compliance with these two principles of the constitution is mutually reinforcing.

Jawaharlal Nehru's philosophy and vision shaped the tribal policy in the fifties. He enunciated the five fundamental principles of tribal development known as 'Tribal Panchsheel' which included the fundamental principles of respecting the tribal rights in land and forests.

The Scheduled Areas and Scheduled Tribes Commission (1961) evaluated the working of constitutional safeguards for the tribals and tribal development programmes. It recommended that "The Forest Department should be deemed to be charged as a branch of government with the responsibility of participating in the betterment of tribals side-by-side with the development of forest Government should accept as a policy that, as far as possible it will take steps to eliminate the middlemen between the inhabitants of the forest and exploitation of the forest". The Commission felt that a very little attention has been paid to the processing side and the produce is sold in the raw farm. The price line between the raw and processed articles are sometimes as one to three. Processing can be a great source of employment for the tribal people.[22]

The committee on Tribal Economy in Forest Areas (Hari Singh Committee, 1967) observed that for the tribal living in forests, the mere subsistance on part time agriculture and seasonal employment in forest cannot ensure sustenance throughout the year. The best way of diverting the tribals from denuding the forest for the purpose of cultivation is to provide them employment in major and minor forest produce, harvesting and collection by eliminating contractors. In pre-dominantly tribal areas, forest must be managed not basically for protection or only for conservation but for furthering tribal interest. This means the revenue will not be the most important consideration but the welfare of the inhabitants of these areas."[23]

The Central Board of Forestry in 1954, recommended greater attention to be paid to tribal welfare. In its 9th meeting held at Ranchi (1965) and in several other meetings including the 18th meeting (1980) the Board reiterated that early steps should be taken to eliminate forest contractor from forest working under a time bound programme.

The National Commission on Agriculture (1976) 3 bestowed their attention on the inter-relationship of forest economy and tribal economy and urged rationality in forest operations and better utilisation of forest produce. Some of the important recommendations are:

(i) Fair price shops should be opened for assured supply of essential commodities at reasonable rates to tribals, including opening Nistar Bhandars (depots) for the supply of domestic forest produce requirement of tribals.
(ii) Tribals should be allotted homestead land, where programmes of afforestation, pasture and grassland development, introduction of horticulture crops, etc. are taken up.
(iii) Tribals should be trained for absorption in all skilled forestry jobs and in forest-based industries.
(iv) For cackling shifting cultivation, multi-disciplinary approach should be adopted and institutional arrangements for maintenance of shifting cultivators should be ensured.

The Conference of State Ministers of Forests and Tribal Welfare on the "Role of Forest in Tribal Economy (1978)[24] recommended that forest development, instead of being planned in isolation, should become an integral part of a comprehensive plan for development of the area in which the needs of local economy should get high priority and should consequently influence the choice of species for each area. The Conference accepted the need for associating tribals in a big plantation programme giving individual rights on the tree and their usufruct. The Conference underlined the need for establishment, but Tribal Development Department, of a strong cooperative base in conjunction with the Forest Department. Further, that the tribals living in forest villages should be given heritable and inalienable rights over the land which they cultivated without further loss of time. All social and economic development programmes should be expanded to these villages on the same lines as for the residents of other villages and wherever possible, action should be taken to convert these villages, into revenue villages.

The Working Group on Tribal Development during Sixth Plan 1980-85[25] has recommended that the local tribal community which has symbiotic relationship with the forest, should be accepted as partners in the local forestry development efforts in each area. Unless this promise is accepted and built into the system, it may not be possible to avoid conflicting situation at the local level. The best protective devise for the existing forest and new addition is to create interest of the local community in the forest wealth.

"Report of the Committee on forest and tribal development in India"[26] recommended integrated development of forests and tribals. The main recommendations are:

(i) In forest-rich regions forest area (30 per cent or more) forestry-oriented tribal development programmes should be framed. For such Integrated Tribal Development Projects (ITDPs) separate working (management) plans would be necessary for linking forestry programmes with economic development of tribals.

(ii) In forest rich ITDP's landless people should be provided gainful employment in forest working and in forest industries so that tribal migration is prevented.

(iii) Through selection of suitable technology and production pattern, land about a hectare or so can make a family economically viable. Hence choice should be made from capital-intensive coffee plantation, plantation of fruit-bearing trees, host plants for tusar, plantation of fodder trees linked to animal husbandry, fuelwood plantation etc. Tusar cultivation with plantation of host trees is important since the tribal areas have good potential for sericulture.

(iv) On the pattern of Gujarat, social security plantation schemes, tribal families may be involved in plantation work. They may be paid wages during the gestation period and subsequently profits from the usufruct may be shared on fifty-fifty basis between them and the Forest Department.

(v) Tribal farmers should be encouraged to take up farm forestry and agro-forestry under which production and fertility of soil and environment improve.

(vi) Some of the cottage, small and medium forest-based industries are saw-milling, furniture making, toy making, etc. should be locally established to generate employ meat for tribals.

(vii) Bullock-carts should be provided to individuals assigning them transportation work of forest produce on an average for 150 days in a year. These bullock-carts may also be engaged in transportation of seedlings from nursery to the planting sites and consumer goods from market to the tribal areas.

(viii) Beneficiary-oriented programmes in forestry sector should be executed under IRDP, NREP, DPAP, DDP, Hill Area Development Plan, Tribal sub-Plan, etc.

ROLE OF FORESTRY IN THE EXISTING PROGRAMMES OF ALLEVIATION OF POVERTY

The Sixth Five Year Plan has the following among its major objectives:[27]

(i) Progressive reduction in the incidence of poverty (48 per cent living below the poverty line reducing to 30 per cent in 1984-85 and to less than 10 per cent by 1994-95) and unemployment.

(ii) Improving the quality of life of the people in general with special reference to the economically and social handicapped population, through a minimum needs programme.

(iii) Strengthening the redistribution bias of public policies and services in favour of the poor, contributing to a reduction in inequalities of income and wealth.

(iv) A progressive reduction in regional inequalities in the pace of development and in the diffusion of technological benefits.

(v) Promoting the active involvement of all sections of the people in the process of development through appropriate education, communication and institutional strategies.

The new 20-Point Programme lay emphasis on effective implementation of following programmes for poverty alleviation:

(i) Strengthen and expand coverage of integrated rural development and national rural employment programme.

(ii) Implement agricultural land ceilings, distribute surplus land and complete compilation of land records by removing all administrative and legal difficulties.

(iii) Review and effectively enforce minimum wages for agricultural labour.

(iv) Rehabilitation of bonded labour.

(v) Accelerate programmes for development of scheduled castes and scheduled tribes.

(vi) Allot house sites to rural homeless families and expand the programmes for construction assistance to them.

(vii) Pursue vigorously the programmes of afforestation, social and farm forestry and the development of bio-gas and other alternative energy sources.

In order to improve and expand employment opportunities for rural landless with a view to provide guarantee of employment to atleast one member of every landless labour household upto 100 days in a year the new scheme of 'Rural Landless Employment Guarantee Programme' was announced by the Prime Minister on 15th August 1983.

The important programmes drawn for the help of the rural poor include:

(i) The Integrated Rural Development Programme (IRDP) extended to all the 5011 blocks of the country for economic assistance to 15.03 million poorest families to bring them above the poverty line. Under this programme, a total subsidy of Rs. 1500 crores, shared equally between the Centre and the State, will supplement credit facilities of Rs. 3000 crores during 1984-85. In about 2011 blocks which are in hilly and forested regions the adopted programme could not improve the income of poorest families because they were neither economically viable nor sustainable. Forests and forest industries in these blocks can play an important role in the economic development of poor families.

(ii) The National Rural Employment Programme (NREP) is expected to generate 300 million to 400 million mandays employment every year. A total of Rs. 1620 crores has been provided by the Centre and the States for this programme. Apart from employment maximisation, the programme aims at strengthening the rural infrastructure which in turn would boost rural economy. Under this programme the projects of social forestery, soil conservation, minor irrigation and basic amenities to the scheduled castes and scheduled tribes communities have been assigned high priority.

(iii) The Drought Prone Areas Programme and the Desert Development Programme (DPAP and DDP) aim at optimum utilisation of land, water, livestock resources and stabilisation of incomes of people particularly the weaker sections of the society. The OPAP covers 511 blocks spread over 69 districts and DDP 18 districts in Rajasthan, Haryana and Gujarat and cold desert areas in Jammu and Kashmir and Himachal Pradesh. Ecological degradation is of far greater consequence to the community in these areas and rehabilitation work has to be taken up with far greater urgency and on a priority basis.

(iv) The Tribal sub-Plan Programme (TSP) operates in 19 States/2 Union Territories having concentration of Scheduled Tribe population. Special programmes have been taken up for the primitive tribes. Besides flow from State Plans and Central Ministeries, special Central assistance of the order of Rs. 470 crores has been provided in the Sixth Plan period. Forestry occupy the Central position in tribal economy; hence integrated development of scheduled tribes and forests, is ecologically and economically desirable and deserves priority.

(v) Hill Area Development Programme (HADP) cover 11 districts in Assam, Uttar Pradesh and West Bengal and 132 talukas in the States of Maharashtra, Karnataka, Tamil Nadu, Kerala and the Union Territory of Goa. Forestry development is essential not only for eco-preservation but also for supply of fuel, fodder, timber and raw material for industries. Afforestation of catchment areas is of very high priority for preventing soil erosion as well as regulating water supply. There is an immediate need for fostering agro-forestry techniques in such areas.

(vi) Component plans have been formulated for development of scheduled castes. The flow of fund from the State Plan to the scheduled castes component plan during the Sixth Plan period is estimated to be more than Rs. 4000 crores. In addition, a provision of Rs. 600 crores of special Central assistance has been made for 1980-85. 17 Scheduled Castes Finance and Development Corporations are expected to channellise inputs and credits. Social Forestry, MFP development and forest-based cottage industries are expected to play a major role in their development.

(vii) The National Dairy Development Programme aims to cover about 15 million families in the country during the Sixth Plan to provide additional income and employment in addition to assisting in improvement of nutrition. Priority is given to landless labour families and women belonging to weaker sections of the community in imparting training in dairy farming. Success of this programme largely depends on pasture, fodder and fuel development on marginal and sub-marginal areas.

(viii) Handicraft, handloom, sericulture and other cottage and small industries programmes, etc. aim to provide additional income and employment to the rural poor.

Forestry has to play an important role in supporting these programmes.

(ix) Rural Landless Employment Guarantee Programme (RLEGP) aims to provide employment to atleast one member of every landless family upto 100 days in a year particularly during the lean agricultural period. Social forestry and development of Minor Forest Produce can generate desired employment in the rural areas.

The concept of Minimum Needs Programmes (MNP) emerged and crystallised out of the experience of the previous plans that neither growth nor social consumption could be sustained much less accelerated unless they are mutually supportive. The programme is essentially an investment in human resource development. The MNP lays down the urgency for providing social services according to nationally accepted norms within a time bound programme. Time and again, it has been felt necessary that fuelwood and fodder production should be included in MNP.

Land in the rural areas continues to be an important asset and measure of social and economic strength. The mainstay for the majority of the rural population is agriculture, forestry, animal husbandry and allied activities. There is a continuous decline in the proportion of cultivators of own land and corresponding increase in the proportion of labourers. Thus, agriculture is not in a position to absorb landless rural masses on sustained basis.

In the past, the management of forests was restricted to timber resources management and the wood industries were concerned with maximum returns on invested capital. Now, social benefits from forestry are constantly being stressed. It has been estimated that about one million man years of work is created for an annual plantation of one million ha. Nearly 100 million ha. of land is in dire need of afforestation and it is physically possible to afforest about 3 million ha. every year which shall generate 3 million man years of work. This along with development of MFP and establishment of forest industries would generate employment for all the rural unemployed.

The interface between forestry and agriculture is being fully recognised. Farm Forestry is acting as an important catalyst for rural development leading to employment in the primary, secondary and tertiary sectors. Farm Forestry should not restrict to growing of trees alone. Degraded forests, wasteland, marginal and sub-marginal areas under the private ownership may also be brought under social forestry and farm forestry. A minimum objective is to enable poor people to gain, secure decent livelihood in ways they welcome without impairing the ecological security. Other supporting objectives should be increasing productivity level, equity in access to the resources created and long-term resource stability.

The country has to harness forestry which must act as a catalyst for rural and community development. The high demand for forest products particularly from low income groups and the pronounced linkage effects of forest industries with other sectors of economy provide such industries the potential to contribute to rapid economic growth. Through selection of suitable technology and production pattern, about one ha. land can make a family economically viable. Forest needs strengthening in large investments and use of new technology so that it can yield a higher surplus of forest produce for consumption locally, regionally and at national level besides exporting selected items.

BENEFICIARY SCHEMES IN FORESTRY SECTOR

The other programmes which support and compliment forestry programme include:

(i) Present Sixth Plan outlay of Rs. 4520 million for all plantation activities;
(ii) A minimum of 10 per cent outlay of funds for social forestry under the National Rural Employment Programme;
(iii) An outlay of about Rs. 400 million as special central assistance under Tribal Sub-plans;
(iv) Extensive tree planting under Hill Area Development Programme;
(v) Afforestation programmes under DPAP and DDP;
(vi) Plantation programmes under tusser and mulberry sericulture;
(vii) Forest industries motivated and supported joint/private plantation;

(viii) Individual beneficiary-oriented programmes of afforestation under IRD programmes; and

(ix) Afforestation programme under Rural Landless Employment Guarantee Programme.

Poor people living in the rural areas mainly include landless labourers, small and marginal farmers, rural artisans, scheduled castes and scheduled tribes. These people have either no assets or assets with very low productivity, few relevant skills and no regular full time jobs or very low paid jobs.

Land in the rural areas continues to be an important asset and measures of social and economic strength. The mainstay for the majority of the rural population is agriculture and allied activities. There is a continuous decline in the proportion of cultivators of own land and corresponding increase in the proportion of labourers.

Forests and wastelands cover about one-third of the geographical area of the country. Perhaps some 50 million tribals depend totally or in part on the use of forests for their livelihood, as do many million of other poor rural people. A minimum objective is to enable more poor people to gain secure and decent livelihoods in ways which they welcome. To this end, other supporting objectives are increasing productivity of resource, equity in access in them, and long-term resources stability.

The role of forests has been recognised in generation of employment, improving environment, upgrading economy of forest dwellers and providing fuelwood energy to the masses. As a national policy it has been stressed that:

(i) Forests need strengthening through rationality in operation, large investments and use of new technology so that it can yield a higher surplus;

(ii) Social forestry programme should be a programme of true plantations by ensuring involvement of people;

(iii) Conjoint efforts of government, cooperative, community and corporate sectors are necessary to increase production of forest product; and

(iv) Forestry practices should make the lives of forest-dwellers happier by adopting:

(a) elimination of contractor agency from all forestry operations;
(b) involvement of people in different forestry operations for earning their livelihood;
(c) by launching a special drive for collection, procurement, processing and marketing of minor forest produce; and
(d) by implementing programmes such as 'a tree for every child', 'nutrition gardens', 'forest farming' and 'the raising of energy and industrial plantations'.

Forestry Schemes for People Assistance

Elimination of contractor agency from harvesting of major forest produce has been given top priority. State-wise achievements made may be summed up as under:

(i) Andhra Pradesh State Government took a policy decision to replace the contractor agency by departmental working of all timber, fuel-wood and bamboo coupes. The State Forest Department and Forest Development Corporations, have since been harvesting the forest coupes by directly employing people on regular basis as well as on job basis and the contractor agency has been eliminated. Forest labour cooperative societies are yet to be organised. Bamboo coupes leased out to the paper mills should be harvested through departmental agency.
(ii) Bihar State took a decision to eliminate contractor agency by 1982-83. Departmental working has been introduced in the State as a whole. One of the important policies of the State Government is the formation of cooperative societies of the tribal people with the sole purpose of giving them economic benefit. Timber coupes upto a value of Rs. 30,000 are settled with these cooperatives at reserve price. There are about 120 cooperative societies in the State and during 1980-81, 91 forest coupes worth Rs. 15 lakhs were given to them for working. Forest Department has established 19 depots for supply of fuel and bamboo to the local people.
(iii) Gujarat State has viable Forest Labour Cooperative Societies (FLCS) structure in the State for undertaking

exploitation, logging and transport of all major forest produce. There are about 141 FLCSs in the State of which 132 are in tribal areas. Almost all forest coupes of timber, fuelwood and charcoal are being worked through the FLCS. Tribals derive from FLCS a fair wage and a share in the profits. This share alone comes to nearly one crore of rupees every year. The societies are permitted to 10 per cent material derived from the coupes to local tribals and members of the society at 60 per cent of the prevailing market rate for domestic use.[28]

(iv) Madhya Pradesh has nationalised timber, bamboo and Khair wood trade under the provision of a special Act "Madhya Pradesh Vanupaja (Vyapar Viniyaman) Adhiniyam, 1969" and has started departmental working of the coupes by engaging tribals and others on job basis. The department is exploiting annually 40 lakh cubic metres of wood employing tribals on job basis and distributing annually Rs. 15.7 crores as wages. The Forest Department has also started about 3,982 Nistar depots from where constructional timber, small timber, fuelwood, charcoal and other forest produce are supplied. Urban population is also supplied fuelwood, charcoal and bamboo at concessional rates.[29]

(v) In the State of Maharashtra, there are 442 FLCS with a total membership of 59,000 of which 53,000 are tribal members. The annual turnover of the societies is about Rs. 9 crores. The total share capital is of the order of about Rs. 15 lakhs. However, this movement has not gathered desired momentum in the tribal districts of Chandrapur and Bhandara. The State is making efforts to organise more societies in these districts where presently the major part of the work is being done by the departmental agency and the Forest Development Corporation. About 25-30 per cent of the coupes are being leased out to contractors. It is expected that the contractor agencies will be totally eliminated by the end of Sixth Plan.

(vi) In Rajasthan, timber, fuelwood and Khairwood are at present exploited through departmental agency by engaging tribals on job basis and the contractor agency has been eliminated. Further, the State Government is organising five Forest Labour Cooperative Societies annually and they expect that FLCS should be able to handle all the forest coupes towards the end of the Sixth Five Year Plan.

(vii) The State of Jammu and Kashmir has eliminated contractors and replaced them by departmental working.

(viii) In Uttar Pradesh, State Forest Department has agreed to give maximum number of coupes to the Forest Development Corporation, and the Tribal Development Corporation. However, the contractors agency is still in vogue and needs to be replaced on priority.

(ix) West Bengal Forest Development Corporation has taken up a massive programme of mechanised logging in Darjeeling-Kalimpong hills. Departmental working has been started in a few coupes in the plains.

(x) Sikkim and the Administration of Andaman and Nicobar Island have eliminated the system of contractors and replaced it by departmental agency.

(xi) Some other States viz., Assam, Kerala, Karnataka, Manipur, Nagaland, Orissa, Tripura and Tamil Nadu have initiated the process of elimination of contractor agency. The constraints appear to be organisational and financial.

According to the National Commission on Agriculture various items of Minor Forest Produce (MFP) have the potential to bring about an economic revolution for tribals and other rural people in the country. To provide economically viable schemes of MFP collection, processing and marketing, State-wise attempts made may be summed up as:[30]

(i) In Andhra Pradesh, the Girijan Cooperative Corporation (GCC) has monopoly rights over procurement and marketing of MFP. The GCC is an apex cooperative institution with 29 primary marketing societies at the operational level as its members. The GCC was doing normal procurement of MFP worth Rs. 150 lakhs per year which is proposed to be raised to Rs. 540 lakhs. Annual employment generation was estimated to be 60 lakh man-days since 1982-83 onward Forest Department has taken up State trading in *tendu* leaves.

(ii) In Bihar, Forest Department has taken up State trading in *tendu* leaves since 1973. An ordinance to regulate the trade of 34 MFP items was issued in 1977 but it has not been possible to organise State trading in all the 34 MFP items. Forest Development Corporation has taken up the trade of oilseeds of tree origin viz., *Sal, Mahuwa, Kusum, Karanj, Palas* and *Harra, Bahera* and *Aonla* on monopoly basis by involving LAMPS and other cooperatives. The Bihar State Cooperative Lac Marketing Federation oraganises procurement, processing and marketing of lac and its products. The State Cooperative Development Corporation organises procurement, processing and *Barbatti* (Beans), tassar, cocoon and a few other MFP items.

(iii) The Gujarat State Forest Development Corporation is directly involved in MFP collection since 1977. During the first year only 3 MEP items namely *Timru* leaves (Tendu leaves), *Mahuwa* flowers and *Mahuwa* seeds were collected. From 3rd year onward i.e., 1979, the Corporation started collection of 34 MFP items. The Corporation has identified whole-sellers in MFP and actual user of MFP. The Corporation has also started processing of MFP.

(iv) In Kerala, 27 Girijan Service Cooperative Societies carry out procurement and processing of MFP items.

(v) MFP leases in Karnataka are given to the tribal Societies (LAMPS) at a concessional rate with 33 per cent exemption on total lease value. Some societies are reported to have done good work.

(vi) *Tendu* leaves, *Sal* seed, *Harra,* gums (five types), Khair-wood and Bamboo are nationalised items in Madhya Pradesh for monopoly State trading. The remaining MFP items (about 34 in number) are handled by contractor agency. The State has now created MFP Federation for eliminating contractor agency.

(vii) The Forest Department of Maharashtra has taken up *Tendu* leaf trading since 1969. Maharashtra State Cooperative Tribal Development Corporation procures gums, *Harra* and *Mahuwa* seed. Contractor agency is carrying out other MFP collection.

(viii) Orissa is the only State in the country where *Kendu* (Tendu) leaf is directly collected by the Forest Department and marketed by Orissa Forest Corporation. *Sal* seed trade has also been nationalised. Simplipal Forest Development Corporation and Tribal Area Development Cooperative Federation organises collection of number of MFP item.

(ix) Tendu leaves in Rajasthan trade is handled by Forest Department on monopoly basis. Tribal Area Development Cooperative Federation organises collection of other MFP items.

(x) MFP collection is maximised through departmental collection by Forest Department in Tamil Nadu and by Girijan Cooperatives.

(xi) In Uttar Pradesh, Forest Department Corporation is generally taking up MFP collection. The State has also to encourage collection of MFP through Tarai Anusuchit Janjati Vikas Nigam and Garhwal and Kumaon Tribal Development Corporations.

(xii) The Tribal Development Cooperative Corporation organises the collection of all MFP items by involving LAMPS in West Bengal.

(xiii) Other states are also planning collection, procurement, processing of MFP items in a planned manner.

(xiv) The NCDC and NAFED extend suitable support to different Corporation/Federations and LAMPS for increasing procurement and processing of MFP items. For greater support, creation of 'TRIFED' is under active consideration.

Trees have an important place in the economic and cultural lives of forest dwellers. It is necessary to strengthen these ties by involving the people in development and conservation of forest resources. The new programmes developed may be summed up as under:[31]

(i) Gujarat State has introduced following beneficiary schemes in forestry sector:

(a) Social Security through Plantations

The Gujarat Forest department has started social security, afforestation schemes for tribal families. In the absence of sustained employment, landless tribals indulge in illicit fellings or migrate to far-off places every year in search of manual work resulting in dislocation of economic and social life for them. The Forest Department has developed a scheme through which an assured monthly income is to be provided by permanently engaging a tribal family on forest plantation work by earmarking plots of certain size say of 2.5 hectare on yearly basis, i.e., 37.5 hectares for 15 years. Plantation of suitable forest species is raised in this land by the family under the supervision and guidance of the forest department. The required materials viz., polythene bags, seeds, etc., are supplied by the forest department. The family is responsible for all operations for successful raising of the plantation, i.e., digging of pits, soil conservation measures, planting, weeding, fencing and protection of the planted crops. For the labour put in, each family is paid a monthly remuneration of Rs. 50 for a period of 15 years. The family is also given small timber, bamboo, etc., for constructing temporary hut near the plantation site and is allowed to cut grasses and collect MFP free of charge. At the end of rotation period of 15 years, the family is to be given 20 per cent share in the profit derived from the sale of the material making him partner in the profits. The measure is aimed at helping the family to stabilise and in the process ensures protection of the new plantation and existing forest resulting in production of scarce fuel wood and small timber. The scheme is expected to improve the socio-economic condition of landless tribals.

(b) Afforestation of Marginal and Sub-marginal Areas

In Gujarat the lands of most of the tribals of Dangs and Dharampur regions, are on steep slopes in hilly terrain with sandy soil having poor fertility. The ecological conditions are also unsuitable for good agriculture and remunerative returns. Income from such areas is generally not more than Rs. 250 per hectare per year. Often due to floods or famine conditions there is complete failure of crop. In such agricultural areas the tribals are being persuaded to raise teak and bamboo plantations under community forestry schemes by the forest department. The farmer is given a subsistence allowance of Rs. 250 per hectare per year which is equivalent to his expected average annual earning from agronomic cultivation of such land up to the time of exploitation of forest crop. At the end of about 15 years period the trees will be exploited by the Forest Department and sold on behalf of the landholder, deduct the cost of plantation and subsistence allowance paid to him over the intervening years without charging any interest and handover the balance to the landholders. According to an estimate, the forest crop is likely to give them a much higher return than what farmers were getting under agriculture. The scheme is expected not only to benefit the farmer but also protect the precious soil from erosion and improve the environment.

(c) The farmers of Gujarat have realised the economic importance of tree farming and other benefits accruing from it. Nearly 18,000 farmers have raised trees in their farms either as peripheral plantations on bunds or block plantations. Farmers have been motivated to raise tree seedlings as an economic activity. During 1982-83 in all 567 'Kisan Nurseries' were established which raised 22.80 million seedlings.

(d) The school children were encouraged to raise seedling in their schools by supplying polythene bags, seeds and giving them all technical guidance. During 1982-83, 722 schools were motivated for raising 9.72 million seedlings and are likely to earn more than Rs. 2.6 million.

(e) Under I.R.D. schemes, Rural Development Department has sanctioned a scheme for irrigated as well as rainfed plantations to be raised by the small and marginal farmers by providing them subsidy of 50 per cent of the cost of formulation upto Rs. 3000 to Rs. 5000 depending on the category of beneficiary. The commercial bank and other agencies provide loans to the farmers.

(ii) In Madhya Pradesh, individual farmers were motivated to raise 'Private Nurseries'. The Social Forestry Department provided seeds, polythene bags, technical know-how and cash advances. The seedlings were purchased by department which provided attractive earning to the people. Already about 150 'Private Nurseries' are operating and their number will increase as Social Forestry Programme gains momentum.

(iii) In Rajasthan, following beneficiary schemes were started in forestry sectors:[32]

(a) Scheduled castes and scheduled tribes farmers were motivated to raise tree seedlings on their farms. Nearly 100 S.C. and S.T. families were identified and provided seeds, polythene bags and technical know-how. During 1980-81 about 6.34 lakh seedlings were produced which were purchased by the Forest Department.

(b) Under 'Tree farming' scheme, the farmers are required to dig pits and plant a unit of 100 plants in a group in his 'khatedari' land and provide needed protection to the plants. In order to recompensate the farmers for the labour and the possible bit of crop foregone, they are paid incentive of Rs. 10 per plant in 3 instalments as follows:

1st year: Rs. 5.00 per plant (Rs. 2.50 are paid in October and Rs. 2.50 in March) after verifying the survival of plant.

2nd year: Rs. 3.00 per plant on surviving plants of first year.

3rd year: Rs. 2.00 per plant on surviving plants.

(c) 'Social Security through Plantation' scheme of Gujarat has also been introduced in the Tribal sub-Plan area at instance of Ministry of Home Affairs, Government of India.*

(iv) In Bihar, Forest Department, raised social forestry plantations on the holdings of farmers and bears total cost of plantation. The species being raised are mixture of quick growing fuelwood, small timber, fodder and fruit trees. About 20 to 25 per cent of fruit trees are planted on the tribal land.

(v) In Tamil Nadu, the Swedish International Development Authority[33] (SIDA) aided Social Forestry Project and has introduced "the tree cultivation incentives Programme".

*The plants and other inputs are made available to the farmers at the site of planting by Forest Department free of cost.

The programme is designed to make possible and encourage the small farmers and landless to take up tree cultivation. The component aim at the objective "to help economically weaker sections to raise plantations in their land holdings which are unsuitable for agriculture". Majority of the participants, on account of their small land holdings are expected to plant 1—100 seedlings. An individual hosehold is entitled to a free supply of 500 seedlings of suitable fuel, small timber, fodder and fruit yielding species. In order to compensate the participants, cash incentives are paid on the basis of surviving plants at the end of first and second year on a sliding seate as under:

Surviving Plants	*Rate of incentive Plant (Rs.)*	*Total amount of incentive (Rs.)*
1-10	1.60	10.00
11-30	0.50	10.00
31-100	0.25	17.50
101-500	0.10	40.00
		77.50

Thus, a family planting 500 seedlings, if all the plants survive, will be entitled to get incentives as follows:

1st year	*2nd year*	*Total*
Rs. 77.50	Rs. 77.50	Rs. 155.00

(vi) In the World Bank aided West Bengal Social Forestry Project three forestry schemes have been introduced to assist the beneficiaries:

(a) To encourage poor farmers with small holdings of wasteland to take up tree planting of a maximum of 750 seedlings. A minimum plantation of 50 seedlings would enable the farmers to qualify for a cash payment of 40 paise per seedling to be paid in three yearly instalments. Seedlings and inputs shall be provided at the planting site.

(b) Distribution of free seedlings with cash incentive

similar to scheme (a) shall be extended to landless people by apportioning 0.5 ha. of State owned wasteland to them for raising tree crop.

(c) Social Forestry wing would distribute a total of 50 million seedlings free of cost (approximately 2.500 seedling per ha.) to farmers for planting on privately owned wastelands.

(vii) To motivate the farmers to take up afforestation programmes on their marginal and sub-marginal lands, Andhra Pradesh State has prepared a special scheme of private forestry for raising fuel and small wood trees on their holdings. The scheme is already under implementation and has received good response in may areas.

Forest industries particularly pulp and papers are finding it extremely difficult to meet their raw-material requirement. The industries are now coming forward to support farm forestry programmes for raising industrial plantations.[34] Attempts made so far are summed up as under:

(i) The Titaghur Paper Mills Co. Ltd. motivated people of rural areas adjacent to the Mill locations to grow bamboo and wood in their homestead lands or in unused farm lands. The 12 centres were selected within the period of 1978 to extend the idea of farm forestry.

(a) The theme of extension work was:

- Growing of bamboo, wood, etc. in homestead or in unused lands are profitable was explained to the people and facts and figures were presented to them.
- Assurance was given by the Paper Mill Authorities, that production will be lifted by payment of cash price, i.e. offtake guarantee was given at a reasonable price. The purchase price of raw-material was quoted as the minimum price payable.
- That the growing of bamboo and wood will create certain amount of employment in plantation, cutting, feeling, bundling and transport of the produce. That if people are

enthusiastic, centres will be located in their village and nursery creation and other ancillary job will need the help of young under-employed farmers and unemployed students.

(b) The incentives that were offered included:

- The seedlings of bamboo and wood, etc. were given free by the company at the nursery site located in the rural centre.
- A total of about 5,00,000 seedlings were distributed in course of 3-1/2 years.
- The persons giving the land for nursery were given a reasonable rent. Gardens were selected locally and employed.
- The unemployed students were given work to contact individual families and to extend the idea of farm forestry. These students were given pocket allowances.

(c) The results have been moderately good so far. The success as has been assessed in terms of the number of seedlings growing is around 35 per cent. For better success greater inputs have been felt necessary.

(ii) To increase the production of raw material Sree Rayalseema Paper Mills Ltd. has started implementing a farm forestry scheme. The salient points of this scheme are:

The ill raises nursery and supply seedlings free to the farmers (ryot) willing to raise quick growing pulpwood species in their farms. The mill also gives assurance to the farmers that all pulpwood will be purchased when it is ready at Rs. 200 per tonne of standing crop. The Mill will get the trees debarked, and transport pulpwood (upto 5 cms diameters at the top) upto the mill site.

The farmers prepare their field and raise the plants on their field bunds or in the farm in rows intermixed with their agricultural crops, tend the plants and sell the standing wood to the mills when it is mature. The farmers also undertake the works of fertilising and applying insecticides and fungicides as required under the guidance of the mills.

- During the gestation period the Syndicate Bank gave an annual loan of about Rs. 500 per hectare for rainfed plantation over a period of 7 years and Rs. 1000 per hectare on irrigated plantation crop for five years to the farmers on the recommendation of the mill with the assurance that the mill will remit the amount to the bank at the time of purchasing wood. The bank after deducting the loan with interest reimburses the residuary amount to the farmer. The scheme has been successfully implemented over an area of 170 ha. till 1981. From 1982 onward, it was proposed to raise about 1000 ha of plantation on yearly basis subject to a total area of 10,000 hectares to be covered.

(iii) The Sheshaya Paper Mills, Erode, have been implementing a scheme to raise Eucalyptus on private farms for the last four years. To motivate the farmers, besides providing inputs for raising of plantations, monetary incentive have been provided. A rupee for every surviving seedling on a specific size at the end of second year and at the end of four years been provided. A seven year rotation has been fixed for harvesting the planted crop. A tripartite agreement has been entered between the participating farmer the industry and the commercial bank. One of the conditions stipulated is that first crop is earmarked for the industry concerned at the same rate at which the Forest Department, supplies Eucalyptus to the industry. Out of the total amount payable incentive amount is deducted from the farmers by the Bank. From second rotation, the farmer is free to sell the raw material to the industry at a competitive market price.

CONCLUSIONS

Since forest is about half the agriculture area in the country, forestry should be able to generate employment for about 20 million standard person year. Out of 5011 community development blocks nearly 2011 are in the forest areas. This means out of about 15 million households to be assisted under IRD programme during the Sixth Plan period nearly 6.33 million households may require direct or indirect support from forestry sector.

Rural economy and forest development are actually interdependent. More beneficiary-oriented programmes in forestry sector should be identified and implemented. Assistance should be given to tribals and landless people for developing income generating programmes based on managing and marketing of forest produce on a sustainable basis.

Notes and References

1. Statistics on Soil Conservation in India, Ministry of Agriculture, New Delhi, 1982
2. Report of the Fuel Wood Study Committee, Planning Commission, Government of India, New Delhi, March, 1982.
3. Report of Committee on Forest and Tribals in India, Government of India, Ministry of Home Affairs, New Delhi, 1982.
4. "Forest Conservancy in India" (extract from the Handbook of Exhibits of the Indian FD at the Chicago Exhibition, 1895), md. For 19 (189 p. 26d.)
5. N.L. Bor, "Manual of India Forest Botany," Oxford, 1963, p. 18.
6. E.P. Stebbing, 'The Forests of India', pp. 61-62, Large areas of mountain forests were also given away for tea and coffee plantion.
7. G.I. Pearson, 'Sub-Himalayan Forests of Kumaon and Garhwal', in "Selections from the Records of the Government of the North Western Provinces", second series, Volume II, Allahabad, 1869, pp. 132-33, emphasis in original.
8. K.P. Sagreiya, "Forests and Forestry", Delhi, 1979, p. 8.
9. T.W. Webber, "The Forests of Upper India and Their Inhabitants", London, 1902, pp. xii-xiii.
10. N. Hearle, "W.P. of the Tehri Garhwal Leased Forests, 7 Jaunsar", For Div. Allahabad, 1888, p. 16.
11. A.K. Lameson, Settlement Officer of Midnapur district quoted in S. Dasgupta, "The Local Face of Non-cooperation: the Santhal Movement in Midnapur (1918-1923)", (unpublished paper). Another documented case is of the British districts Ajmer and Mewar, where the government had at the time of the 1850 land settlement, explicitly relinquished its rights over the wastes and jungles which were handed over in entirety to the villagers (Brandis, "Indian Forestry," pp. 15-16)
12. C.F. Army, 'On Forest Rights in India", in D. Brandis and A. Smythies,

ed., "Report on the Proceedings of the Forest Conference held at Simla, October 1875", Calcutta, 1876, p. 27.

13. Superintendent, Dehra Dun, to Commissioner, Meerut Division dated 22-5-1897 No. 1997/IV, 244 of 1897), File No. 244. List No. 2 (UPRA).
14. V. Elwin, "A Philosophy for NEFA", Calcutta, 1960, p. 86 f.
15. J.A. Voelcker, "Report of Indian Agriculture," Calcutta 1897 (first published 1893), p. 16, emphasis in original.
16. GCI, Revenue and Agricultural Department (Forests) Circular No. 22 F dated October 19, 1894 (File No. 244, List No. 2UPRA).
17. GOI, Report of the Forestry Committee, Simla, 1929, p. 30.
18. E.A. Smythies: Indian Forest Wealth, pp. 13, 82, 84 etc.
19. K.M. Tewari, "Social Forestry in Uttar Pradesh", Forest Conference, Lucknow, January 25, 1981.
20. Report of the Scheduled Areas and Scheduled Tribes Commission appointed by President of India in 1960, UN Dhebar, Chairman of this Commission presented the report to the president of India.
21. Report of the Committee on Tribal economy in forest areas under the chairmanship of Shri Hari Singh, Inspector General of Forest, who presented the report in 1967.
22. Report of the National Commission on Agriculture, para 9, Forestry—1975-76.
23. Conference of Ministers incharge of Forests and Tribal Welfare on the 'Role of Forests and Tribal Economy' inaugurated by the Prime Minister of India at New Delhi, 1978.
24. Report of the Working Group on Tribal Development during Sixth Plan 1980-85 submitted to the Planning Commission of India.
25. Report on the development of a tribal Areas by National Committee on the development of backward areas, Planning Commission, Government of India, June, 1981.
26. Sixth Five Year Plan, Planning Commission, Government of India; 1980.
27. Tribal sub-Plan document of Gujarat, 1981-82.
28. Information furnished by the Chief Conservator of Forests (Production), Madhya Pradesh, Bhopal.
29. Tribal Sub-Plan document of States and Union Territories.
30. Principal Chief Conservator of Forests, Gujarat, letter dated 22-9-1982.
31. Chief Conservator of Forests, Rajasthan, letter dated 6-12-1982.
32. Chief Conservator of Forests, Tamil Nadu, letter dated 26-9-82.
33. Additional Chief Conservator of Forests, letter dated 27-9-82.
34. Report of the Committee on the Forest and Tribals, Government of India, Ministry of Home Affairs, 1982.

APPENDIX

TABLE 1

Forest Statistics
Land Area, Forest Area and Population of some Countries of the World

Sl. No.	*Country*	*Total land area (thousand sq. km.)*	*Total Forest area (thousand sq. km.)*	*Per cent of land under forests*	*Mid year Population 1969 (in thousand)*	*Per capita area*	
						All land (ha.)	*Forests (ha.)*
1	*2*	*3*	*4*	*5*	*6*	*7*	*8*
1.	U.S.S.R. (1971)@	2,24,02	91,00	40.6	2,42,700	9.23	3.75
2.	Canada (1971)@	99,76	44,30	44.4	21,400	46.61	20.70
3.	United State (1971)	93,63	29,61	31.6	2,05,300	4.56	1.44
4.	Australia (1971)@	76,87	3,48	4.5	12,200	63.00	2.15
5.	India (1971)@	32,81	7,46	22.7	5,57,950	0.60	0.14
6.	Argentina (1967)	27,77	6,33	22.8	23,255	11.34	2.72
7.	Sudan (1954)	26,06	9,15	36.5	14,355	17.46	6.37
8.	Algeria (1967)	23,32	30	1.3	12,154	10.50	0.25
9.	Congo Republic (1959)	23,45	10,00	42.6	16,353	14.34	6.11
10.	Maxico (1971)@	19,72	4,37	22.1	50,600	3.89	0.86
11.	Indonesia (1954)	14,92	9,08	60.9	110,899	1.34	0.81
12.	Peru (1965)	12,85	8,70	67.7	12,385	0.37	8.03
13.	Ethopia (1965)	12,22	90	7.3	23,400	5.22	0.38

14.	Pakistan (1965)	9,47	42	4.4	120,685	0.79	0.03
15.	Burma (1971)@	6,78	4,53	66.8	25,500	2.46	1.64
16.	Afghanistan (1967)	6,78	20	3.1	16,045	1.04	0.13
17.	France (1966)	3,47	1,27	23.2	49,966	1.10	0.25
18.	Japan (1971)@	3,69	2,55	69.1	19,35,00	3.56	0.25
19.	Italy (1967)	3,01	61	20.3	52,334	0.50	0.11
20.	U.K. (1971)@	2,44	18	7.4	55,700	0.44	0.63
21.	Nepal (1966)	1,41	45	32.2	10,492	1.34	0.43

@ "Bharat ke Van—1974"—Published by Central Forestry Commission.

Source : Forest Statistics, Bulletin No. 11 (Area Statistics) April 1971—Central Forestry Commission, Government of India.

TABLE 2

Forest Land in Relation to Total Land and Population in India

(Area in thousand hectares)

Sl. No.	*Name of State*	*Total geographical area (a)*	*Total forest area*	*Percent of land under forests*	*Popula-tion in thousand*	*Density of population*	*Forest area per Capita in ha.*
1	2	3	4	5	6	7	8
1.	Andhra Pradesh	27,682	6,480	23.41	45,428	1,641	0,14
2.	Assam	7,852	2,855	36.36	15,984	2,035	0,23
3.	Bihar	17,388	2,923	16.85	58,696	3,375	0,05
4.	Gujarat	19,598	1,697	8.66	28.227	1,440	0,06
5.	Haryana	4,422	152	9.66	10,546	2,384	0,01
6.	Himachal Pradesh	5,567	2,167	38.93	3,547	637	0,61
7.	Jammu and Kashmir	22,224	2,072	9.32	4,831	2,173	0,43
8.	Kerala	3,887	1,127	28.99	22,474	5,781	0,05
9.	Madhya Pradesh	44,284	16,835	38.01	44,010	993	0,38
10.	Maharashtra	30,776	6,613	21.49	59,950	1,947	0,12
11.	Manipur	2,236	602	26.92	1,126	503	0,53
12.	Meghalaya	2,249	699	31.08	1,059	470	0,66
13.	Karnataka	19,177	3,608	18.82	30,646	1,598	0,12
14.	Nagaland	1,653	688	17.42	533	323	0,54
15.	Orissa	5,578	6,793	43.61	22,989	1,475	0,30
16.	Punjab	15,036	2,13	4.23	14,136	2,806	0,01

17.	Rajasthan	34,221	3,589	10.49	27,154	793	0,13
18.	Tripura	1,048	605	57.73	1,631	1,556	0,37
19.	Tamil Nadu	13,007	2,234	17.17	43,035	3,308	0,05
20.	Uttar Pradesh	29,441	5,013	17.03	91,732	3,115	0,05
21.	West Bengal	9,785	1,183	13.47	46,594	4,761	0,03
22.	Andaman and N. Islands	829	746	89.99	1,21	145	6,16
23.	Dadar and Nagar Haveli	49	20	40.82	78	30,302	0,26
24.	Delhi	149	4	2.68	4,515	2,359	0,03
25.	Goa Daman Diu	311	131	34.38	899		0,14
26.	Mizoram	2,109	8,87	24.06	Included under Assam		
27.	Arunachal Pradesh	8,358	5,154	61.67	490	58	10,52
28.	Sikkim	730	265	36.30	364	498	0,73
29.	Others	63	—	—	795	1,261	—
30.	All India	328,779	74,964	22.80	574,580	1,747	0,13

Others : Include geographical area of Pondicherry, Chandigarh, Lakshadeep for which statistics returns are not available.
Source: "India's Forests 1976" issued by Central Forestry Commission.

TABLE 3

Division-wise Area of Forests

(*Area in ha*)

Sl. No.	*Name of Division*	*District*	*Reserved Forests*	*Protected Forests*	*Unclassed Forests*	*Total*
1.	Deoghar	(i) Santhal Parganas	—	31,400	—	
		(ii) Bhagalpur	2,866	42,522	—	76,788
2.	Dumka	Santhal Parganas	12,853	1,48,136	—	1,60,989
3.	Monghyr	Monghyr	24,242	41,077	—	65,319
4.	Shababad	Rohtas	—	1,79,762	—	1,79,762
5.	Gaya	(i) Gaya	937	31.357	—	
		(ii) Nawadah	6,378	57,038	—	1,49,573
		(iii) Aurangabad	5,895	47,968	—	
6.	Jamui Affn.	Monghyr	28,971	34,760	—	63,731
7.	Extension	Purnea	—	1,305	—	1,305
		Total	82,142	6,15,325	—	6,97,467
8.	Hazaribagh West	Hazaribagh	672	1,76,525	340	1,77,537
9.	Hazaribagh East	(i) Hazaribagh	1,743	63,566	—	1,25,700
		(ii) Giridih	—	60,331	—	
10.	Chatra South	Hazaribagh	752	1,01,828	—	1,02,580
11.	Chatra North	-do-	—	93,372	—	93,372
12.	Kodarma	-do-	15,630	73,408	—	89,038
13.	Giridih	Giridih	8,776	1,43,268	—	1,52,044
14.	Dhanbad	Dhanbad	10,825	15,621	—	26,446
		Total	38,398	7,27,979	340	7,66,717

15.	Saranda	Singhbhum	81,808	3,988	86	85,882
16.	Kolhan	-do-	58,716	11,258	68	70.042
17.	Pora hat	-do-	50,628	15,816	98	66,542
18.	Chaibassa (South)	-do-	31	50,875	—	50,906
19.	Chaibassa (North)	-do-	6,486	61,540	—	68,026
20.	Dhalbhum	-do-	53,050	51,963	—	1,05,018
21.	Ranchi East	Ranchi	11,742	80,182	—	91,924
		Total	2,63,461	2,75,627	252	5,38,340
22.	Ranchi West	Ranchi	26,290	73,753	—	1,00,043
23.	Gumla	Ranchi	12,102	1,18,717	16	1,30,835
24.	Latehar	(i) Ranchi	3,417	10,652	—	1,32,366
		(ii) Palamau	17,213	1,01,084	—	
25.	Daltonganj South	-do-	58,081	46,044	45	1,04,170
26.	Daltonganj North	-do-	3,987	1,26,661	—	1,30,648
27.	Garhwa South	-do-	549	1,23,586	—	1,24,135
28.	Garhwa North	-do-	—	78,705	—	78,705
		Total	1,21,639	6,79,202	61	8,00,902
29.	Gaya Affn.	(i) Gaya	—	165	—	11,132
		(ii) Nawada	—	6,327	—	
		(iii) Nalanda	—	4,640	—	
30.	Giridih Affn.	Giridih	485	16,318	—	16,803
		Total	485	27,450	—	27,935
31.	Biological Park	Patna	—	—	56	56
32.	Champaran	(i) East Champaran	—	70	—	91,815
		(ii) West Champaran	—	91,745	—	
		Grand Total	5,05,125	24,17,398	709	29,23,232

TABLE 4

District-wise Area of Forests

Sl. No.	*Name of District*	*Geographical area in sq. km.*	*Forest area in sq. km.*	*Percent of land under forests*	*Human popula-tion in thousand*	*Per Capita forest area in ha*	*Live-stock in lakh @*	*Forest area per head of livestock in ha*
1	2	3	4	5	6	7	8	9
1.	Patna	3,182	+1	2,00	22,51	—		
2.	Nalanda	2,346	46	—	13,06	004	9.59	0.004
3.	Gaya	4,288	325	7,6	19,24	0.0117		
4.	Aurangabad	4,409	539	12,2	12,93	0.042	21.17	0.72
5.	Nawadah	3,648	697	191	12,44			
6.	Bhojpur	4,024	—	—	19,95	0.056		
7.	Rohtas	7,296	1,798	24,6	19,44	0.092	16.25	0.111
8.	Sasaram	3,241	—	—	20,35	—		
9.	Siwan	3,711	—	—	12,44	—	13.48	—
10.	East Champaran	4,334	—	—	19 56	—		
11.	West Champaran	4,862	9.17	18,8	15,87	0.058	17.64	0.052
12.	Muzaffarpur	3,160	—	—	19,09	—		
13.	Vaishali	2,019	—	—	43 49	—	16 63	—
14.	Sitamarhi	2,659	—	—	15,83	—		
15.	Darbhanga	2,296	—	—	15,17	—		
16.	Samastipur	2,856	—	—	18,25	—	16.69	—
17.	Madhubani	337	-	—	18,92	—		

18.	Monghyr	7,928	1,291	16,2	27,55	0.047	15.21	0.050
19.	Bhagalpur	5,656	454	8,0	29,91	0.022	10.03	0.050
20.	Santhal Parganas	11,129	1,921	13,5	31,87	0060	28.59	0.067
21.	Begusarai	1,809	—	—	11,47	—	11.35	—
22.	Saharsa	5,885	—	—	23,50	—		
23.	Purnea	11,013	13	0,1	39,43	0.003	2198	—
24.	Palamau	11,677	5,560	43,8	15.04	0.370	14.00	0.399
25.	Hazaribagh	1,1153	5,278	47,3	16,46	0.321		
26.	Giridih	6,908	2,292	33,1	13,74	0.167	21.30	0.853
27.	Ranchi	18,331	3,368	16,4	26,11	0.129	22.39	0.149
28.	Dhanbad	2,994	264	8,8	14,66	0.018	16.45	0.279
29.	Singhbhum	13,447	4,464	33,1	2,430	0.193	16.15	0.976
	Total	1,73,876	29,22	16,6	5,63,53	0.052	289.66	0.276

Source: Census of India 1971, Primary Census Abstract @ Provisional figures of 1972-census by Directorate of Animal Husbandry, Bihar.

TABLE 5

Forest Roads

(Length in km)

Sl. No.	*Name of Division*	*Length of Roads*			*Expenditure (Rs. in 1.000)**	
		Up to 1976-77	*During 1977-78*	*Up to 1977-78*	*New*	*Repairs*
1.	Deoghar	201	—	201	24	45
2.	Dumka	350	—	350	—	30
3.	Monghyr	620	—	620	115	55
4.	Champaran	292	—	292	—	—
5.	Shahabad	759	—	759	—	66
6.	Gaya	681	—	681	—	48
7.	Hazaribagh West	744	—	744	—	55
8.	Hazaribagh East	796	—	796	—	55
9.	Chatra South	592	—	592	—	34
10.	Chatra North	508	—	508	—	41
11.	Giridih	751	—	751	10	109
12.	Kodarma	760	—	760	—	36
13.	Dhanbad	140	—	140	—	23
14.	Suranda	544	—	544	—	—
15.	Kolhan	538	—	538	—	89
16.	Porahat	487	—	487	15	28
17.	Chaibassa South	262	—	262	—	28
18.	Chaibassa North	295	—	295	—	29
19.	Dhalbhum	427	—	427	—	—

20.	Ranchi East	283	—	283	—	—
21.	Ranchi West	463	—	463	14	55
22.	Gumla	201	—	204	8	25
23.	Latehar	513	—	513	—	55
24.	Daltonganj South	710	—	710	—	45
25.	Daltonganj North	537	—	537	10	45
26.	Garhwa South	457	—	457	—	—
27.	Garhwa North	392	—	392	—	8
28.	Giridih Afforestation	32	—	32	—	—
29.	Jamui Afforestation	—	—	—	—	11
30.	Gaya Afforestation	53	—	53	—	—
	Total	13,391	—	13,391	1,30	10,35

* Includes expenditure on culverts, etc.

TABLE 6

Forest Building

Sl. No.	*Name of Division*	*Building constructed upto 1976-77*				
		D.F. O.S. office	*F.R. H.*	*R.I. H.*	*D. F. O.*	*R. O.*
1	2	3	4	5	6	7
1.	Deoghar	—	5	3	—	2
2.	Dumka	1	2	11	1	7
3.	Monghyr	1	10	13	1	6
4.	Champaran	1	7	8	1	5
5.	Shahabad	1	4	9	1	5
6.	Gaya	—	6	8	1	6
7.	Extension	—	—	—	—	1
	Total	1	34	52	5	32
8.	Hazaribagh West	1	10	8	1	6
9.	Hazaribagh East	1	4	5	—	5
10.	Chatra South	1	3	8	1	4
11.	Chatra North	—	4	6	—	4
12.	Kodarma	1	6	4	1	4

13	Giridih	1	14	9	1	6
14.	Dhanbad	—	3	9	1	6
	Total	5	44	49	5	33
15.	Saranda	1	12	22	1	5
16.	Kolhan	1	11	16	1	4
17.	Porahat	1	12	20	1	6
18.	Chaibassa South	1	3	19	1	3
19.	Chaibassa North	1	3	8	1	4
20.	Dhalbhum	1	7	16	1	4
21.	Ranchi East	1	15	5	—	6
	Total	7	53	116	6	32
22.	Panchi West	—	8	15	1	5
23.	Gumla	1	8	10	1	4
24.	Latehar	1	7	14	1	5
25.	Daltonganj South	1	14	12	1	7
26.	Daltonganj North	1	6	8	—	5
27.	Garhwa South	2	7	14	1	4
28.	Garhwa North	—	1	—	—	—
	Total	6	51	73	5	30

(*Contd.*)

TABLE 6 (*Contd.*)

1	*2*	*3*	*4*	*5*	*6*	*7*
29.	North Bihar Affn.	—	—	—	—	2
30.	Gaya Affn.	1	2	1	1	—
31.	Giridih Affn.	—	1	2	—	2
32.	Singhbhum Affn.	1	1	3	1	1
33.	Chatra Affn.	—	1	1	—	4
34.	Hazaribagh Affn.	1	—	1	1	4
35.	Forest Reseorch Dn.	1	—	—	1	6
36.	D.F.M. Morghyr	1	—	—	—	2
37.	Utilisation	—	—	—	—	2
38.	Working Plans Office Northern Circle	—	—	—	1	—
	Total	5	5	7	5	23
	Grand Total	27	187	297	26	148

(*Contd.*)

TABLE 6 (*Contd.*)

Sl. No.	*Name of Division*	*Quarters*				*Constructed during 1977-78*	*Total up-to 1977-78*
		B. O.	*F. G.*	*Clerk*	*Others*		
1	*2*	*8*	*9*	*10*	*11*	*12*	*13*
1.	Deoghar	12	2	8	7	—	39
2.	Dumka	17	17	8	1		65
3.	Monghyr	20	85	8	4	others-1	199
4.	Champaran	12	43	6	2	—	85
5.	Shahabad	8	33	8	12	—	82
6.	Gaya	14	37	6	6	others-1	86
7.	Extension	1	16	5	9	—	32
	Total	84	234	49	41	2	588
8.	Hazaribagh West	16	51	18	37		148
9.	Hazaribagh East	12	56	7	9	others 1	100
10.	Chatra South	6	23	8	8		62
11.	Chatra North	10	30	4	5	—	63
12.	Kodarma	11	35	8	1	—	71
13.	Giridih	20	71	8	13		314
14.	Dhanbad	14	39	6	8	—	84
	Total	89	305	59	81	1	671

(*Contd.*)

TABLE 6 (*Contd.*)

1	*2*	*8*	*9*	*10*	*11*	*12*	*13*
15.	Saranda	11	48	8	127	—	235
16.	Kolhan	8	52	8	82	—	184
17.	Porahat	12	57	8	30	—	144
18.	Chaibassa South	8	51	10	8	—	104
19.	Chaibassa North	1	65	—	—	—	93
20.	Dhalbhum	16	113	4	15	—	177
21.	Ranchi East	11	46	4	14	—	102
	Total	77	433	42	276	—	1039
22.	Ranchi West	13	55	4	14	others-2	117
23.	Gumla	12	44	8	2	—	90
24.	Latehar	15	71	8	18	others-1	141
25.	Daltonganj South	16	24	14	61	—	150
26.	Daltonganj North	13	58	9	5	—	105
27.	Garhwa South	11	64	14	7	—	124
28.	Garhwa North	—	77	4	3	—	85
	Total	80	383	61	106	6	812
29.	North Bihar Affn.	2	10	4	—	—	18
30.	Gaya Affn.	3	7	6	2	—	22
31.	Giridih Affn.	11	29	1	6	—	52

32.	Singhbhum Affn.	8	42	—	9	—	66
33.	Chatra Affn.	5	14	2	4	—	31
34.	Hazaribagh Affn.	5	16	6	8	—	42
35.	Forest Research Dn.	24	27	12	26	—	97
36.	D.F.M. Morghyr	—	6	3	2	—	14
37.	Utilisation	3	2	—	—	—	7
38.	Working Plans Office Northern Circle	—	—	—	17	—	18
	Total	69	153	34	74	—	367
	Grand Total	389	1507	238	578	6	3477

TABLE 7

Progress of Afforestation

(Area in Hectares)

Sl. No.	*Name of Division*	*Bamboo*		*Teak*		*Sisoo*		*Eucalyptus*	
		During	*Upto*	*During*	*Upto*	*During*	*Upto*	*During*	*Upto*
1	2	3	4	5	6	7	8	9	10
1.	Singhbhum Affn.	—	10671	—	—	—	—	9	3785
2.	North Bihar Affn.	—	1697	—	300	—	4501	—	103
3.	Giridih Affn.	—	3014	—	2	—	1834	46	852
4.	Gaya Affn.	—	618	—	1168	98	5570	6	566
5.	Hazaribagh Affn.	—	2226	—	55	—	3172	99	2660
6.	Chatra Affn.	—	685	—	1102	35	4123	36	780
7.	Jamui Affn.	—	—	—	—	—	—	—	—
8.	Palamau Affn.	—	—	—	—	—	—	—	193
	Total	—	18911	—	2627	133	19200	196	8939
9.	Daltonganj South	—	1088	—	752	—	2	—	285
10.	Daltonganj North	—	320	—	64	—	1058	—	1431
11.	Latehar	—	509	—	246	—	—	—	1103
12.	Garhwa South	—	57	—	—	—	19	—	1936
13.	Garhwa North	—	227	—	—	—	—	—	1963
14.	Gumla	—	—	—	—	—	—	—	8
15.	Ranchi North	—	90	—	—	—	—	—	470
	Total	—	2291	—	1062	—	1079	—	7196

No.	Division								
16.	Ranchi East	—	—	—	—	—	—	—	96
17.	Saranda	—	—	104	2241	—	—	—	—
18.	Kolhan	—	—	116	1555	—	—	—	—
19.	Porahat	—	—	2	1656	—	—	—	—
20.	Dhalbhum	—	—	—	—	—	—	75	757
21.	Chaibassa North	—	—	—	—	200	200	—	85
22.	Chaibassa South	—	—	—	—	—	—	—	—
	Total	—	—	222	5452	200	200	75	948
23.	Giridih	—	12	—	60	—	42	—	—
24.	Kodarma	—	48	—	—	—	65	—	216
25.	Chatra South	—	46	—	—	—	40	—	196
26.	Chatra North	—	77	—	—	—	191	—	119
27.	Dhanbad	—	965	—	—	—	596	—	237
	Total	—	1148	—	60	—	934	—	768
28.	Monghyr	—	—	—	—	—	—	—	—
29.	Shahabad	—	1826	—	—	—	20	—	165
30.	Extension	—	—	—	—	—	—	—	—
31.	Deoghar	—	1533	—	20	—	2185	—	983
32.	Champaran	—	—	—	—	—	—	—	—
33.	Dumka	—	—	—	—	—	—	—	—
	Total	—	3359	—	20	—	2205	—	1148
	Grand Total	—	25709	222	9221	333	23618	271	18999

(Contd.)

TABLE 7 (*Contd.*)

Sl. No.	*Name of Division*	*Semal*		*Others*		*Total*	
		During	*Upto*	*During*	*Upto*	*During*	*Upto*
1	*2*	*11*	*12*	*13*	*14*	*15*	*16*
1.	Singhbhum Affn.	—	—	1907	13,249	1916	27705
2.	North Bihar Affn.	—	487	—	2162	—	9250
3.	Giridih Affn.	—	—	318	7917	364	13619
4.	Gaya Affn.	—	4	1832	9294	1936	17220
5.	Hazaribagh Affn.	—	17	1119	9252	1218	17382
6.	Chatra Affn.	—	—	689	5984	760	12674
7.	Jamui Affn.	—	—	1512	2762	1512	2762
8.	Palamu Affn.	—	—	1563	2246	1563	2439
	Total	—	508	8940	52866	9269	103051
9	Daltonganj South	—	32	—	—	—	2159
10.	Daltonganj North	—	—	—	1239	—	4112
11.	Latehar	—	76	—	1354	—	3288
12.	Garhwa South	—	31	—	363	—	2406
13.	Garhwa North	—	—	—	365	—	2555
14.	Gumla	—	—	—	45	—	53
15.	Ranchi North	—	—	—	495	—	1055
	Total	—	139	—	3861	—	15628

16.	Ranchi East	—	—	—	—	—	96
17.	Saranda	—	463	—	13	104	2717
18.	Kolhan	—	135	—	—	116	1690
19.	Porahat	—	332	—	—	2	1988
20.	Dhalbhum	—	262	18	291	93	1320
21.	Chaibassa North	—	—	—	—	200	285
22.	Chaibassa South	—	—	159	159	159	159
	Total	—	1192	177	463	674	8255
23.	Giridih	—	—	—	583	—	697
24.	Kodarma	—	—	—	91	—	420
25.	Chatra South	—	—	—	101	—	383
26.	Chatra North	—	—	—	526	—	913
27.	Dhanbad	—	—	—	2572	—	4370
	Total	—	—	—	3873	—	6783
28.	Monghyr	—	—	—	307	—	307
29.	Shahabad	—	—	—	1288	—	3299
30.	Extension	—	—	—	130	—	130
31.	Deoghar	—	—	—	4038	—	8759
32.	Champaran	—	—	—	6	—	6
33.	Dumka	—	—	—	276	—	276
	Total	—	—	—	6045	—	12777
	Grand Total	—	1839	9117	67108	9943	1,46,494

TABLE 8

Major Forest Produce

(Quantity in m^3)

Sl. No.	Name of Divisions	Timber	Firewood	Total
1.	Deoghar	420	1,176	1,596
2.	Dumka	6,517	3,234	9,751
3.	Gaya	6,621	14,802	21,423
4.	Monghyr	25,404	10	25,414
5.	Jamui Affrn.	2,531	—	2,531
6.	Shahabad	1(100	26,345	27,445
7.	Champaran	16,386	31,020	47,406
8.	Hazaribagh West	15,787	11,640	27,427
9.	Hazaribagh East	2,651	6,588	9,239
10.	Chatra South	28,406	45,918	74,324
11.	Chatra North	21,833	19,152	40,985
12.	Giridih	15,555	640	16,195
13.	Kodarma	15,899	8,269	24,168
14.	Dhanbad	1,146	108	1,254
15.	Saranda	40,700	16,245	56,945
16.	Kolhan	37,509	2,985	40,494
17.	Porahat	17,448	13,370	30,818

18.	Chaibassa South	18,461	5,060	23,521
19.	Chaibassa North	1,904	2,924	4,828
20.	Dhalbhum	19,222	8,698	27,920
21.	Ranchi East	5,625	21,538	27,162
22.	Ranchi West	36,424	9,209	45,634
23.	Gumla	13,429	12,315	25,744
24.	Latehar	42,887	776	43,663
25.	Daltonganj South	8,404	1,096	9,500
26.	Daltonganj North	26,494	5,322	31,816
27.	Garhwa South	26,494	32,293	58,787
28.	Garhwa North	741	17,023	17,764
29.	Singhbhum Affrn.	7,769	7,299	15,068
30.	Giridih Affrn.	34	2,211	2,245
31.	Hazaribagh Affrn.	340	93	433
	Total	4,64,141	3,27,359	7,91,500

TABLE 9

Out-turn of Forest Produce

Sl. No.	*Name of Divisions*	*Bamboo*		*Kendu-Leaf*	
		Quantity in Tonnes	*Value in 1000 Rs.*	*Quantity in Standard Bags*	*Value in 1000 Rs.*
1	2	3	4	5	6
1.	Deoghar	—	—	9,348	333
2.	Dumka	983	31	21,618	1,843
3.	Monghyr	5,146	608	16,527	654
4.	Shahabad	905	82	40,328	2,273
5.	Gaya	602	119	60,930	2,748
6.	Extension	1,634	103	—	—
7.	Jamui Affrn.	1,789	173	16,188	665
8.	Saranda	5	—	5,015	293
9.	Kolhan	—	—	12,177	706
10.	Porahat	3,441	2,250	15,534	796
11.	Chaibassa South	—	—	7,157	551
12.	Chaibassa North	40	200	14,476	910
13.	Dhalbhum	—	—	19,857	1,411
14.	Ranchi East	—	—	16,994	785
15.	Hazaribagh West	3,172	291	23,067	849

16.	Hazaribagh East	5,267	9	12,284	531
17.	Chatra South	2,954	476	39220	1,737
18.	Chatra North	15,559	2,661	66,351	3,099
19.	Giridih	2,517	322	30,547	1,333
20.	Kodarma	2,213	469	31,688	1,418
21.	Dhanbad	823	114	1,273	47
22.	Ranchi West	2,173	307	5,930	217
23.	Gumla	—	—	30,469	2383
24.	Latehar	65,320	1486	67,777	3571
25.	D'ganj (S)	19,856	1922	15,653	1074
26.	D'ganj (N)	10,831	1140	66,675	3632
27.	Garhwa (S)	26,176	7,03	59,830	4377
28.	Garhwa (N)	1,46	48	55,945	4112
29.	Gaya Affrn.	—	—	—	—
30.	Giridih Affrn.	—	—	2,750	90
31.	Chatra Affrn.	—	—	—	—
32.	H'bagh Affrn.	—	—	—	—
33.	Singhbum Affrn.	20	5	—	—
	Grand Total	1,71,572	13,522	7,77,708	42,438

(*Contd..*)

TABLE 9 (*Contd.*)

Sl. No.	*Name of Divisions*	*Sabai Grass*		*Grazing Fodder*		*Other M.F.P.*	
		Quantity in Quintals	*Value in Rupees*	*Quantity in Quintals*	*Value in Rupees*	*Quantity in Quintals*	*Value in Rupees*
1	*2*	*7*	*8*	*9*	*10*	*11*	*12*
1.	Deoghar	—	—	—	—	—	—
2.	Dumka	9,690	2,20,458	—	—	—	—
3.	Monghyr	1,510	12,300	—	—	—	350
4.	Shahabad	—	—	—	—	—	6,000
5.	Gaya	720	2,500	—	—	—	7,51,570
6.	Extension	—	—	—	—	—	—
7.	Jamui Affrn.	—	—	—	—	—	—
8.	Saranda	7	200	—	—	—	1,01,518
9.	Kolhan	1	20	—	—	—	1,13,000
10.	Porahat	—	-	—	—	—	80 000
11.	Chaibassa South	—	—	—	—	—	25,877
12.	Chaibassa North	—	—	—	—	—	11,000
13.	Dhalbhum	—	—	—	—	—	11,950
14.	Ranchi East	—	—	—	—	—	65,750
15.	Hazaribagh West	1,371	32,405	—	—	—	14,949
16.	Hazaribagh East	-	—	—	—	—	39,862
17.	Chatra South	—	—	—	—	—	3,49,095

18.	Chatra North	—	—	—	—	—	—
19.	Giridih	—	—	—	—	—	19,500
20.	Kodarma	—	—	—	—	—	23,99,400
21.	Dhanbad	—	—	—	—	—	2,29,000
22.	Ranchi West	—	—	—	—	—	16808
23.	Gumla	—	—	—	—	—	7797
24.	Uthar	—	—	—	—	—	23,000
25.	D'ganj (S)	—	—	—	—	—	74,800
26.	D'ganj (N)	—	—	—	—	—	10,01,059
27.	Garhwa (S)	—	—	—	—	—	35,875
28.	Garhwa (N)	—	—	—	—	—	2,700
29.	Gaya Affrn.	—	—	—	—	—	—
30.	Giridih Affrn	—	—	—	—	—	—
31.	Chatra Affrn.	—	—	5,78	1,500	—	46,000
32.	H'bagh Affrn.	—	—	—	—	—	17,391
33.	Singhbum Affrn.	—	—	—	—	—	—
	Grand Total	13,299	2,67,883	1,278	1,500	—	5,447,251

TABLE 10

Forest-Based Industries and Supply to various Organization of the State Government and Government of India

			Quantity (m^3)	Value (Rs.)
A. Sleepers				
Supply to				
(a) Railway	(i) B.G.	—	1472	44,31,299
	(ii) M.G.	—	1373	
	(iii) N.G.	—	513	
	(iv) Specials	—	2640	
(b) N.C.D.C.	(i) B.G.	—	78 m^3	16,204
B. Logs				
Supply to				
(a) D.G.S. & D.			Quantity (m^3)	Value (Rs.)
New Delhi—	(i) Laure	—	832	13,2,8135
	(ii) Haldu	—	593	
	(iii) Sal	—	373	
C. Poles :			Quantity (m^3)	Value (Rs.)
Supply to				
(a) B.S.E.B.	(i) Treated Poles	—	696	14,62,331
(b) Irrigation Deptt.	(i) Poles	—	1367	998,264
(c) Eighth Engineering Ragiment	(i) Untreated Poles		—	3,618
(d) Fencing Post: Palamau Affrn.				
	(i) Fencing Post (Treated)	—	163	54,797

TABLE 11

Revenue and Expenditure

(Rs. in '000)

Sl. No.	Name of Division	Revenue	Expenditure		
			Non-plan	Plan	Total
1	2	3	4	5	6
1.	Chief Conservators of forests	8,42	6,65	59	7,24
	Total	8,42	6,65	59	7,24
2.	Conservator of Forests Southern Circle	—	1,60	—	1,60
3.	Saranda	1,17,96	11,36	1,63	12,99
4.	Kolhan	87,23	12,41	2,10	1,451
5.	Porahat	36,04	5,31	5,35	10,66
6.	Chaibassa South	27,18	6,94	2,75	9,69
7.	Chaibassa North	30,73	13,39	4,12	17,51
8.	Dhalbhum	46,51	17,29	4,91	22,20
9.	Ranchi East	15,69	14,41	3,98	18,39
	Total	3.61,34	82,71	2.4,84	1.07,55
10.	Conservator of Forests Western Circle	—	1,67	—	1,67
11.	Daltonganj South	69,40	12,54	1,22	13,76
12.	Daltonganj North	74,50	23,83	3,40	27,32

(Contd.)

TABLE 11 (*Contd.*)

1	2	3	4	5	6
13.	Latehar	1,19,56	3,12	23,59	26,61
14.	Garhwa South	1,37,99	23,42	2,92	26.34
15.	Garhwa North	43,58	4,40	1,98	6,38
16.	Gumla	45,70	16,98	2,14	19,12
17.	Ranchi West	60,97	10,64	18,71	29,35
	Total	5,51,60	96,60	53,96	1,50,56
18.	Conservator of Forests Hazaribagh Circle	—	195	—	195
19.	Hazaribagh West	47,61	23,04	347	26,51
20.	Hazaribagh East	10,36	10,48	53	11,01
21.	Chatra South	1,05,02	17,69	6	17,75
22.	Chatra North	11,997	21,13	33	21,46
23.	Kodarma	40,90	15,14	, 20	15,34
24.	Giridih	45,14	20,40	1,98	22,36
25.	Dhanbad	5,66	10,89	37	11,26
	Total	36900	10983	657	11638
26.	Conservator of Forests Magadh Circle	50,00	2,33	1	2,34
27.	Deoghar	11,13	7,06	7.55	14,61
28.	Dumka	36,88	20,51	6,39	26,81
29.	Gaya	50,99	10,54	15,25	25,79

30.	Monghyr	18,51	13,82	—	14,81
31.	Shahabad	27,67	18,26	6,67	24,93
32.	Extension	1,33	4,72	10,07	14.79
33.	Jamui Affrn.	13,07	7.82	13,11	20,93
	Total	2,0858	8,506	5896	14501
34.	Coservator of Forests				
	Development Circle	—	1,81	—	1,81
35.	H'bagh Affrn.	38	17.71	3,48	21,19
36.	Chatra Affrn.	1,32	6	16,23	16,29
37.	Giridih Affrn.	2,91	10,59	2,55	13,14
38.	Gaya Affrn.	17	1,23	19,21	20,44
39.	Singhbhum Affrn.	9,88	20	18.18	18,38
40.	Palamau Affrn.	—	3	8.03	8,06
41.	Ranchi Affrn.	—	—	1,33	1,33
	Total	1466	31,63	6646	10064
42	Conservator of Forests				
	Special Circle	—	4.87	—	4.87
43.	Departmental Working Division				
	Hazaribagh	3672	—	3829	38.29
44.	Do Do Monghyr	26,40	1	4,46	4,47
45.	Forest utilization Division	17,10	4,23	—	4,23
	Total	80,22	9,11	42,75	51,86

(Contd.)

TABLE 11 (*Contd.*)

1	2	3	4	5	6
46.	Conservator of Forests W.P. & R. Circle	—	10,7	—	1,07
47.	W.P. Hazaribagh Circle	2	2,19	—	2,19
48.	W.P. Southern Circle	—	1,72	—	1,72
49.	Working Plan Western Circle	1	1,73	—	1,73
50.	W.P. Magadh Circle	—	3,12	—	2,12
51.	Forest Research Division	7,66	6,02	9,28	15,30
52.	Forest Resources Survey Division	6	1,48	—	1,48
53.	Biological park	17	—	11,72	11,72
	Total	792	1633	21,00	37,33
54.	Conservator of Forests Kendu leaf —	1,91	—	1,91	
55.	Project Tiger	2,65	4,65	10,02	14,67
56.	Wild life	8	—	1,93	1,93
	Grand Total	1596,15	4,44,48	2,87,08	7,35,17

TABLE 12

Estimated Growing Stock, Percentage Availability and Average Annual Production by Species in Bihar Forests

Name of Species		*Growing Stock in '000 m³ (in round)*	*Average annual availability in '000 m³ (in round)*	*Percentage availability*
Local Name	*Botanical Name*			
Sal	Sborea sobusta	1,65,49	2,54	55.0
Salai	Boswallia serrata	1,33,64	1,01	13.1
Asan	Terminalia tomentosa	31,92	32	4.2
Mahua	Madhuca indica	27,71	—	3.9
Dhawra	Anogeissus latifolia	24,30	19	2.4
Bija	Pterocarpus marsupium	11,02	13	1.7
Jamun	Syzygium cumini	6,50	5	0.5
Sandan	Ougeinia oojeineinsis	5,83	7	0.9
Semal	Salmalia belerica	5,39	4	0.5
Karam	Adina cordifolia	3,02	10	1.3
Gamhar	Gmelina arborea	1,36	7	0.9
Misc.		2,94,50	3,18	15.5
Total		7,10,68	7,70	—
Bamboo	Dendro-calamus strictus (1000 tonnes)	9,30	1,45	

TABLE 13

Statement of Research Plots

Sl. No.	*Name of Division*	*Sample plot (no.)*	*Expt. plot (no.)*	*L. T. I. plot (no.)*	*S. T. I. plot (no.)*	*Preservation plot (no.)*	*Obs. plot (no.)*
1	*2*	*3*	*4*	*5*	*6*	*7*	*8*
1.	Saranda	24	—	12	1	—	—
2.	Kolhan	19	–	1	—	—	—
3.	Porabat	16	3	3	—	—	—
4.	Ranchi West	5	5	—	—	—	—
5.	Ranchi East	1	7	1	—	—	22
6.	Daltonganj South	7	13	4	—	—	—
7.	Daltonganj North	—	—	1	—	—	—
8.	Hazaribagh East	3	—	—	—	—	5
9.	Hazaribagh West	—	5	—	—	—	4
10.	Kodarma	2	—	—	—	—	—
11.	Chatra South	3	2	—	—	—	—
12.	Chatra North	1	—	—	—	—	—
13.	Latehar	7	6	—	—	—	1
14.	Champaran	5	—	—	—	—	—
15.	Extension	3	—	—	—	—	—
16.	Gaya	4	1	—	—	—	—

17.	Dhalbhum	7	7	—	—	—	—
18.	Garhwa South	2	1	—	—	—	—
19.	Garhwa North	6	4	—	—	—	—
20.	Monghyr	1	—	—	—	—	—
	Total	116	42	10	6	1	32

TABLE 14

Personnel

Sl. No.	Category	In the year					
		1951-52	1955-57	1961-62	1966-67	1969-70	1977-78
1	2	3	4	5	6	7	8
1.	Chief conservator of Forests, Bihar	1	1	1	1	1	1
2.	Addl. chief conservator of Forests, Bihar	—	—	—	—	—	2
3.	Deputy chief conservator of Forests, Bihar	—	—	1	1	1	—
4.	Conservator of Forests	2	2	4	6	6	9
5.	Deputy conservator of Forests	20	29	34	42	43	46
6.	Assistant conservator of Forests	10	11	20	26	28	88
7.	Accounts Officer	—	—	1	1	1	1
8.	Lac Development officer	—	—	1	1	1	1
9.	Forest Economist	—	—	1	1	1	1
10.	Personal Asstt. to the chief Conservator of Forests, Bihar	1	1	1	1	1	1
11.	Junior Forest service officer	—	—	—	17	17	1
12.	Forest Statistical Officer	—	—	—	—	—	1
13.	Forest statistician	—	—	1	1	2	2
14.	Statistical Supervisor	—	—	—	—	—	1

15.	Range officer of Forests	94	102	153	160	216	272
16.	Senior Statistical Asstt.	—	—	—	—	—	2
17.	Junior Statistical Assistant	—	—	—	—	—	4
18.	Statistical computer	—	—	1	1	2	5
19.	Statistical compiler	—	—	2	2	2	4
20.	Ministerial staff	212	332	416	474	484	600
21.	Forester	393	417	598	629	6 0	715
22.	Forest Guard	2322	2425	2979	2962	3096	4100
23.	Lac Inspector	—	—	4	4	5	8
24.	Lac Demonstrator	—	—	25	25	25	25
25.	Lac Attendant	—	—	40	40	40	10
26.	Others	224	258	406	437	494	530
	Total	3279	3578	4689	4832	5106	6430

TABLE 15

Forest Administrative Unit

(Area in Sq. Km.)

Sl. No.	*Name of Division*	*Area of Division*	*No.*	*Range Av. area*	*No.*	*Beat Av. area*	*No.*	*Sub-beat Av. area*
1	*2*	*3*	*4*	*5*	*6*	*7*	*8*	*9*
1.	Deoghar	768	6	128	14	54	96	8
2.	Dumka	1610	6	266	19	84	97	16
3.	Gaya	1496	6	249	19	78	123	12
4.	Monghyr	653	7	163	12	54	73	8
5.	Shahabad	1798	6	299	16	112	96	18
6.	Champaran	918	5	183	16	57	100	9
7.	Extension	13	3	5	8	1	36	—
8.	Jamui Affn.	637	3	212	24	27	107	6
	Total	7893	42	1504	128	457	721	77
9.	Hazaribagh West	1775	6	295	20	88	131	13
10.	Hazaribagh East	1257	5	251	16	78	119	10
11.	Chatra South	1026	4	44	8	128	65	15
12.	Chatra North	934	4	233	10	93	61	15
13.	Giridih	1520	6	253	23	66	165	9
14.	Kodarma	890	4	222	14	63	62	14
15.	Dhaobad	264	3	88	9	29	61	4
	Total	7666	32	2086	100	545	664	10

16. Saranda	859	4	284	12	71	39	12
17. Kolhan	700	4	175	8	87	45	8
18. Porahat	665	5	133	5	60	36	11
19. Chaibassa South	509	3	12	9	42	64	6
20. Chaibassa North	680	4	223	9	75	62	10
21. Dhalbhum	1050	5	210	15	70	100	1
22. Ranchi East	919	6	153	13	70	126	7
Total	5312	31	1282	71	475	472	55
23. Gumla	1308	4	327	12	109	82	15
24. Daltonganj South	1042	5	208	9	115	51	20
25. Daltonganj North	1306	6	217	14	93	81	14
26. Garhwa South	1241	5	248	13	95	53	19
27. Garhwa North	787	3	262	7	112	52	15
28. Latehar	1324	5	264	14	94	72	18
29. Ranchi West	1000	6	200	13	76	109	9
Total	8008	34	1726	82	694	500	110
30. Giridih Afforestation	168	6	28	18	9	93	1
31. Gaya Affn.	111	5	22	16	—	64	1
32. Hazaribagh Affn.	—	5	—	19	—	84	—
33. Chatra Affn.	—	4	—	13	—	50	—
34. Singhbhum Affn.	—	5	—	19	—	60	—
35. North Bihar Affn.	—	4	—	10	—	48	—
Total	279	29	50	95	9	399	2

(Contd.)

TABLE 15 (*Contd.*)

1	2	3	4	5	6	7	8	9
36.	Forest Research	—	9	—	30	—	45	—
37.	Forest Resources	—	2	—	2	—	—	—
38.	Working Plans, Southern Circle	—	4	—	1	—	—	—
39.	Working Plans, Magadh Circle	—	5	—	—	—	–	—
40.	Working Plans, Northern Circle	—	3	—	1	—	—	—
	Total	—	23	34	45			
41.	Depttl. Working, Hazaribagh	—	5	—	—	—	—	—
42.	Depttl. Working, Monghyr	—	4	—	11	—	30	—
43.	Forest Utilization	—	6	—	13	—	14	—
	Total	—	15	—	24	—	44	—
	Grand total	29232	206	6598	534	2190	2852	324

TABLE 16

Conversion Table

1 Pole = 1.5 cft = 0.042 m³	1 B. G. Sleeper — 0.088 m³
1 Cogging, fencing Post or Khuta = 0.5 cft. = 0.014 m³	1 M. G. Sleeper — 0.039 m³
15 cft Stock Volume fire wood = 1 Quintal	I N. G. Sleeper — 0.031 m³
3 cft Stock Volume = 1 cft Solid Volume	1 T. L. Sleeper — 0.019 m³
(As per Addl. C.C.F. (Dev)'s letter no. 1813 d./3/11/78	Special Sleeper — 0.125 m³

Volume/Weight :

Cubic meter	Cubic feet	Tonne of wood
1	35315	0.706
0.028	1	0.02
1.415	50 (usually)	1

TABLE 17

Yield for one Acre of Sal—III Quality

Age	*Main Crop*					
	Average diameter	*Average height*	*Total basal area*	*Number of trees*	*Stem timber from factor*	*Small wood from factor stem & branch*
Years	*Ins/cm*	*Ft./m*	*sq.ft/m²*	—		
1	2	3	4	5	6	7
20	25 (6.3 cm)	31 (9.45 m)	52 (4.8 m²)	—	0.0	0.149
30	4.5 (11.4 cms)	43 (13.11m)	72 (6.7 m²)	652	0.0	0.349
40	6.7 (17.0 cms)	51 (15.54 m)	88 (8.1 m²)	359	0.052	0.363
50	8.6 (21.8)	59 (17.98 m)	101 (9.4 m²)	250 0.214	0.163	0.264
60	10.2 (25.9)	65 (19.81 m)	109 (10.1 m²)	192	0.212	0.186

(*Contd.*)

TABLE 17 (*Contd.*)

Age	*Main Crop*				*Thinning*	
	Standing volume stems timber	*Standing volume small wood*	*Total standing volume, stem timber & small wood*	*Stem timber*	*Small wood, stem and branch*	*Total stem timber and small wood*
Years	*C.ft/m*^{3}	*C.ft/m*^{3}	*C.ft/m*^{3}	*C. ft/m*^{3}	*Cft/m*^{3}	*t.ft/m*^{3}
1	*8*	*9*	*10*	*11*	*12*	*13*
20	0	240 (6.7 m^2)	240 (6.7 m^2)	0	0	0
30	0	1080 (30.2 m^3)	1080 (30.2 m^3)	0	440 (12.3 m^3)	440 (12.3 m^3)
40	230 (.6 m^3)	1630 (45.6 m^3)	1860 (52.0 m^3)	0	440 (12.3 m^3)	440 (12.3 m^3)
50	965 (27.0 m^3)	1575 (44.1 m^3)	2540 (71.1 m^3)	0	445 (12.4 m^3)	445 (12.4 m^3)
60	1,500 (42.0 m^3)	1,320 (36.9 m^3)	2820 (78.9 m^3)	65 (1.8 m^3)	255 (7.1 m^3)	320 (8.9 m^3)

Note : Figures in Brackets are in Metric Unit.
Source: Forest Pocket Book, by S.H. Howard, I.F.S. (Former) Inspector General of Forests, 5th Edition, 1941, pp. 200-201.

TABLE 18

Wild Life Sanctuary

Sl. No.	*Division*	*National Park/Game Sanctuary*	*Year of creation*	*Area in sq. km.*	*Government notification No. & Date*
1	*2*	*3*	*4*	*5*	*6*
A. National Park					
1.	Hazaribagh West	Hazaribagh National Park	—	184	—
2.	Daltonganj South	Palamau National Park	—	161	—
B. Game Sanctuary					
Existing sanctuaries					
1.	Gaya Affn.	@ Rajgir Game sanctuary	1969	36	1877R dt. 10.11.69
2.	Dhanbad	@ Topchanchi game sanctuary	1970	9	S0900 dt. 22.9.70
3.	Chatra South	@ Lawalong game sanctuary	1969	207	1173 dt. 17.12.69
4.	Champaran	@ Ganauli game sanctuary	1960	149	1918R dt. 29.8.60
5.	Champaran	@ Madanpur game sanctuary			
6.	Champaran	@ Udaipur game sanctuary	1960	6	-do-
7.	Shahabad	@ Kairmur game sanctuary	1959	1342	C.F. 22012/59
8.	Shahabad	@ Adhaura game sanctuary	—		
9.	Kolhan	@ Ramiaburu game sanctuary	1931	130	C.F. Bihar's No. 8276 dt. 17.12.34
10.	Porahat	@ Tebo game sanctuary	1932	132	1066111 ESR dt. 14.10.32

11.	Daltonganj South	@ Lat game sanctuary	—	7	—
12.	Daltonganj South	@ Bagechampa game sanctuary	—	8	—
13.	Daltonganj South	@ Baresandguru game sanctuary	—	9	—
14.	Daltonganj South	@ Netarhat 'A' game sanctuary	—	2	—
15.	Daltonganj South	@ Netarhat 'B' game sanctuary	—	1	—
16.	Kadarma	@ Kodarma game sanctuary	—	176	—
C. Proposed Sanctuary					
1.	Saranda	Saranda game sanctuary	1968-72	313	—
2.	Garhwa South	Bisrampur game sanctuary	1968-72	269	—
3.	Garhwa South	Tilighari game sanctuary	1968	73	—
4.	Garhwa South	Gawan Range game sanctuary	—	86	—
5.	Hazaribagh	Parasnath game sanctuary	1973	53	—
6.	Daltonganj South	Betla game sanctuary	1969	268	—
7.	Chatra North	Hindia game sanctuary	1970	70	—
8.	Ranchi East	Horahap game sanctuary	1970	66	—
D. Sanctuary to be Proposed					
1.	Gaya and Kodarma	Gautam Budha Abhayaranya	—	353	—
2.	Shahabad	Black Buck sanctuary		Not available	
3.	Shahabad	Rohtas Abhyaranya	1959	1484	—
4.	Monghyr	Bhim Bandh Abhyaranya	—	676	—
5.	Daltonganj South	Sarkadih game sanctuary	—	63	—
6.	Dhalbhum	Dalma game sanctuary	—	202	—
7.	Hazaribagh East	Konhary game sanctuary	—	—	8

Note : There are 226 shooting Blocks in the State, which cease to function as such as a measure for conservation of wild life.

TABLE 19

(A) Census Report of Wild Animals in National Parks

Sl. No.	Species	Betla National Park	Hazaribagh National Park
1.	Bison	550	@
2.	Spotted Deer	20,500	70
3.	Sambar	900	1350
4.	Tiger	32	@
5.	Leopard	65	@
6.	Barking Deer	800	250
7.	Peafowul	@	@
8.	Wild Boar	19,500	3,770
9.	Blue Bull	120	290
10.	Bear	300	@
11.	Elephant	37	@
12.	Wild dog	@	90
13.	Hyena	34	60
14.	Wolf	@	110
15.	Peacocks	@	@
16.	Fourhorned atelope	@	210
17.	Chinkara	@	110
18.	Sloth Bear	@	240
19.	Mangoose	@	@

@ Not covered in the Census during the year.

(B) No. of Visitors to the National Parks

Sl. No.	National Parks	Visitors			Revenue realised (Rs.)
		Indian	Foreigners	Total	
1.	Hazaribagh	24,975	623	25,598	44,798
2.	Palamau	19,519	224	19,743	1,43,324

Index